Laurel & Hardy

The British Tours

A. J. Marriot

with a foreword by Lord Delfont

Laurel & Hardy: The British Tours
by A. J. Marriot

with a foreword by Lord Delfont

Text copyright © A. J. Marriot, 1993

Published by A. J. Marriot, 6 Gainsborough Road, Blackpool
Typeset by Carnegie Publishing, 18 Maynard St., Preston
Printed and bound in the UK by The Bath Press, Bath

ISBN 0-9521308-0-7

Laurel & Hardy

The British Tours

A. J. Marriot

with a foreword by Lord Delfont

Foreword

WHEN asked to write this foreword, I was only too happy to be able to pay my respects to two comedians who have always held a special place in my affections. Watching the films of Laurel and Hardy was a staple part of my boyhood years, and one of the most enjoyable. Little did I realise that in later years, when their film career was finished, I would be able to repay the loyalty and devotion I felt by inviting them to play in British theatre. What followed exceeded everyone's expectations, and lifted both our careers.

Unfortunately, within a few years of adapting so successfully to this medium, they were forced by illness to withdraw, and the British public were denied further opportunity to see, in the flesh, the world's two most fascinating funny men. Fate, though, had decreed that I play one more part in ensuring that they weren't readily forgotten.

While over in New York, on a business trip, I was approached by the producers of the American TV programme, *This is Your Life*. It was November 1954, and Laurel and Hardy were by now 'resting', and living their separate lives. Ralph Edwards, the show's host, wanted the two comedians to be his next subjects, so needed an excuse to get them together without suspicion being raised. Knowing of my past relationship with the Boys, the production team hit upon the idea that I should phone Stan and Babe individually, inform them I was in town, and invite them to the *Knickerbocker Hotel*.

Lord (Bernard) Delfont

On 1 December the plan was put into operation and the comedy duo were surprised by a camera crew, and a voice-over from Ralph Edwards announcing: 'Stan Laurel and Oliver Hardy – This is Your Life.'

Stan Laurel and Oliver Hardy were two lovable, gentle men, and to have been instrumental in increasing the amount of time they were able to impart laughter to their legion of adoring fans was indeed a time of great pride for me. A. J. Marriot has excellently documented these years, and in reading the book I was reminded of the many happy hours spent in the wonderful company of the two comedians. They are sadly missed by all who had the honour and pleasure to meet them or see them working live, but within these pages is captured the spirit of those times.

Preface

W HEN my good friend Roy Sims – expert on Laurel and Hardy memorabilia – started to turn up ephemera which showed the two comedians to have made stage appearances in Britain, I began to ask questions which neither he nor any other Laurel and Hardy students could answer. Turning to the authoritative, biographical works on the comedy duo I was further frustrated by their lack of coverage of these tours.

Determined to seek out exactly when and where Laurel and Hardy had played their theatre engagements, I began to do research. The deeper I went, the bigger the mystery became. Why hadn't Laurel and Hardy's tours been documented by their biographers? Why didn't people want to talk about the tours? Was something being hidden? Had Laurel and Hardy wanted to forget about the tours?

Bit by bit, I began to piece together their movements over in Britain, and contacted several acts who had worked with them. A handful were helpful in the extreme, but the majority of responses were disappointing: a few didn't wish to help; some were able to remember nothing; and others related only nonsense.

Four people who could have solved the great, untold mysteries of the British tours – Stan and Ida Laurel, and Oliver and Lucille Hardy – were, sad to say, departed from this world, long before my research began. There were others who could have helped, but chose not to. It was then that newspapers became a great source of information. Although often guilty of printing fabrication, this medium at least allows one the freedom of contradiction. Tell a newspaperman he's full of baloney and you'll escape unscathed. Say the same to someone you are interviewing and you risk severe retribution.

Newspapers were also invaluable in providing reliable dates, along with interesting comments and reviews from the time. Personal accounts often become embellished or distorted over the years, whereas the contemporary viewpoints in newspapers remain unaltered – hence the prominence of quotations from this medium in this book. In most cases, those articles containing inaccuracies or fabrication have been commented upon and corrected, where possible.

This book, as a story, is not complete, and never could be – not even if the original manuscript, which was twice as long as this book, had been published. It is meant only to supply details of the theatres at which Laurel and Hardy played; the hotels at which they stayed; the acts with whom they worked; some of the people they met; the functions they attended; their modes of transport; and the impact they made on the British public, both off-stage and on, during the British tours.

In setting the scene for the tours it was felt necessary, and of interest, to document many unpublished facts about Laurel's early life; his father's career; his apprenticeship in the British theatre; and his pre-Hardy days in America; and to correct mistakes from previous sources.

After hearing many myths and rumours, and very little else about Laurel and Hardy's British tours, readers will, I hope, find within these pages the information they are looking for. As this is a first time effort, additional material will be welcomed for a proposed second edition.

Those who withheld information will get only the bizarre satisfaction of looking for tiny holes in this account. To all others, I hope you get as much fun out of reading it as I got out of researching it.

Bouquets and brickbats to the author, care of the publisher.

Contents

Chapter One

The British Connection

On 3 June 1954 two ageing comedians went unnoticed as they waved goodbye to England from the stern of a ship bound for America. The skinny, red-haired one had first made a similar journey over forty years earlier and, watching the shoreline fast disappearing, could not help but reflect on the intervening years – years that had seen him rise from a struggling music-hall artiste, to one of the world's best loved film comedians. This accolade was shared by the huge man standing at his side; his inseparable business partner for the last twenty-seven years.

In 1932, almost at the peak of their film career, the two had popped over to England for a supposed holiday, but between leaving home and getting back were under continuous siege from masses of fans. Fifteen years later came a return to Britain, to work in variety theatre – the medium in which the skinny one had learned the basics of his trade. This visit too had people turning out in their thousands just to see them in person. In the early 'fifties two more British tours had followed, but the status of the two stars had diminished, and the public's urge to fight and jostle to see them was limited to the front rows of theatres.

To understand why these two world-renowned comedians – both now in their sixties, and of ailing health – had gone from making films in America to working in British theatres, we must first go back to England in the mid-nineteenth century, and trace the roots of the skinny one.

In the America of the 1850s, the Jeffersons *were* the drama theatre, with Joseph Jefferson playing Lord Dundreary over eight hundred times. In later life, Englishman Arthur Jefferson claimed to be a close relative of the American Jeffersons but, in truth, had no family connection. When Arthur himself chose the stage as a profession he received strong disapproval from his parents, and so ran away from his Manchester home. He toured the music halls for a while, as a comedian, before taking up a resident position at the *Hippodrome Theatre*, in Ulverston, Lancashire (now Cumbria). In

Arthur Jefferson in his guise of comedian 'Bobby Baxter – Fra Manchester'. The working-class man in the shabby gent's suit, wing-collar shirt and bowler hat, were all trademarks adopted by his son. (By kind permission of John Cooper.)

1884 Arthur married local girl Madge Metcalfe, whom he had first seen singing in the church choir in nearby Millom. The newly-weds stayed at the home of Madge's parents, George and Sarah Metcalfe, where, eleven months later Madge bore a son, George Gordon Jefferson (see page 266). After lending her support to her husband's activities at the theatre, Madge also developed a desire to make a career in acting, but when she too received disapproval from her parents, who had not even wanted an actor as a son-in-law, the Jeffersons left the Metcalfes' house and moved to County Durham. Together, they then spent a couple of seasons touring with drama companies, during which time Madge fulfilled her ambition and became an accomplished actress.

In 1889 a move from their first home in Tenter Street, Bishop Auckland, to South View, coincided with their settling down and Arthur starting a long-lasting working relationship with the local *Theatre Royal*. When Madge became pregnant again, she feared there might be complications with the birth, and decided to return to Ulverston to have the child under her mother's supervision. The decision was well taken as the baby was born a weakly child, having survived a difficult delivery during which the mother's health was also impaired. As the baby was not expected to live, a christening was quickly arranged in the home.

The birth certificate recorded the child's name as Arthur Stanley Jefferson; date of birth 16 June 1890. The place of birth was given as Foundry Cottages which, confusingly, was the name of at least two other terraces in the area; the actual address is 3 Argyle Street. Madge feared that because of her health and lifestyle she would be unable to give proper care to the baby so, having to return to her husband's side, left him to be raised by his grandparents. This then was the beginning in the life of a little red-haired baby, who in later years would become one of the world's most famous comedians – STAN LAUREL.

When he was sixteen months old Stanley was taken to be with his mother, who was now living at 66 Princes Street, Bishop Auckland. It wasn't long, though, before he was returned to his grandparents' home in Ulverston, as Madge's skill and assistance in refurbishing the interiors of Arthur's two current theatres was far more valuable to her husband than her services as a mother.

The *Theatre Royal*, Consett, with Arthur Jefferson as lessee and manager, was reopened at the beginning of the 1892 Autumn season, followed two months later by the unveiling of the year-long transformation of the

Theatre Royal, Bishop Auckland, renamed *The Eden* (see page 267). One year later, Jefferson bought the lease for the *Theatre Royal* in Blyth where, as with the theatre at Bishop Auckland, its re-establishment as a prestige venue was regarded as a serious attempt to lift the depression which existed in the town.

Whilst 'A. J.' (the most familiar of Arthur Jefferson's forms of address) was keeping his theatrical image alive, Madge had temporarily to forsake hers when in December 1894 her only daughter, Beatrice Olga, was born. Stanley was brought over for the christening and, in a double ceremony, was received into the church. This might also have been the time he finally left his grandparents to go and live with his parents in Bishop Auckland.

From what has been written so far, one can see that those accounts containing all the old clichés about Stan Laurel's being born in a trunk and carried from theatre to theatre, were total fabrication. For the first five years of his life, the roar of the crowd and the smell of the greasepaint could not have been further from him. His influences had been from a very stiff and formal, elderly couple, who were keen to ensure that the profession of their son-in-law would not rub off on their daughter's child. Instead of being cast into the environment of bars, bawdy ladies and backstage gossip, Stanley had been kept under the strict disciplinarian eye of his grandfather and, whenever he misbehaved, had been whacked with a leather strap, or banished to the gloom of the out-house.

A. J.'s next acquisition was the *Theatre Royal* in North Shields, Tyneside, for which he staged a grand re-opening in August 1895. Within just a few months, A. J.'s talents as manager, producer, writer and comedy actor were to become firmly established in the minds of all his patrons, as the *Shields Daily News* of 31 December will testify:

> Last night the house at Mr Jefferson's cosy theatre, was crowded in every part to witness a new production by the popular lessee, entitled *The Orphan Heiress*. Mr Jefferson himself undertakes one of the characters, that of 'Ginger', and is responsible for most of the fun. His eccentricities and comicalities were very entertaining, and appealed to the risible faculties of the audience. We also see Mrs Jefferson (Madge Metcalfe – a Shields' favourite), prominent in the cast, and she proved herself an able exponent of the part allotted to her.

By October 1897 the Jeffersons were themselves living in North Shields, at Gordon House, 8 Dockwray Square. Here Stanley spent what he was later

THE NORTHERN
Fine Art Photo Co.

TURNBULL'S BUILDINGS,
MARKET PLACE,
BLYTH.

After a poor start in life, the weakly baby grew into a beautiful child.
(By kind permission of Nancy Wardell.)

to describe as the happiest days of his life. As well as Dockwray Square being his play area, he was also schooled in a kindergarten in the basement of one of the houses. His next place of education was a private school called Gordons, in the neighbouring town of Tynemouth, after which (according to letters written by Stan in his retirement years)

> I was sent to boarding school in Tynemouth. I believe it was called Tynemouth College, the reason my folks had me board there was due to my always being in mischief & trouble at home, like setting fire to the house, (accidently of course) & falling into a barrel of fish guts in my best Sunday suit on the fish quay near the 'Wooden Dolly', again having my Sunday-best Eton suit ruined, when a local street urchin hit me with a soot bomb on my way to a birthday party, Drinking Gin (thought it was water) got cockeyed & many more escapades too numerous to mention. Think this was the forerunner of my film character!

Just when Arthur Jnr had found happiness, and Arthur Snr's empire was flourishing, the family was struck by the tragedy of the loss of Madge's newly-born son, Sydney Everitt, who died aged only five months. How lucky for the world that Madge had been so prudent at Stan's birth. The following year her heartbreak was somewhat softened when she bore another son, Edward Everitt (Teddy).

In May 1900, news headlines worldwide were proclaiming the 'Relief of Mafeking'. Mafeking – a small town in South Africa, under British protector-ship during the Boer War – had been besieged by the Boers for over seven months before finally being freed. This caused widespread celebrations, especially throughout Britain, which rivalled those for any coronation or royal wedding. Commencing on Saturday morning, 19 May, work was suspended and people of all ages filled the streets. Everywhere was alive with colour; flags flew from every window ledge; and red, white, and blue bunting criss-crossed the streets.

In North Shields, three bands and a choir paraded in Dockwray Square. Swelled by hundreds of local residents, the whole entourage moved in procession out of the square and through the main streets of the town. For his enterprise in leading the pony on which was seated 'Lord Roberts', one young showman was to receive the first of thousands of articles written about him throughout his life.

Stan Jefferson (standing) and pal (Walton or Davidson) prior to the 'Relief of Mafeking' celebrations. Dockwray Square. Inset: Roland Park as 'Lord Roberts'. 19 May 1900.

(By kind permission of Jefferson Woods.)

A conspicuous feature was seen at the head of the procession. Master Roland Park attired in full regimentals representing Lord Roberts, and mounted on a pony, was the central figure; he was attended by Masters [Stanley] Jefferson, Walton and Davidson attired in the uniform of the Imperial Yeomanry, and they made a perfect little picture, which excited much comment.

(Shields Daily News.)

That evening every house in the borough was illuminated, and in Dockwray Square the residents assembled to watch a mock battle between a hundred soldiers of the Civil Imperial Volunteers. This was followed by a huge bonfire and firework display, and dancing until the early hours.

During 1899 A. J. had been fully occupied with building a new theatre near the site of the old *Theatre Royal* in Blyth, for which he staged a grand opening in February 1900. By July of that year Jefferson was showing projected moving 'living-pictures'. These were short subjects, about two hundred feet in length, shown preceding the plays at his theatres. He had gone all the way to London to see, with his own eyes, the stupendous machine, the 'Royal Randvoll', which projected the films, and, suitably impressed, taken it back to the North – the first of its kind. 'And did the North like it?' asked the *Picturegoer* in a 1932 interview. 'Not a bit!' replied Arthur. 'And did Stan get excited?' ' Not a bit! I don't remember a single display of enthusiasm on his part. In that black box lay his future fortunes, and he wasn't even interested.'

A. J.'s empire was at its largest in 1901. To the lesseeship of the *Borough of Tynemouth Circus and Novelty Hippodrome*, and the *Theatre Royals* in Blyth, Wallsend, Hebburn and North Shields, he added the *Metropole Theatre*, Glasgow. This was looked upon with great excitement by those members of the local populace who were aware of his theatrical achievements. For those unaware, he placed the following newspaper announcement in the *Glasgow Daily Record*:

August 5th 1901
THEATRE METROPOLE, GLASGOW.
Ladies and Gentlemen, – Having secured a long lease of this
Theatre, permit me to assure you that I shall strive hard not only to
prove worthy of the patronage accorded to and so justly deserved
by my predecessors, but to augment same to the extent to which –

MR. ARTHUR JEFFERSON,

LESSEE AND MANAGER OF THE METROPOLE THEATRE, GLASGOW.

IT would be difficult to find a better example of theatrical enterprise than is apparent at the Metropole Theatre in Stockwell Street, Glasgow, since it came under the sway of Mr. Arthur Jefferson, the present lessee. Originally built by Mr. Baylis, and carried on for many years as a music hall, the house has always been a popular one with the people ; but a higher destiny was in store for it, and while it may have appeared a bold and venturesome stroke on the part of those who succeeded the Baylis family to determine upon and complete such an absolute metamorphosis subsequent events have amply justified the wisdom of the undertaking. Altered, re-arranged, and brought thoroughly up-to-date in every particular, the Metropole is one of the most comfortable and capacious temples of the drama in Scotland. Quite recently the whole interior has been again overhauled, and the auditorium fresh from the hands of the decorators, Messrs. J. and R. Anderson, of Bath Street, Glasgow, improved in a manner beyond recognition, the style of treatment and harmony of colours being in every instance both appropriate and artistic.

"In 'London Day and Night,' which is being performed at our local theatre by the author's No. 1 company, there are many features that do not fail to give the utmost satisfaction and pleasure. Humour and pathos are admirably blended, and whilst the latter is not too painfully evident the former is not overdone. At the same time the plot is arranged in such a way as to allow for the enactments of numerous thrilling incidents and *denouement*, and though it is complicated as melodramatic plots usually are its leading movements can be easily followed by the unsophisticated playgoer."

To sum up Mr. Jefferson's conquests in the theatrical world would fill a goodly volume, so we must be content with a mere summary of the leading points in a career of undeviating energy and usefulness which may serve to convey some idea of "the man and his work." He has entered upon his seventh year of management of the Theatre Royal, North Shields, lessee and manager of the Theatre Royal, Wallsend, New Theatre Royal, Hepburn, and New Theatre Royal, Blyth, which latter was erected at a cost of £14,000, and prior to this he was lessee of the old Royal in that town for a period of eight years. Mr. Jefferson is also proprietor of the Borough of Tynemouth Circus and Novelty Hippodrome, and managing director of the North British Animated Picture Company. As Captain Slingsley remarks

MR. ARTHUR JEFFERSON.

MRS. JEFFERSON.

Since the advent of Mr. Jefferson some weeks ago, it became quite evident that his intention was to maintain for the Metropole the very highest standard of excellence, and in this he has eminently succeeded by securing the leading London and Provincial Touring Companies in one continuous line of succession. This, added to his energetic and skilful management and the strong influence of his own personality and experience in the professional world, have crowned the undertaking with unparalleled success, and for this alone we feel constrained to add the whole theatre-going population of the west of Scotland owe him a debt of gratitude. Of Mr. Jefferson it may truly be said : "He came, saw and conquered" ; but, like Peter the Great, his unimpaired energies are still seeking for further outlet and other worlds to conquer. As a playwriter and author he has already made a name for himself, and those two well-known plays at present on tour, "The Orphan Heiress" and "London by Day and Night," are the creation of his pen. Of this latter we might quote a short extract from the *Rochdale Times* of 11th July last.

in the *Yorkshire Sport*, "A truly wonderful man is this Mr. Jefferson. He has just opened another theatre in Glasgow, in Stockwell Street. I may inform my Bradfordians who are visiting the Exhibition—this being his fifth so far—he is only forty years of age, and the author of the 'Orphan Heiress' and many other dramas."

Mr. Jefferson is ably assisted by his good lady, under whose supervision the decorations have been so handsomely carried out in the Metropole this summer. We have much pleasure in including their photos in our "Portrait Gallery," and wishing to the pair a long career of happiness and prosperity.

Victualling Trades' Review, *15 August 1901*
Articles on Arthur Jefferson are numerous, but acknowledgement of Madge's contribution to one of her husband's enterprises is an extreme rarity.
(Courtesy of the British Newspaper Library.)

after a fair trial – you may consider my efforts are entitled.
My Respectful Compliments
ARTHUR JEFFERSON

A. J. left the *Metropole* in the hands of an acting manager, and continued to run his businesses from North Shields. Late the following year the Jeffersons moved from Dockwray Square to Ayton House, a substantial property on the edge of North Shields, where they were to stay for two and a half years. As some compensation for Stan's disappointment in having to leave Dockwray Square, A. J. had his stage-hands build a theatre in the attic of their new home. This allowed Stan to carry out his ambition to run his own repertory company, and acted as a social gathering place for all the family, including cousins Mary and Nellie Shaw. Nellie recalled: 'Stan used to play the drums – not very well – and this served as the orchestra.' The project designed to enable our subject to learn his craft from an early age was, however, short lived. During one play an oil lamp was accidentally kicked over, and a fire started. Luckily, it was soon contained, but A. J. decided the theatre should be closed.

Stan soon found an audience elsewhere. While attending the King James I Grammar School, Bishop Auckland (January 1902 to July 1903), he learned to his delight the perks one can receive from the art of making people laugh. Most comedians will tell you that the way they escaped being bullied at school was by keeping their would-be attackers amused. This also pays dividends with teachers, as they are unlikely to punish a child who enlivens the dull routine of school existence with genuine amusement. Stan was soon recognised as having this quality, and his services as an entertainer were sought after by pupils and masters alike. In this instance, though, his popularity went against him as A. J. felt that Stan wasn't learning enough, due to the teachers' leniency, and had him transferred to Gainford Academy.

In 1905 the Jeffersons moved to Glasgow, because (Arthur said) of Madge's ill-health. A. J. left his North East theatres in the hands of acting-managers, and concentrated on running the *Metropole*. The Jeffersons' first address in Scotland was Buchanan Drive, Rutherglen, followed (it is thought) by a move to 185 Stonelaw Road. Stan's education again suffered, but yet another move – from Stonelaw High School, Rutherglen, to Queen's Park Secondary – proved futile, as he was forever playing truant. One of his hideaways was an old shed in Rutherglen, where he would play-act with other members of the entertainment troupe run by his friend, Willy Walker.

When Stan left school, A. J. put him in full-time employment at the *Met.*' There, often finding himself on stage in front of a deserted auditorium, Stan would imagine himself to be one of his idols: Dan Leno, George Robey, or Tom Foy. Finally, during one such enactment, Stan decided he had had enough of all this pretence, and determined to launch himself as a comedian. He spent several weeks building up an act and then, unknown to his father, gave himself a couple of tryouts at the nearby *Britannia Theatre*, of which the *Victualling Trades Review* said, 'The Britannia, the oldest music hall in town, presents a bill of fare equalled by few. Their amateur night every Friday is held in great repute by budding Dan Lenos.'

On about the third occasion, when he again sneaked out of the *Metropole* to go to the *Britannia*, Stan was keener than ever to avoid being caught by his father, for in a parcel under his arm was a pair of his father's check trousers, cut down to fit Stan; a long frock coat, also A. J.'s; the cover off his father's umbrella, which had been fastened to a cane to make a comic gamp; and a stick of red grease paint. The latter was for painting Stan's nose red, of which he said, 'You couldn't be funny in those days, unless you had a red nose.' As if the contents of the parcel weren't causing him enough worry, the thought of appearing at the *Britannia* was even worse. All comedians get attacks of nerves before a show but, like electrical impulses, they usually discharge from the comedian once he is at ease with his audience. Stan's nerves, however, were to remain with him for the duration of his act, for there, standing at the back of the room, was no less a person than his father.

Chapter Two

Solo - So low

STAN had obviously overplayed his hand, for it needed no Sherlock Holmes to locate him that night. A. J.'s suspicions would have been aroused as to his recent Friday-night disappearances, and a casual word with Madge or the proprietor of the *Britannia*, A. E. Pickard, would easily have solved the mystery.

The *Britannia Theatre of Varieties*, to give it its full title, was situated on the first floor of a four-storey entertainments complex known as the *Panopticon*. As the latter name would suggest, the building incorporated the widest spectrum of attractions, including wax tableaux; a gypsy palmist; bioscope pictures; slot machines; electric rifle-shooting machine; a zoological collection of live animals; roof gardens; an American museum; and a freak show which, at various periods, boasted such curiosities as The Bear Lady, The World's Fattest Boy, and The Armless Lady Midget. Opening hours were 6 a.m. till 10 p.m., and admission was a mere 2d. If the exhibits weren't enough to justify the entrance fee, consider that there were four shows daily from a music-hall revue company.

Stan managed to stay coherent during his act, and resisted the temptation to flee the stage. More importantly, whether due to sympathy or talent, he received a good round of applause from the audience, after which, in his own words:

> I removed my make-up and rushed back to the *Met'* to hide from my father's wrath, but he was already there. He called me into his office

*The Panopticon, photographed in about 1898, incorporating, on the first floor, the
Britannia Music Hall. Lessee: A. E. Pickard, 1906–1920.*
(By kind permission of Strathclyde University Archives.)

where, for what seemed like several minutes, neither of us spoke.
Finally he glanced up at me and said, 'Not bad, son, but where on earth
did you get all those gags?' Fearfully, I told him the whole story and

waited for the storm to burst. Slowly, he rose to his feet, 'Have a whisky-and-soda?' he asked quite casually. At first I could not believe my ears, but when it dawned upon me I seemed to grow six inches in as many seconds. My boyhood was behind me – dad was accepting me as a man! Then I did the silliest thing – I burst out crying.

Putting his arm around me he led me into the theatre bar and, with eyes glistening, introduced me to his friends as 'My son, Stan – the new comedian'. Was I proud? I still think it was the greatest moment of my life.

That the young Jefferson emerged unscathed from this traumatic evening, made it one of the most significant occasions in the development of Stan Laurel, the comedian. Experiencing, in front of his father, public humiliation from the usually derisive audience would have caused irreparable damage to the boy's ego, and halted progression into the next stage of his metamorphosis. As it was, A. J. now knew that his son was against following in his footsteps as a theatre manager, and was set on touring the halls – a profession he had hoped Stan would avoid after being warned of all the pitfalls and heartaches involved.

Jefferson senior may also have been aggrieved that his son was leaving the drama theatre to go into Music Hall.[1] Drama had a long history and was socially acceptable at most levels; Music Hall, however, was a fairly recent entertainment form, and could scarcely be called cultural. Its roots lay in the pubs of London in the early nineteenth century, and it was to be as late as 1912, only after the first *Royal Variety Command Performance*, before it was considered to be truly legitimate. Up until then it was frowned upon by the Church and Establishment alike. Also, audiences in the early music halls, where some of the venues were little more than taverns, drank throughout the evening and were thus unable to appreciate the finer points of quality entertainment.

Accepting that Stan was determined to pursue his career in this medium, his father decided it was better to get him off to a good start than to make him stumble at the outset, and used his status to obtain for Stan an introduction into the Levy and Cardwell Juvenile Pantomime Company. Putting someone on a team does not guarantee their keeping their place, so Stan would still have to prove his worth if he were to stay. This he did for

---

1   Later to become known as 'Variety' and, in America, as 'Vaudeville'.

two Christmas seasons, his first one being in 1907 in the pantomime *Sleeping Beauty* (see page 268).

In this production the scene opens upon a nursery. A small boy (twelve-year-old Wee Georgie Wood) is sitting up in bed, surrounded by several mechanical toys. A nurse is by his bedside reading to him the story of Sleeping Beauty. The boy falls asleep, and in his dream his toys come to life. One of these was a golliwog, behind the black face of which was one Stanley Jefferson. Even in this guise, the comic genius of the young Jefferson could not be stifled, and his natural talents not only shone through, but actually competed with the tough competition of Wee Georgie Wood's comedy spots, and the well-polished routines of senior double acts The Brothers Armstrong, and Graham & Barron. Confirmation of this is contained in the review in *The Stage* for *Sleeping Beauty* at, among other venues, *His Majesty's Theatre*, Carlisle, which acknowledged:

> Jack Adamson and Stanley Jefferson caused considerable laughter as the two golliwogs 'Julius Caesar' and 'Ebeneezer'.

Trixie Wyatt, who was in the cast, added, 'Stan was as daft off-stage as on'.

It would appear that Stan's talent for scriptwriting had already surfaced at this early stage in his career as, on 16 April 1908, Arthur Jefferson placed an advert in *The Stage* informing readers about the five sketches he and his son had written (see page 271), and that one of them, *Home from the Honeymoon*, was shortly to go on tour. In *Home from the Honeymoon*, two tramps enter a house which is temporarily empty whilst the owner is away on holiday. When the owner returns home early and calls the police to have the tramps evicted, they try to convince the policeman that the owner is a lunatic, and should be taken away and locked up.

This piece of farce was to prove invaluable to Stan. Instantaneously, it promoted him to working the number one circuit of theatres in the country, then, much later, it did wonders in establishing his credibility as a film-maker, both in front of and behind the camera, as the basis of one of the earliest Laurel and Hardy films, *Duck Soup*. When, a few years later, *Duck Soup* was remade as a 'talkie' (*Another Fine Mess*), Jefferson Jnr received a third bite of the cherry, even though credit for the original storyline was given to his father.

Home from the Honeymoon was long thought to have been a play, but it was, in fact, a short sketch and, as such, was performed as one of several turns on a music-hall bill. The *Leicester Daily Mercury* said of it:

Good comedy sketches are always acceptable, and that introduced by Mr Arthur Jefferson's Company, *Home from the Honeymoon*, is excellent. It is smartly written, and last night's audiences thoroughly enjoyed the many comical situations with which the sketch abounds.

Stan joined *Home from the Honeymoon* towards the later end of its tour, August 1908 (see page 271), after leaving a company touring with *The Gentleman Jockey*. Here, whilst playing the *Stoll-Moss Empires*, he wasn't surrounded by drunken louts who would as soon pillory him as applaud, but was able to perform to nice people, who had paid good money to sit in comfort and be entertained. Secondly, although taking only a minor role, this is where he would have first begun to feel exactly what kind of performer he wished to become. Here our apprentice stage performer was trained, not to the use of the risqué joke and the bawdy song, but, to observe and practise the art of the comedy character – his true forte. An audience of several hundred listening to every word and reacting to every expression of the players on stage, could not help but work wonders on the ego of one so impressionable.

Just as Stan seemed to be heading in the right direction, he was knocked sideways by the death of his mother (1 December 1908). Madge had been ill for quite a while, but now that she was gone A. J.'s domestic standards were seriously questioned. Being able to manage theatres is one thing, but being able to run a household and bring up children is quite another. So, after the funeral, it was felt best that Teddy be removed from the Jeffersons' home at 17 Craigmillar Road, and be looked after by his Aunty Nant and Uncle John (Shaw).

Aunty Nant was Madge's sister Sarah Ann, 'Nant' being a distortion of 'Aunt', which she inherited when the baby Stanley could not pronounce her name properly. After Sarah married John Shaw, she continued to live in her hometown of Ulverston, where she bore him six children, the two oldest of whom, Mary and Elsie, were Stan's playmates during his earliest upbringing and the times he spent holidaying in Ulverston. But then, in 1906, the Shaws moved to Batley, Yorkshire, near John's hometown of Dewsbury, where they were shortly followed by Madge's parents who set up home in a house opposite, in Lady Ann Road. In 1907 the two families merged to live as one eleven-strong family in a large house at South View, Soothill; but then, needing a bigger house, all moved in 1908 to 85 Warwick Road. But, no matter where they were, Stan always found time to go and visit them, and thus they were able to stay such a close family.

Immediately after his mother's funeral, Stan had to hide his grief and go into rehearsal with the Levy and Cardwell Company for their 1908 Christmas pantomime, *The House that Jack Built* (see page 272). Though again given only a small role, Stan continued to shine. The story was part nursery rhyme, part fantasy, based on 'The Old Woman Who Lived in a Shoe', but managed to inject some topical humour about the usage of the 'modern day' motor car. *The Stage* at the *Theatre Royal*, Castleford credited:

> Levy and Cardwell's Company are proving a good attraction. The company give an excellent all round performance and the piece is well mounted . . . Mr Stanley Jefferson and Mr Ireland Cutter as 'Harold' and 'Percy', contribute greatly to the fun.

And from the *Theatre Royal*, Darwen:

> Mr Stanley Jefferson and Mr Ireland Cutter as the motor tourists create much laughter.

A review in *The Performer*, from the *Dudley Opera House*, hints at further business in which the above duo were involved:

> The company contains some most charming and accomplished children who have been trained to a high standard of achievement, and the pantomime is one which, from its all-round merit, is sure to gain success. Messrs. Jefferson, Adams, and Cutter, are excellent in animal studies.

On finishing the pantomime run, Stan tried his luck around the music halls as a solo comedian, for which he billed himself as 'Young Stanley Jefferson – He of the Funny Ways'. In later life, though, he was to confess:

> My act was an unashamed imitation of the great Harry Randall – make-up, songs, patter and all – but as most of the audiences in the cheaper halls I was working had never seen the original, I was never accused of plagarism.
>
> I wasn't too successful. I'd had no experience and no material [of my own]. I hadn't 'found' myself. I just didn't know what kind of comedian I was. I guess I was at an awkward age. All I know is that I enjoyed being in front of the footlights.

Stanley Jefferson – 'He of the funny ways'.

George Robey, another comedian from whom he borrowed his 'funny ways'.

The phrase 'awkward age' sums up exactly what was wrong with Stan's act. Although a few boy-comedians were popular at that time, the trend has never continued. Audiences are not willing to take from adolescents what they will accept from an adult. A boy-comedian is automatically limited as to material; sex, wives, mothers-in-law, drink, etc., obviously being excluded from his repertoire. What remains almost always emerges with the little fellow sounding smug – and nobody likes a smart aleck. One critic was to say of Wee Georgie Wood, 'He's so clever, I could smack his face.' Comedians need time to mature, and are normally at their best around forty, at which age they can relate to both ends of the age spectrum without talking up, or talking down, to either. So Stan Jefferson was pursuing the right course for, through his trials, he ensured that when he attained forty he was indeed the master of his trade.

Some of his experiences he could laugh off in later years, but at the time tears were the probable outlet. Before starting on a life of touring Stan had always had his family around him. Now he was forced to live with people whose company he hadn't chosen; that is, the other acts in the shows. Many of these artistes were foreign-speaking, and those who *could* speak English weren't always willing to console a kid who was still wet behind the ears. Consequently Stan spent many a lonely and uncomfortable hour in his quest for stardom. One story he narrated about these times, went as follows:

> I was staying in digs in Manchester, and money was so tight we had to sleep four to a room. I was only a small boy and the other three were all fat, and very smelly, as they had a seal act. The seal slept in a basket at the bottom of the bed, and made a terrible noise all night. I paid the landlady an extra 2s. 6d. to put me in another room. I didn't fare much better here. Although I only had to share with one man, the room was much smaller. He was a trick cyclist, and had six bikes which took up most of the room. Every time I got up to go to the toilet, which was outside in the yard, I tripped over the damn things.

Realising that stand-up comedy wasn't for him, and wanting further experience as an actor, Stan joined the Percy Williams Company for a tour with *Alone in the World*. The story was about a deserted New York newsboy whose mother (when later married to her father's bank manager) takes an absorbing interest in waifs in the hope of eventually finding her child. Stan's description of the bank scene, as given to biographer John McCabe, was of a set which comprised (in direct misrepresentation of the advertising poster) 'a tiny box-set, a rickety table, a kitchen chair, and a cardboard safe'. The set for the opening scene sounded little better. The curtains opened to reveal a backcloth on which was painted a levee, spanned by a bridge which seemingly stretches to infinity. This was meant to portray the Deep South and, further to aid the illusion, an off-stage chorus can be heard singing, 'Way Down upon de Swannee Ribber'. That the bridge strongly resembled the Brooklyn Bridge (in New York), though, rather destroyed the illusion. Here, with his back to the audience, Stan was seen to be fishing, a role of which he recollected:

> I played an American 'hobo', if you please. Speaking through my nose with a broad Lancashire accent, I fondly imagined that I was giving a perfect impersonation of a true son of Uncle Sam. After a suitable length

of time, I had to put down my fishing rod and say: 'Wal, I guess 'n calculate I can't catch no fish with that tarnation mob a-singin'. (Pause) Gee whizz'.

I did a lot of guessin' and calculatin' in the part, but I'm sure the audience had to do a great deal more [guessin' and calculatin'] to discover what I was talking about.

In remembering this great line, and nothing else of the plot, Stan did himself a great disservice, for the *Todmorden Herald* revealed a second role he played, a role for which he earned high praise:

Mr Stanley Jefferson, as 'P.C. Stoney Broke' is a first-rate comedian and dancer, and his eccentricities create roars of laughter.

Despite other such excellent reviews for Stan and for the play itself – including the surprising comments: 'excellently mounted'; 'efficiently staged'; and 'over 3 tons of new scenery carried' – this inauspicious 'light drama' soon hit trouble. Booked on the prestigious Broadhead Circuit of north-west theatres, it was withdrawn after just one week, and scratch bookings had to be taken at short notice (see page 275). The efforts to keep it afloat, though, proved too much and, with the bookings disappearing fast, this 'Beautiful and Pathetic Play' sank without trace. To add insult to injury, the manager skipped with the receipts, leaving Stan to live out his greatest role to date – 'Stoney Broke'.

Things could not have taken a better turn for Stanley Jefferson when, next, he secured a place in the Fred Karno Company of Comedians. Karno was a showman of extraordinary magnitude. *His* name on billboards, rather than those of the players, was enough to fill theatres. When bookers asked of Karno 'Who's your star name?', he would reply, 'My name's up there, and that's good enough'. And how right he was! Karno also had a brilliant comedy mind, and, although he could never adequately put his ideas down on paper, his personal coaching always ensured the crafting of hilarious sketches.

In November 1909 this legendary promoter was producing *Mother Goose* at the *Grand Theatre*, Glasgow where, Stan recalled:

I presented my card with a request for an interview, and was promptly ushered onto the stage where a gentle-voiced little man came forward to meet me. 'Well, Mr Jefferson Junior,' he said, 'What can I do for you?' I told him I wanted to see Mr Karno. 'You're seeing him now,' he replied quietly. It was quite a shock and such a relief to find him such a pleasant, friendly man. Briefly I explained that I wanted a job as a comedian. 'Are you funny?' he asked. I told him of my youthful experience. He nodded. 'Very well,' he said, 'I'll try you out at £2 a week. Report to Frank ONeill, who is running my *Mumming Birds* company in Manchester. Push yourself forward, and I'll see you in London in a few weeks' time.'

Bewildered at the suddenness of it all, I blurted out my thanks and staggered into the street in a daze. I had achieved the height of every budding comedian's ambition – I was one of Fred Karno's Comedians.

Of his debut in *Mumming Birds* at the *Hippodrome and Floral Garden*, Hulme, Manchester on 6 December 1909, Jefferson Junior related:

I was given a badly-fitting dress suit to wear and told that I was to play 'a member of the audience' in a [fake, theatre] box, on stage, and told to study the methods of the other performers. In due course I was given a small part to play but, before I could make my first big appearance, I received a set-back. The wardrobe mistress told me, 'There's a new comedian just joined us from one of the other companies. He's taking over Mr O'Neill's part as "the drunken swell". I haven't a suit to fit him, except the one you are wearing, so I'm afraid you will have to take that off and hand it over'.

Reluctantly, I removed the suit and took it along to the new comedian's dressing room. I found him to be a pleasant little fellow with dark, curly hair, blue eyes, very white teeth, and a friendly smile. I took to him right away, and in the course of time we became close friends, sharing rooms together on tour. His name – Charlie Chaplin.

Karno had as many as ten different touring companies at any one time, some with duplicate productions, and it was common practice for him to pull out the lead comic from a show which was established, and transfer him to one which needed a boost. *Mumming Birds* [2] had Sydney Chaplin (older brother of Charlie), Billy Reeves, Jimmy Russell, Albert Weston, and

---

2   *Mumming Birds* was Karno's most famous sketch and ran on and off, in various forms, for forty-five years. The many variances in cast and production in this, and other sketches, make it almost impossible for historians to plot the movements of any one particular player, but the lists on pages 276–80 are as near as probability allows to an accurate plan of Stan Jefferson's appearances within the Karno Company.

the earlier-mentioned Frank O'Neill playing the lead comic role of 'the drunk' within a very short space of time – some concurrently. Research would suggest that Chaplin's debut in the principal role in *Mumming Birds* was on 10 January 1910, at the *Pavilion Theatre*, Liverpool.

The following week Charlie was given the lead role in the No. 2 company of a new sketch called *Skating*, written by, and starring (in the No. 1 company), Sydney Chaplin. Stan Jefferson is thought to have been with Charlie throughout its twelve-week run. The entire sketch of *Skating* was featured at a roller-skating rink. Part of the on-stage business (on a specially laid floor) was the dancing of the Lancers, on roller-skates; but it was the collisions and falls caused by the flirtation between the two lead characters which caused the biggest laughter. The *Sheffield Daily Independent* was respectful enough of the players' achievement to mention them by name:

> Fred Karno's sketch *Skating* is one of the funniest ever staged at the *Sheffield Hippodrome*. Not only are the crowded audiences kept in a continuous roar of laughter, but the members of the troupe – including Johnny Doyle as 'Zena Flapper' and Charlie Chaplin as 'Archibald Binks' – sandwich some excellent fancy skating in with their burlesque performance.

The *Sheffield Daily Telegraph*, too, was quick to give praise, where praise was due:

> *Skating* – an entirely new and original pantomimic absurdity on the latest craze – is typical of Fred Karno's sketches, with its broad, rollicking fun. The large house was kept in continuous laughter from start to finish, and the skating scene in the second act included a clever quadrille dance.
>
> Charlie Chaplin, as 'Archibald', was in great form, his tumbling and foolery being extremely funny. With Johnny Doyle as 'Zena Flapper', he was particularly nimble on his skates, and fell with a ludicrous freedom that all learners must have envied.

Undoubtedly, this sketch was the inspiration for the second reel of Chaplin's 1916 picture *The Rink*, with Charlie resuming his role and Edna Purviance playing 'Miss Flapper'.

Stan and Charlie were next put into rehearsal for a new Karno sketch, *Jimmy the Fearless*, the plot for which went as follows:

Jimmy, the son of a collier, stays downstairs after his parents have retired to bed, and reads a particularly bloodthirsty comic magazine (the 'Penny Blood' or 'Penny Dreadful'). Upon falling asleep in front of the fire, he dreams himself to be in 'Deadman's Gulch', a Wild West town. Entering the Dog's Nose Saloon, he becomes embroiled in a fierce gun battle, involving everyone in there, and promptly clears the place with his impressive gun-play. Discovering his 'tart' has been kidnapped he heads for the Rocky Mountains to confront her captor, Alkali Ike, and dispenses the outlaw gang with similar aplomb.

Next he confronts a pirate band, to whom he demonstrates his prowess with the cutlass, before returning in triumph with his fairy princess and a hoard of treasure and gold coins which he uses to keep his parents from the workhouse. His dreams are shattered when, next morning, his father finds him asleep in the chair, clutching the forbidden comic, and, placing the boy over his knee, gives him a thorough whacking.

A few days into rehearsals at the *Hippodrome Theatre*, West Ealing, an incident happened which led to Jefferson's temporarily ousting Chaplin as the company's star comedian. Stan explained:

> When we started rehearsals, Charlie was playing the leading part and I was just one of the cowboys in the background. Fred Karno popped in to rehearsals and didn't like Charlie's interpretation of the role. Thereupon, Charlie replied that he didn't like the part anyway, and that he would rather not play it. To my amazement Frank O'Neill immediately put me up for the part, and Karno nodded his assent.
>
> The opening night arrived. We were appearing at two theatres – Willesden and Ealing – and had to travel between them by one of Karno's private buses. The show was a terrific hit. I had to take five curtain calls. You can imagine how I felt. I was a 'star comedian', at last, and a Karno one at that!

Such an enthusiastic response was too much to bear for Chaplin who, after watching the sketch, stated he liked the potential of the part, and decided he would do it after all. Others might prefer to say he took the part after witnessing *Stan's* potential. Thus, with Chaplin in the eponymous role of 'The Boy 'Ero', it was back to being a lowly cowboy for Jefferson.

The review for the *Stratford Empire* ran:

As it stands at present, *Jimmy the Fearless*, is hardly likely to emulate the success of its predecessors. The best work is done by Chas. Chaplin in the name part.

And from the *Swansea Empire*:

Fred Karno's latest production causes much laughter. The name part is cleverly acted by Charles Chaplin.

And a third review, for the *Ardwick Green Empire*:

Somehow the performance is not so amusing as it ought to be, but the swank of the invincible hero makes one laugh fitfully.

Fred Karno, as well as being a great ideas man where comedy sketches were concerned, was a great one for finding and coaching unknown talent to the point of stardom. He believed that comedians should always be doleful, and able to command deep-rooted sympathy as well as laughter from the audience. It was the influence these ideas had on Stan which were to stand him in such good stead during his film career, and help model his character. As late as 1903 the company had been billed as 'Karno's Speechless Comedians', for music halls were licensed for singing and dancing only, and the spoken word was, unbelievably, not permitted. Although Karno did flaunt the rule, his sketches were almost totally mime, and when this law was annulled he began to include dialogue; *but* only to heighten the visual aspect, and not to act as substitute. This very policy was adhered to by Stan throughout his career in theatre and film, and thus, in years to come, when he was making silent films, the lack of dialogue in no way inhibited him; and when 'talkies' arrived, he did not start to create situations where the use of dialogue could be exploited but, from lessons learned, used it only for enhancement.

After a long run throughout the UK with *Jimmy the Fearless* (see page 279), Stan and Charlie played just two weeks in *The Wow-Wows*, a sketch concerning the setting up of a secret society amongst a party of youths on a camping holiday, and the subsequent initiation of the leading character, 'Archibald Binks'. For their next presentation, the two aspiring comedians were amongst those chosen to continue in establishing the name of Karno slightly farther afield – America.

Chapter Three

From Stage to Screen

AFTER missing the liner which would have taken them across the 'great pond' in comfort, the intrepid Karno Company[3] ended up on the British steamer the *Cairnrona*. This had two major drawbacks: it was a converted cattle-boat; and, instead of going direct to New York, their destination, was going to Montreal. From leaving Southampton on 22 September 1910, the passengers had to endure a rough eleven days at sea, during which time widespread sea-sickness made rehearsals for the sketch, *The Wow-Wows*, impossible.

Finally disembarking on 2 October, at least three days late, and taking a train ride via Toronto, the travel-stained company arrived with just enough time to open on 3 October at the *Colonial Theatre*, New York. Reviews for *The Wow-Wows* (re-titled, for American audiences, *A Night in a London Secret Society*) were disastrous. One newspaper described the sketch as 'a lot of blithering, blathering Englishmen', and advised people to stay away. They took the advice. Dropping the latter sketch in favour of the acclaimed *Mumming Birds*[4] (re-titled *A Night in an English Music Hall*) the players fared much better, and the initial six-week tour was extended.

---

3   Karno troupes had previously toured America with *Mumming Birds* in 1907 and 1908, and included manager Alf Reeves, his wife-to-be Amy Minster, and his brother Billy as principal comic. In total, *Mumming Birds* played eight years in America

4   The company had a third sketch, *A Night in a London Club* (subtitled *The Amateur Entertainers*), in their repertoire, which was very similar to *Mumming Birds*, and was sometimes performed in place of it.

The Karno Company aboard the SS Cairnrona,
bound for a new life in America, 22 September 1910.
Back: Albert Austin, Fred Palmer, Bert Williams, George Seaman,
Frank Melroyd.
Centre: Stan Jefferson, Fred Karno Jnr, Charlie Chaplin, Arthur Dandoe.
Front: Muriel Palmer, Mike Asher, Amy Minster.
Missing from picture: Emily Seaman, Alf Reeves, Charles Griffiths.
(Courtesy of the British Film Institute.)

The experience young Jefferson was gaining with the Karno Company, plus the ideas for gags, were to become invaluable to him but, at the time, the lack of a decent wage seemed too high a price to pay. So, along with fellow comedian Arthur Dandoe, he quit, and the two home-sick Britons took a train to New York and sailed home steerage on the *Lusitania*. Back in London they formed The Barto Brothers, and with a sketch written by Stan, *The Rum 'Uns from Rome*, began to find regular well-paid work. 'Then, like a couple of silly school girls, Dandoe and I had a slight difference of opinion – and our partnership fizzled out like a seidlitz powder,' confessed Stan. 'After that I was out of work for a whole year.'

In 1912, Stan joined a production of *The Wax-works*, which he soon left, and re-formed *The Rum 'Uns* with new partner Ted Leo. The double-act was short-lived as Bob 'Tubby' Reed offered them a place in his company.

When not distorting his facial features into comical grimaces, the twenty-year-old comedian touring America with the Karno Company revealed a handsome visage.
(By kind permission of Nancy Wardell.)

This consisted of Bob Reed himself, his wife and daughter, his son Jim, Ted Leo and his wife, a runaway youth, and Stan; who together became The Eight Comics. In Spring 1912 the troupe set off for a tour of Holland, playing the sketch *Fun on the Tyrol*. At the *Circus Variété* in Rotterdam (week commencing 25 May), a week of 'no play – no pay', caused by non-stop rain, led to the ladies' being sent home, and the men staying on to try to retrieve the situation. With no theatre work around, Stan took on a temporary job in a restaurant as a comic waiter where, for the price of his food alone, he entertained customers with comic business. Moving on to the *Palace* in Liège, Belgium, the depleted company were plagued by more bad luck, which left them stranded with no work, and no money.

Whilst Stan had been running around America and Europe, his brother Gordon had stayed on at the *Metropole* in Glasgow but then, in December 1911, transferred as acting-manager to the newly-built *Princes Theatre* in London. It was here that Stan turned up after scraping his way back to

England from Belgium, with money borrowed from an English comedian who had been appearing in Brussels. By the time he arrived he looked more like a tramp than Chaplin could ever have hoped. Calling on fraternal charity, he was asked the question which every comedian has been asked at some stage of his career: 'Why don't you get yourself a *proper* job?' Like most other comedians Stan's pride forbade him, and the belief that stardom was just around the corner led him to accept a stop-gap job at the *Princes* – a small part in *Ben My Chree* (Manx for *Girl of My Heart*). The production ran from 3 July to 7 September 1912, but Stan's part must have indeed been small, for in the programme he is not listed amongst the players. During the day, he earned extra money by typing scripts.

The next booking seemed to be financially sound, and was obtained when Stan bumped into Alf Reeves, now back in England with the rest of the Karno company, after their tour of America and Canada. In Leicester Square Reeves enquired of Stan, 'What are you doing, nowadays? Starring in the West End?', to which Stan quickly replied, 'Starving in the West End, more like it'. There and then Reeves offered him a pay-rise, and one week later, on 18 September 1912, Stan Jefferson set sail for America once again. This time the trip was from Southampton direct to New York and, being on the British White Star passenger ship the *Olympic*, was a much more comfortable crossing. Stan expected his stay in America to be for one season only. This actually became a life-time residence, during which time he was to plumb the lowest depths and reach the highest peaks.

The fellow actors on Jefferson's second trip to the States were Alf Reeves (manager), Mrs Alf Reeves (Amy Minster), Mike Asher, Arthur Dandoe, Albert Austin and Charles Chaplin, plus new members Edgar and Ethel Hurley, Ted Banks, Billy Crackles, and Whimsical Walker. With most of the cast having played America before, the company knew what the audiences wanted, so there was no initial hiccup. Chaplin again began to attract rave reviews and, in November 1913, was lured away by Mack Sennett to make films. With their star player gone, the Karno company folded.[5]

Seeing no advantage in returning to England, Stan decided to stay on and make a go of it. Enlisting Edgar and Ethel Hurley from the disbanded Karno company, Stan formed The Three [English] Comiques, for whom he wrote *The Nutty Burglars*, a sketch about two burglars breaking into a lady's

5   Although Alf Reeves was to become Chaplin's manager, and Albert Austin was to become one of Chaplin's stock players, their split from the Karno Company was yet a few years away.

apartment (almost certainly a version of *An Unwilling Burglar*, a sketch he and his father had written in 1908 – see page 271). After being accepted on one of the better circuits the act was revamped and the name changed, firstly to Hurley, Stan, and Wren, then to The Keystone Trio. The characters in the latter were an out-and-out steal of those of Chaplin and his assistants, Chester Conklin and Mabel Normand, who by this time were well known to cinema-goers. Stan seemed blissfully unaware of the lack of ethics in this, and in an interview in a 1940 *Picture Show*, is quoted as saying

> If imitation be the sincerest form of flattery then I surely proved to Charlie the depth of my admiration in my vaudeville take-offs of his clowning pantomime. Since I had played with him for so long a time, and since, as his understudy, I had learned to copy every trick of his movements and speech, I found it easy. Charlie admitted that I made a pretty good job of it. I should have, after seven [sic] years' study, shouldn't I?

Around 1915, after an internal disagreement had led to The Keystone Trio separating, Stan formed The Stan Jefferson Trio, with man-and-wife team Baldwin and Alice Cooke. This combination stayed together for two seasons, playing *The Crazy Cracksman* – a hybrid of Stan's two previous sketches. Although Stan had been the first to realise the potential in the Chaplin character, he wisely dropped the impersonation for the latest act, as so many others were now doing it.

Whilst touring, Stan met Mae Charlotte Dahlberg – half of an Australian duo called The Hayden Sisters. Being besotted with her, even though the girl was married, he started a relationship which was to last several years, and dropped the Cookes to pursue a career with her. The change of partner also brought about a change of name, and from now on Stan Jefferson would be known as Stan Laurel. With yet another burglar sketch, *No Mother to Guide Her* – in which Stan played 'Baffles', a burglar mistaken for a dentist – Stan and Mae Laurel hit the vaudeville circuit.

Whilst appearing at the *Hippodrome* in Los Angeles, Stan was approached backstage and asked if he wished to be in pictures. Receiving an answer in the affirmative, film promoter Adolph Ramish followed up his enquiry by financing Laurel in the making of *Nuts in May* (1917). A short series of films for Universal followed (unfortunately thought to be lost), with Laurel in the guise of 'Hickory Hiram', before a return to vaudeville with Mae. The next approach was from director Alf Goulding who, in May

Stan Jefferson and Mae Charlotte Dahlberg (his common-law wife) during their American vaudeville days as 'Stan & Mae Laurel'. The photographs were taken in about 1918.
(Photograph of Mae Dahlberg by kind permission of Brian Clarry.)

Stan to the Hal Roach Studios where he made five films, but was then released. Laurel's next spell in front of the camera was in three films with comedy star Larry Semon, at the Vitagraph Studios, after which G. M. 'Broncho Billy' Anderson made a pilot film, *The Lucky Dog*, to promote Stan to would-be backers. The 'heavy' in the film was none other than Oliver Hardy, but such was the briefness of the meeting that no-one had a chance to assess the chemical mix between the two that was so evident in later years.

Oliver Norvell Hardy, to give him his full name, was born in Harlem, Georgia on 18 January 1892. His father died while Oliver was still in his first year, and his mother, Emily, took over management of a boarding house in Madison. Six years and a few stops later, the Hardys took up residence at the *Baldwin Hotel* in Milledgeville, Georgia. Oliver loved singing and, no matter where he was during his upbringing, always found an audience to whom he could air his beautiful voice. 'At sixteen I made my first public appearance with a minstrel troupe, and managed to earn a few dollars,' related Hardy. 'In 1910, I started work at Milledgeville's first movie-theatre

– checking tickets and helping to clean the projector, and of course, singing in the evenings. Then I went on tour with a vocal quartette.'

One year of observing film comedies convinced Hardy he could do as well as any of the actors in them, so he set out for their place of origin – Jacksonville, Florida. He first found work as a singer in cabaret and vaudeville, and in the latter also found himself a wife, Madelyn Saloslien, who was the pianist in the pit orchestra at the *Orpheum Theatre*, Jacksonville. They were married on 7 November 1913, in Macon, Georgia. Whilst appearing at the *Grand Theatre*, Jacksonville, Hardy was contacted backstage by a representative of the Lubin Motion Picture Company and, like Laurel, was addressed with the immortal line: 'Would you like to be in pictures?' Said Hardy, 'I turned up at the studios in Atlantic City, New Jersey, rather fancying the idea of becoming a screen hero, but ended up as a fat villain in a modest one-reel Wild West picture. This was long before Hollywood had ever been heard of.'

The movie bug had bitten him, however, and he stayed with Lubin for two and a half years, during which he worked his way up to star comic. He also gained a nickname which was to stay with him the rest of his life and, although he was proud of his family name – in his own words, 'all of it' – he eventually succumbed to being addressed as 'Babe'. Next came a trip to New York with friend and fellow actor Raymond MacKee. Hardy, though, soon packed up and left, there being no work available, and went to Florida, where he made out by singing songs in theatres to accompany such newsreel footage as that of the First World War. Said Hardy:

> My friend MacKee then sent word from New York that he had obtained an engagement with a film company who were producing a twelve-reel series of 'Get-Rich-Quick-Wallingford' stories, for which I was [subsequently] used as 'comic relief'. This consisted mainly of my being the target of custard pies, and having my false beard painfully tugged. I did however learn the art of taking a tumble, which stood me in good stead for what was to come later.

On returning to Jacksonville, still 1915, Hardy sang in cabaret, then did film work with Vim Comedies. The greater part of 1916 found him playing in a series of films known as the 'Plump and Runt' comedies, with Billy Ruge – a partnership which foreshadowed that of Laurel and Hardy. In 1917 Hardy paired with Vim comedienne Kate Price, then played supporting roles with Billy West, for King Bee Film Corporation (1917–1918) and

Jimmy Aubrey (1919-1921). In November 1921 he divorced Madelyn, after a four-year separation, and within days married Myrtle Lee Reeves, whom he had met during filmwork. 'I was in drama, and he was in comedy, and so we met and were married,' she was later quoted as saying. Now regarded as one of the best foils in the business, Hardy became part of the stock company of highly-rated comedian Larry Semon, with whom he played the 'heavy', on and off, between 1921 and 1925, and made around ten films.

Whilst Babe remained in continual employment in films, Stan and Mae made only sporadic entries, so by far the greater part of the period between the making of *The Lucky Dog* and the beginning of 1922 the Laurels spent back on the vaudeville circuit. It took G. M. Anderson all of that time to come up with a backer for the series of films he then made with Stan, and released through Metro. Although Laurel had starred in the latter series, and was keen to stay in films where, in his own words, 'I didn't have to work seven days and seven nights a week, and could live like a human,' he was again forced back into vaudeville – a medium he had come to hate. He was grateful therefore when, in 1923, Roach recalled him and launched him in a series of one- and two-reelers. Within two years he had been released again, but almost immediately was picked up by film producer Joe Rock. Rock felt that Laurel's film career was being hampered by Mae, and helped him to encourage her to return to Australia. On the day the deed was done, Rock arranged a social distraction for Stan in the form of a young lady named Lois Neilson. This was no temporary distraction, for on 26 August 1926 the two were married.

Through a legal wrangle with Rock, Laurel was left unable to work in films. On hearing of his dilemma Warren Doane, General Manager at the Roach Lot, offered him a job as writer and gag-man; a position which Stan was happy to accept, as he'd never rated himself as a film comedian in any case. Of this sudden change in direction Stan was to say in a 1957 interview:

> I wasn't too successful as a [film] comic. They told me my eyes were too blue to photograph. There was a kind excuse. I didn't feel I was so hot myself, so I was very happy to get into some other end of the business.

Stan commenced work on the Roach Lot in May 1925, and a short time later, after he had shown interest in everything about film-making, was rewarded by supervisor F. Richard Jones offering to train him as a director. By 1926 Stan had co-directed a handful of films, including three with Oliver

Inside twelve months, Stan Laurel and Oliver Hardy had metamorphosed from the two solo actors above (1927), to the world's most famous double act, below (1928).
(Roach Studios.)

Hardy, who was now also working on the Lot. When, one day, Hardy was unable to turn up for filming, having badly scalded his arm, Laurel was reluctantly coaxed back in front of the cameras to fill the vacant role. Roach liked Stan's contribution in the film *Get 'Em Young*, and gave him the go-ahead to write himself a part in the next picture. Hardy had by then recovered sufficiently to return, whereupon the two of them inadvertently appeared in the same film, *45 Minutes From Hollywood*. For Stan Laurel and Oliver Hardy, the wheels of fortune had been set in motion. It was now only a matter of time! Further films ensued in which the two of them appeared, until, almost by a process of natural selection, the potential of playing them *against* one another was spotted and exploited.

Twelve months and just as many films later, Laurel and Hardy made *Hats Off* (August 1927). In this film appear for the first time the two characters who became so consistent throughout the next thirteen years in the Roach films and in their later years on stage. Gone are the false moustaches, wigs and costumes from their differing characters in previous films, and in their place was seen what was to become their regular clothing: Laurel's ill-fitting suit, spotted bow-tie, wing-collar shirt, and flat-heeled shoes; and Hardy's dark trousers, jacket, and the inseparable tie. The two of them have also permanently adopted their most famous of trade-marks – the hats.[6]

The Laurel and Hardy characters were almost totally believable, and surrounded themselves with almost totally believable characters; and, because the comedy of the screen Laurel and Hardy was based on the two characters and the situations in which they found themselves, and not on actual gags, audiences could easily relate to them. Their popularity grew rapidly and, even with the advent of talking pictures, their style of comedy was not hindered, but advanced. Here then were two men, now in their middle-age, who had gone from stage, to silent screen, to talkies, just as easily as a duck travels through air, on land and in water. By July 1932, through sheer audience demand, Stan Laurel and Oliver Hardy had turned out over thirty silent films and almost as many sound films. It was time to take a break.

---

6   'Twin bowlers' is a misnomer used to describe the headgear worn by Laurel and Hardy. Hardy wore an English-type Bowler, whereas Stan wore an Irish Derby, which is rounder, taller, and has a flat brim.

Chapter Four

A Few Weeks'
Golfing and Fishing

STAN had been over to England to see his father in July 1927, but since then had had no time off; so when it came to taking a holiday, England was an obvious choice. That Babe chose to go with him, though, when he could have gone literally anywhere in the world, speaks volumes for the high regard the two partners had for one another. After all, they had lived in each other's pockets for those five years, so one could be forgiven for thinking that the last thing they would want to do, would be to go on holiday together. But Hardy was also proud of the fact that his ancestors were British (see page 132) so, as he was fond of the British, and Britain in general, his desire to go there was increased. That Britain boasted many fine golf courses also had some bearing on the matter.

His affair with an attractive divorcee by the name of Viola Morse having recently been discovered, Babe thought that having his wife Myrtle accompany him on the vacation might help to patch things up, and save their eleven-year marriage. Stan, though, left his wife Lois at home, insisting 'She doesn't like crowds and travelling, and is not over strong, so preferred not to make the trip.' The truth was that the Laurels' marriage was on the rocks, and Lois could not face the ordeal of making the trip in order to keep up appearances. Also in the party were Dr and Ethel Falconar, friends of Myrtle's, who were to remain with them throughout the holiday.

As Stan and Babe understood it, the trip was purely a social call to the 'Old Country', where they could take in a few weeks' golfing and fishing. MGM (the film company Metro-Goldwyn-Mayer, who released the Laurel and Hardy films) had different ideas, though. Having themselves drawn up the travel plan for their rising comedy stars, they organised around it a massive publicity campaign in both Britain *and* America. Consequently, when Laurel and Hardy came to change trains at Chicago, on their four-day train journey from California to New York City, thousands of fans and photographers confronted them. At first they thought there was someone in an adjacent compartment whom the fans were seeking but, when the mob continued to clamour more and more for attention, it soon became frighteningly obvious that this wasn't the case.

Wanting to get away from the situation as quickly as possible, Stan and Babe fought their way through the swarm, to their connection for New York City. Once on the train, they had much cause to speculate as to the reason for the recent scene, and in the end may well have dismissed it as a publicity stunt, manufactured by MGM, to raise interest in the release of their latest film. The reason Laurel and Hardy couldn't believe that all the adulation was for them was that, as far as they were concerned, all they had done for the last five years was make short, supporting films for the main cinema features. In the Hollywood star system this meant they didn't shine very brightly. The public, though, had other views.

Convinced that the nightmare reception was over, Stan and Babe settled back and thought only of enjoying the peacefulness of the British countryside, and the hospitality of its people. Little did they know that their nightmare had just begun, and the sort of reception they had encountered at Chicago was to be repeated at every stop. Mob number two, on New York Broadway, was even bigger. The press were in force, and the presence of the two newly-discovered stars, plus the newsreel cameras, whipped the crowd to the point of hysteria. It took more than a little subterfuge, and a great deal of assistance from the New York Police, before Laurel and Hardy were able to board the Cunard liner the *Aquitania* and set sail for England.

Boarding ship did not afford them instant relief, as they still had to contend with the attentions of the two-thousand-plus passengers and crew – as did fellow travellers Douglas Fairbanks Jnr and his wife, Joan Crawford. After repeated appeals from the captain for the celebrities to be left alone, Babe came out of enforced isolation and joined in with the ship's entertainment. Amongst other invitations, he accepted one to view the ship's engines, and another to referee a boxing match. Stan, however, declined, and seldom came out of his cabin.

Ironically, an incident which could have had very dire consequences occured in the confines of Hardy's quarters. He related:

> Near Cherbourg I heard a noise above my cabin. I put my head out of a porthole to see what was amiss, and a heavy weight came down about three inches from my head. If it had caught me, I don't know what would have happened. At first I thought it was one of Stan's tricks, but the incident was too serious to be funny. It turned out that it was a depth-weight being lowered. It frightened me very much at the time.

On 23 July 1932 the *Aquitania* arrived at Southampton, England, to be greeted by the unbelievable, and totally unexpected, sight and sound of thousands of fans waving, cheering and whistling 'The Cuckoo Song'.[7] Whilst the crowd were showing their delight, and confetti was falling like snow, Laurel was running up and down the passenger deck shouting, 'Where's mi dad?' Hardy, meanwhile, was regaling some of the dozens of pressmen who had swarmed aboard, with stories of their exploits on board the *Aquitania*. These began: 'I'll be glad when I can get Stan off this boat. I have had a terrible time with him, you know . . .'

Shortly, Laurel returned to his partner's side, dragging with him an elderly, nattily-dressed gentleman. 'Babe, meet Dad,' said Stan. A. J. introduced the party to Venetia, his second wife. Whilst the comedians were still on board, the *Sunday Post* recorded the following quotes: 'After our holiday,' said Hardy, 'we go back to Hollywood to complete our contract, which still has about two years to run.' Then, contradicting a statement he had made only a minute earlier, Hardy continued: 'Stan has behaved perfectly on the voyage. He is a thorough little gentleman and the finest fellow in the world. Since 1927 when we first started to work together, we have never had a cross word.' Although the part of this statement concerning Stan's behaviour was said very much with tongue-in-cheek, the latter part, extolling Stan's human qualities, was straight from the heart, and Babe meant every word of it. Stan returned the compliment in an equally sincere

7   The Laurel and Hardy signature tune. Some know it as 'The KuKu Song'; others by the arrangement 'The Dance of the Cuckoos'; but the most favoured is 'The Cuckoo Song'. Stan himself said in *Ideas and Town Talk*: 'We call it "The Cuckoo Song". I don't think it boasts a name really.'

manner: 'Ollie is the kindest man I know. He wouldn't hurt a fly. It's a pleasure to work with him.'

On the dock Laurel was given an invitation, on behalf of the Mayor of Tynemouth, for him and his partner to be guests at a civic lunch during their forthcoming visit to Tyneside. He sent the reply:

> I shall be happy to accept it, I am looking forward tremendously to renewing acquaintance with Tyneside. I have almost forgotten what it looks like, but not quite. I expect that when I go there I shall remember people and places where I spent happy times in years gone by. I shall be delighted to be in North Shields again.

He also sent a message, via the *Sunday Sun*, to his friends in the North East:

> By the time you are reading this I shall be home! Only those who have been away from England for years realise how the Old Country tugs at the heart-strings. No matter how happy, how successful, you may be in new surroundings, your thoughts go back longingly to the friends you left behind. You want to see the old places and old faces again. I have kept in touch with several of my old friends in the North Country, and I am looking forward keenly to seeing the changes and developments that have taken place in the long years I have been absent. With me, of course, comes my great friend and great comedian Oliver Hardy.

Whilst the VIPs were in customs, Hardy was informed that the Minister of Labour had forbidden him to undertake any form of employment, paid or unpaid, during his stay in England. The decision was quickly over-ridden after the intervention of Sam Eckman, managing director of MGM London Pictures, who was on hand to take care of such formalities. Had it not been, Babe could not have made any personal appearances. He was shortly made to wish that permission had not been granted.

Having satisfied the pressmen and the customs officials, Laurel and Hardy had to fight their way through the ever-demanding crowd to board the train for London. Amidst further cheering, flag-waving and confetti-throwing, the train finally pulled out of Southampton docks, one hour late. Arriving at Waterloo station, the two bemused comedians were met by a similar scene to the one at Southampton, with over a thousand pairs of lips whistling 'The Cuckoo Song'. With forty pressmen moving in to take shots, and the crowd getting pushier and pushier, Stan exclaimed, 'What a recep-

Laurel points out his American partner Hardy, on the comedy duo's arrival at
Southampton aboard the Aquitania, *23 July 1932.*
(Note the uncanny similarity with the photograph of the 1947 arrival,
page 85.)

tion. I never imagined anything like this. If my old friends in the North Country are only half as enthusiastic, I shall be thoroughly happy.'

Four hundred porters had volunteered for duty at Waterloo Station but, even so, the pressure of the crowd was so great that the comedians became separated. Hardy couldn't figure out how it happened. He said he just climbed into a taxi and arrived at the *Savoy*, where only the hall porter was on hand to greet him. By the time Laurel arrived, and the confusion was resolved, there was no time for them to rest and freshen up before giving the press reception arranged by MGM. Special interest was held by those newsmen in attendance from the places Laurel and Hardy were expected to visit: Tynemouth, Newcastle, Edinburgh, Glasgow, Birmingham, Blackpool, Leeds, Sheffield, Liverpool, Hull, and Manchester. Asked if they had any business commitments in England, Laurel said, 'No, but we do intend to study audiences with a view to catering for them in future films.'

With the reporters gone, Laurel and Hardy were able to get to their hotel rooms to change. After dinner they retired; Babe to rest, and Stan to talk to his dad, and his sister Olga and her husband, who had now joined the party. The following day, Sunday 24 July, a *Daily Herald* reporter found them in Stan's room, still reminiscing.

> 'Come in and join the family party,' said Stan greeting him with a broad smile. 'I've been waiting for this reunion for five years, saving up all I had to say, and we haven't got past the old times yet. Ollie the great old scout has shuffled off and left us to it. He went to see the "Changing of the Guard" this morning. They must have heard he was coming and were afraid he might get up to something, 'cos they didn't have it,' he announced, and his peal of laughter bounced off the ceiling. 'So he's gone to the *Cheshire Cheese* [a public house in Fleet Street] to have a few cheeses. Reckon he's full of – er – cheese by now.'

As the tea-party continued, the reporter was replaced by one from the *Daily Sketch*, who recorded the conversation as follows:

> 'As for the boy, well . . . ,' said Mr Jefferson, then after a while, 'A good boy. A very good boy. Success hasn't spoiled him. It's something to say that.'
>
> 'He's still the same kid,' said his sister. The boy hung his head modestly. 'Seems to me,' said Jefferson, 'that comedians are born, not made.'

Stan Laurel grins, stepmother Venitia smiles, and father Arthur Jefferson stares blankly at the camera.
Savoy Hotel, *London, 24 July 1932.*
(By courtesy of John McCabe.)

'You said a lot, dad,' said the boy.

'I always go to see him in the pictures,' Mr Jefferson added. 'In our home in Shields in the old days I could see he had something in him. Always being funny, he was. So I made him a little theatre in the attic. Spent the day there, he and his sister Olga. Well what I say is, what's bred in the bone . . .'

Here, the account ends. The amusing observation about this conversation is the way the reporter punctuates it by referring to Stan as 'the boy' – he was forty-two at the time.

Later that evening, Stan and Babe accepted an invitation to go and watch Noel Coward's performance in his play, *Cavalcade*, at the *Drury Lane Theatre*. After receiving a standing ovation from a packed house as they took a bow from their box, the two comedians went backstage for a private party given by Noel Coward. Doug and Joan Fairbanks were also in attendance.

Monday's *Evening Standard* contained an advert for the *Empire Theatre*, Leicester Square, which read: 'Tonight, personal appearance of LAUREL and HARDY at 9 p.m.' As a consequence, two thousand people turned up, giving Leicester Square the appearance of Trafalgar Square on a New Year's Eve. Once again the media had instigated the formation of a huge crowd, into which the precipitation of Laurel and Hardy served as the catalyst for a reaction of hysteria. The whole crowd surged around the comedians' hired car and, in their enthusiasm to get a look inside, caused the door to become torn from its hinges. Inside, Stan and Babe were terrified that they were about to be crushed, for the car appeared to be giving them as much protection as a paper bag. They gained entrance to the theatre only with strong-arm support from a force of policemen. En route, Laurel glanced upwards to see his name in lights above the theatre entrance and remarked to the *Daily Herald* reporter shadowing him:

> Looks great, but kind of wasteful. But you should see the lighthouse in the graveyard at Ulverston in Lancashire where I was born. They put it up when I was a kid, a tombstone with a light on top. It was the Eighth Wonder of the World to me. Ever since then it's been my ambition to have a tombstone like that.

Once inside, after the showing of their film *Any Old Port*, the house-lights went up and the Boys walked on stage. The audience clapped and cheered for several minutes. Once the noise had abated, Hardy expressed their genuine gratitude for the great welcome they had received, whilst Stan interjected some cause for slapstick retribution. Asked, afterwards, how he felt about the welcome, Hardy told a *Daily Sketch* reporter:

> 'I did feel like crying. You see I often get that way. I'm not ashamed of crying, you know,' he added, 'I love to go and see sob-stuff films. I just sit there and cry and cry.'

On Tuesday 27 July, the newspaper radio-programme page announced:

LAUREL & HARDY TO BROADCAST TO-NIGHT.

Laurel and Hardy, the British [sic] film comedians will broadcast for the first time to-night. They are due to appear at the microphone at 10-35, and their performance will last only five minutes. What they talk about will be kept secret until then.

Anticipation of the on-air appearance was causing great excitement as, that week, a huge exhibition of radios was on at the *London Olympia*, and Stan Laurel and Oliver Hardy, being introduced 'live' into people's homes, would be good for publicity. The *Manchester Evening News* said prophetically: 'This will be one of the occasions when Televisors would be really appreciated'. 'Television', to misuse a line from one of Laurel and Hardy's films, was 'still in its infancy', but its predicted development was sufficiently known for Stan's father to speculate, 'Whatever next . . .? Pictures televised direct to our firesides?'

Although no recording of Laurel and Hardy's radio broadcast exists, it is known that Hardy sent greetings to a Mr Bert Tracey. This would seem rather a strange thing to do as, at the time, Bert Tracey[8] was watching Oliver Hardy through a plate-glass window in the studios. Bert's mother, however, received the greetings at her home in Manchester, where Hardy said he was looking forward to meeting her the following Tuesday. Tracey was spending the evening with Laurel and Hardy prior to travelling to the North of England with them.

In a later article in the *Manchester Evening Chronicle*, Tracey described the broadcast as follows:

> The BBC's magnificent new studios astonished Oliver. In spite of the self-possession an actor is supposed to have, the two stars looked like a couple of criminals about to be electrocuted as they seated themselves at the little table before the microphone. Some stuff was written for them to broadcast, but they just slung it away and carried on with one of their little quarrels.

The author surmises that Stan's 'contribution' would have been to interrupt Ollie's speech continually, with some comment as to when he was going to be allowed to say something – as he certainly did in a recording made three weeks later (see page 78).

Immediately after the broadcast Stan and Babe hurried round to the *Strand Theatre*, in Aldwych, where Ivor Novello's play, *Party*, was playing. Backstage they were introduced to members of the cast by Leslie Henson, and again met up with the Fairbanks, plus Ivor Novello himself. Through such late nights the Boys were now extremely tired, so spent Wednesday

---

8   Bert Tracey's connection with Oliver Hardy went back to 1914, when they made comedy films together with the Lubin Picture Company, in America.

morning resting. In the evening they officiated at the opening of the new Screen Artistes' Federation Social Club in Archer Street, after which they were wined and dined by their hosts. Having left early to join up with the rest of their party at the train station, they caught the overnight sleeper and pulled in at Newcastle Central at the unsavoury hour of 5.49 a.m. From there a car took them to the *Grand Hotel*, Tynemouth, where few people other than a keen posse of reporters and a couple of policemen were around. Hardy made no secret of his tiredness, and promptly cancelled the round of golf arranged for later in the day, adding, with an unusual tinge of bitterness, 'I'm just sleepy. Everybody wants me here and there. I'm just like a mannequin on a string.' As one of his main intentions in coming to Britain was to sample her golf courses, he must indeed have been fatigued. Laurel, too, was feeling the pace:

> 'This is supposed to be a holiday, but our tour of England has been extended so that we have to cut out Madrid and Berlin. It's good to be back in Tynemouth,' he yawned, 'but I feel I must have a rest. I'm going to bed.'

By now it was 8 a.m., but at 10.30 both comedians appeared for breakfast, where Stan's niece, Eileen Jefferson, who lived in Newcastle, was able to join her famous uncle. News of Laurel and Hardy's arrival had spread, and a large throng began to gather outside. Inside, a *Shields Gazette* reporter asked Laurel how he was enjoying his return visit to North Shields:

> 'I've just arrived, but I'm pleased to see the place again. Hardy and I came over for a holiday, but we have not had a moment to spare. All the time I was in London I hadn't time to go for a walk. I would like to have had the chance of a walk round the town to see some of the places I remember as a boy, but it cannot be done. We are just rushing about saying "Hello" and then we are gone again. I am looking forward to the luncheon and seeing the councillors. I want to see if I can recognise any of them.'

Breakfast over, the Mayor and Mayoress of Tynemouth, Alderman and Mrs J. G. Telford, arrived to escort them to North Shields Town Hall. On its arrival the mayoral car was surrounded by a crowd of several hundred people determined to get a good look at the local hero. A police cordon some fifty yards long, which had been holding the crowd at bay, snapped like a cheap necklace. Once again, as was now becoming all too regular,

The Boys meet fans, friends and staff at the rear of the Grand Hotel, *Tynemouth, 28 July 1932. Front, centre, is Mrs Roland Park with son and daughter. Third row, centre, is J. G. Ratcliffe, hotel manager.*
(By kind permission of Margery Craig, the little girl in white, front, centre.)

Laurel and Hardy's car was buffeted around like a toy boat in an angry sea. As soon as the police cordon regrouped and ringed the car, Stan and Babe emerged to tremendous cheers. Making their way through hundreds of outstretched hands, they reached the sanctuary of the town hall where, stepping out from his vantage point between the palms and potted plants which bedecked the corridors, a *Sunderland Echo* reporter asked Laurel:

'What do you think of Mr Hardy?'
'He's worth his weight in diamonds,' replied Stan.
Then to Hardy, 'What do you think of Laurel?'
Hardy's eighteen-stone frame quivered with mirth: 'Coming through that crush just now I was mighty glad to be Hardy, but if ever I wish I were anyone else – it's Laurel.'

These were not empty words, spoken to appease a reporter's curiosity, but were a genuine indication of the high regard in which the two partners held each other.

The reception in the mayor's parlour included amongst the guests: the chairman from each of the council committees; local theatre and cinema managers; two representatives from MGM; and members of the press; as well as many of the people whom Stan had known as a boy. After cocktails, the honoured guests were taken across the road to the Albion Assembly Rooms. On the way over they were again mobbed, despite a strong police presence. During luncheon Stan and Babe had constantly to swop their knives for pens, in order to sign the almost continuous stream of papers which were thrust at them, but both men took it in good spirits. In proposing a toast, the mayor recalled when Stan's father was himself a councillor (elected 1 November 1900). In reply to the toast, it was Stan who spoke first. In quiet tones he began:

> Mr Mayor, Aldermen, Councillors, and old pals, I do not know what to say for the marvellous reception. I was not born in North Shields, but I feel that I just belong here. I am proud to be amongst you all. I owe a lot to Mr Hardy for making it possible for me to be in this position to come here and enjoy your wonderful reception. I feel I want to thank everybody personally. God bless you all.

Considering that Oliver Hardy had no roots whatsoever in Tynemouth, and had been afforded its hospitality for only a couple of hours, his tribute would seem to be a bit over the top:

> Mrs Hardy and I want to stay here for ever. You have accepted us and made us feel at home. From the bottom of my heart I wish to thank you. I have never in all my life met with such hearty people, such kindly people, such courteous people, or such considerate people.

Earlier, Hardy had confided to a reporter, 'Mr Laurel wants them to give him the Freedom of the City, but if the Mayor of Tynemouth is wise, he will do nothing of the kind.' The mayor must have taken Hardy's advice, as the luncheon ended with no such ceremony. Feeling non-plussed, Stan sneaked out, and went round to Dockwray Square to survey, in solitude, the home which had meant so much to him as a boy. He was denied the opportunity, however, due to the vast volume of people who had anticipated his move and, though he did manage to get near the house, entry was totally out of the question. He was to say of his lost moment, 'It is a place for sentiment with me. I *belong* to Dockwray Square.'

Unable to get near his former home in Dockwray Square, due to the vast crowd awaiting him, Laurel visits another of his old haunts in North Shields (most probably Ayton House). 28 July 1932. (Roland Park)

Having been picked up by a police escort, which had had to fight a way through the crowd, Stan was driven to his other former home, Ayton House, where he was met by a much smaller gathering. For Laurel it was then back to the *Grand Hotel*, where his comedy partner and the mayor's party had regrouped. On schedule at 3 p.m., Laurel and Hardy made the short walk from the hotel to the *Plaza Cinema*. As soon as Stan emerged, everyone wanted to touch, kiss or shake hands with him. The Tynesiders' show of affection was unbounded, for they were meeting not just any film star, but one whom they regarded as one of their own people. Finally arriving at the terrace at the back of the cinema, the VIPs took their places on a platform specially built to allow the thousands of spectators to see them.

Of the two comedians Ollie was up first, and, after a rather dramatic speech in which he paced up and down the length of the dais, finished with

This view from the Grand Hotel, *Tynemouth, shows the verandah at the rear of the* Plaza, *where Laurel and Hardy were filmed on 28 July 1932.*

the words: 'I will be down amongst you all soon.' With the crowd now baying for him, Stan rose and, in trying to give back the love they were radiating, allowed himself to be pushed, pulled, kissed, hugged, patted on the back and have his hand shaken until it hurt. He signed autographs, and posed for photographs with whoever commanded his presence. When the number of people approaching him didn't seem to be decreasing, he addressed them thus: 'I love you all. I would like to shake hands with you all and say "Thank You". It is the greatest day of my life.' He continued, 'I shall always remember this visit to Tynemouth.' Then, obviously choked with emotion, he regained his seat and proceeded to wipe away real tears of sentiment, whilst his partner could do nothing to console him.

The ranks of people viewing from the terraces, staircases and the adjacent beach, were swelled by six hundred children who came under the charity banner of the Sunshine Fund. In a gesture which only two people with the warm, human spirit that Laurel and Hardy possessed would care to volunteer, they presented gifts (which had been donated to the charity) to all six hundred children. Laughing and joking throughout, Stan and Babe managed this mammoth task with unfailing grace and humour, and brought more pleasure to the children than if Father Christmas himself had given out the presents.[9]

9   Silent film footage taken of the events outside the *Plaza*, for showing in local cinemas, is still in existence (see also p. 76 and p. 302).

At 9 o'clock the two comedians were to be found doing a walk-on at the *Queen's Hall* in Newcastle, which was followed by another at the nearby *Stoll Picture House*. Outside both venues their car was again besieged, and they had to go through the now customary ritual of being manhandled. Laurel was somewhat compensated for his pains by meeting up with Horace Lee, former manager of the *Theatre Royal*, North Shields, of whom he said in a letter written in 1955, 'I used to call him Uncle Horace – a sweet guy. I had the pleasure of seeing him again in '32. It was an emotional meeting; both cried like kids'. Of *his* meeting with Laurel, the reporter from the *Shields Hustler* wrote:

> What struck us all was Stan's sweet naturalness. Success hasn't spoilt him, as it does so many people. He has not developed a swelled head, and his old friends in North Shields were glad of that. There is something sad to witness men who have succeeded in forgetting themselves, and putting on airs – airs that invariably do not become them. Stan is 'being himself' and we like him all the better for it.

After breakfast on Friday, while waiting on Newcastle Central Station, the Boys were kept busy signing autographs and talking to the press. Laurel left the following message for the people of Tyneside:

> 'God bless everybody. I love them all. Tyneside people do not alter – they are as good as ever.'
> Hardy joined in: 'You're all just fine. I feel that America could not have made me feel more welcome.'

Arthur Jefferson was on the platform, but remained behind to continue his own reunion with the people of Tyneside. His wife, however, stayed with the party. Stan hugged and kissed his dad and said goodbye. As the train pulled away, the pair leant through an open window and Stan waved his cloth cap whilst Ollie waved his straw boater. The people of Tynemouth responded by giving them a final rousing cheer. In Scotland, others had yet to stake a claim on the returning hero.

Chapter Five

Scotland for the Brave

RATHER than being an uncontrollable mob, the one-thousand-strong crowd at Edinburgh's Waverley Station could only be described as boisterous. For their restraint, they were treated to a series of antics from Stan and Ollie which resulted in the reception being the jolliest of the whole trip. But allowing the fans freedom of access to the celebrities soon proved too much, so the police force dislodged them from the crowd and escorted them to the *North British Station Hotel*. Inside, both heaved a sigh of relief, pleased to have escaped a bruising for once.

In the afternoon, following a well earned rest, the Boys took an unscheduled walk around Edinburgh Castle, and went unmolested. The evening, though, was to hold a very different atmosphere. With only one public appearance having been arranged in Edinburgh, it was not surprising that crowds had gathered hours before the comedians' arrival. The scenes which followed were caught admirably on film by local amateur enthusiast Alan J. Harpur.[10] As Laurel and Hardy's car pulled up at the *Playhouse Theatre*, pandemonium broke loose. People brushed past the police and ringed the car, jumping, cheering and waving. The fans on the opposite pavement, being denied a view of the comedy duo, surged across the road *en bloc*, prompting Stan and Babe to run for the entrance. The surging mass was then immediately scattered by mounted police.

10   The footage taken at the *Playhouse* is preceded by film of Laurel and Hardy's arrival at the railway station, and also of their leaving the castle.

Fearing their fans have followed them into the North British Station Hotel, *Stan and Babe try to escape over the rooftops.*

Meanwhile, the audience of three thousand inside the *Playhouse* was being kept happy watching the Laurel and Hardy film *Laughing Gravy*. When the house manager introduced Laurel and Hardy on stage there was deafening applause which lasted for several minutes. Filling in with comic interplay, the comedy duo waited for the ovation to subside, and then, when the vast audience became hushed, Hardy started his customary address. In his speech he told the people of Edinburgh how thankful he and his partner were for the wonderful reception they had been given that night, and also for the kindness they had been shown since their arrival in Britain. He went on to say, modestly, that they had been more than adequately rewarded for their little efforts to amuse, and continued:

When I come here again I'm coming in a big limousine, and I am going to 'do' this country properly, even though it may take about three months. I have so many 'Scotch' friends in Hollywood, and I want to see the country from which they came. This visit is all too short, but even so it has meant that we shall have to cut out going to part of the Continent, for which we sail on the 24th of next month.

Laurel then broke into the conversation with his plea to be heard, after which their business ended with Ollie booting Stan off the stage. All things being finished inside the *Playhouse*, Laurel and Hardy had next to work out an escape plan. Looking outside, the pair could see that the crowd had in no way diminished, so police reinforcements were called for and Stan, Babe and Myrtle dashed for the car. Four mounted police then accompanied them down Leith Walk, back to their hotel. By 9.30 p.m. the party was packed and ready on the platform at the Caledonian Station, where fans demanded Stan and Babe's constant attention right up to the last second before the train pulled away. Little did the Boys know, while enjoying the journey west to Glasgow, that this was the lull before the storm, and that in less than ninety minutes their lives, and those of many fans, would be in serious danger.

On 30 July 1932 thousands of people crowded into the Los Angeles stadium, USA, to witness the opening parade of the two thousand athletes in the Olympic games. Countless flags were being waved, and a choir of one thousand people sang the national anthem. The President's Dinner was attended by scores of film stars. On the eve of all this, eight thousand people were crowding around Glasgow railway station, to witness the attraction of just *two* celebrities. Countless flags were being waved, and a massed choir of eight thousand whistled the anthem – not the national anthem, but Laurel and Hardy's anthem, 'The Cuckoo Song'.

This reception was to grab bigger headlines, nationwide, than the Olympics, and the scene to greet Laurel and Hardy was one never seen in Glasgow before, or since. The Central Station was jammed solid with people long before the train was due, and even at that early stage extra police had been drafted in, for it was obvious there were going to be problems. The train drew in at 10.47 p.m. and the comedy duo could be seen standing in the doorway of a Pullman car. The efforts of the police could not prevent those at the front of the crowd from being squashed against the platform barriers, so action had to be taken quickly. A posse of seven policemen ringed the celebrities and tried to lead them out of the station entrance. Such was the pressure of the crowd, though, that an involuntary diversion was made to a side carriage-way. In trying to make headway, Stan and Babe were tossed in all directions, and around them women began to faint, or scream with fright.

As the visitors slowly edged down the alleyway there was a sudden alarming surge towards them from the crowd wedged in the narrow street opposite. So tightly packed was the alleyway that voluntary movement was almost impossible, and many were struggling desperately to escape being crushed. When people started getting hurt, there were serious fears of panic, and the air became filled with shouts and screams. Several people collapsed in a faint and had to be borne over the heads of the crowd to a place of safety, where they could receive treatment. Only the prompt action of the police in holding back part of the crowd helped to relieve the situation.

As the two comedians emerged from the side entrance of the station, a rush was made towards them by the crowd in front of the *Central Hotel*. It was then that, owing to the pressure of numbers, the stone balustrade skirting the wall of the hotel collapsed onto the pavement. The falling masonry bowled over several on-lookers but, luckily, formed in a heap which then prevented others from falling into the basement below. By a miracle only the two people trapped under the debris were injured, but the incident created a wild stampede for safety, and in this a number of persons were hurt. Fifteen minutes after Laurel and Hardy's arrival, the scene was one of devastation. Scores of people were looking around for shoes, hats or coats which had been lost in the mad crush, and others were being treated for minor injuries. Ambulances and police reinforcements had been rushed to the area, and eight men suffering from leg injuries were taken to the Royal Infirmary.

Meanwhile Laurel and Hardy had staggered into the hotel, exhausted and badly ruffled. Stan was deathly pale and looked as if he were about to pass out at any moment. Babe was first to recover and was soon up and wise-cracking. Stan, however, remained badly shaken, and made his feelings of panic known. Outside, so many people were still hanging around that the Boys decided it was best to show themselves. Stepping outside would have been suicidal, so they ascended to a first-floor window ledge, and spent a few minutes 'mugging' to the lustily cheering crowd below. Then Babe, with a slight gesture of his hand, signalled for silence, and, as his call of 'We'll be seein ya!' carried over the heads of the throng, he and his partner gave a final wave and slipped back inside the hotel.

Many pickpockets had taken advantage of the earlier situation, and five had been arrested. Laurel and Hardy had also suffered personal losses when souvenir hunters committed the effrontery of removing articles from their pockets. Stan was most dismayed to find his fifty-guinea wristwatch missing. Fortunately, Mr Hutchinson, the MGM tour rep., had had the foresight to hold the Boys' wallets, which contained huge sums of money. The losses, though, were minor compared with the knowledge that Stan Laurel and Oliver Hardy were now *very frightened* of the prospect of any more public appearances. The first 'reception committee' they had encountered, in Chicago, which they had thought was a one-off, had now become a recurring nightmare, and was getting progressively scarier. Describing the latest ordeal, Stan said, 'I was so tightly wedged in the crowd, I thought my last hour had come. I couldn't breathe, my clothes were torn, and I almost lost a shoe'. And at breakfast he reflected:

> I've never seen anything like it, have you, Babe? The scenes at Southampton and London were just Sunday School picnics compared with that rodeo at the station. Nothing that has happened in the States or elsewhere can compare with our experiences last night.

The Boys themselves were the first to admit that they could do without such demonstrations of appreciation. Even though the crowd's motives were for the pursuit of innocent curiosity, there was a definite risk of people being killed. Laurel himself was to state: 'Honestly, we escaped with our lives only by a miracle'. So, in the early hours of the morning, in a desperate attempt to instill a bit of sanity into their fans, they sneaked over to the offices of the *Evening News* and had the following plea inserted in Saturday's paper:

> Many, many thanks for your very kind welcome. We appreciate your overwhelming reception, but we would like to remind you that we are here on a joy trip for the good of our health. To those who were injured at the station last night, we offer our sincere regrets, and we hope they are now none the worse for their experience. We never expected anything like Glasgow's welcome, and our visit here will be all the happier now, if we are allowed to go around just like a couple of rubber-necks [tourists] on vacation.

The irony of the situation is that the organisers were worried that only a handful of people might bother to turn up at the station at that late hour.

After a limited amount of sleep the Boys managed to make breakfast, where they were joined by A. B. King JP, booker for the *La Scala* Cinema, who had come to take Hardy for a round of golf. A large crowd had gathered outside the hotel hoping to catch a glimpse of the two comedians, but, as Hardy left for Western Gailes Golf Course and Laurel went straight back to bed, they were left disappointed. Later Stan entertained an old friend, William Walker of Tollcross, Glasgow, and together they talked of their school days in Rutherglen, and of the joint shows they'd put on. Willy recollected that when Stan began to earn good money from films, he had written, 'Come out here. It's money for jam.'

On his return to the hotel, Babe, who had won the grand sum of half-a-crown at his game of golf, found Stan answering fan mail. One letter was from a schoolboy requesting a signed photo, and had three-ha'pence enclosed for return of post. The plea was cleverly tagged with words which would be a challenge to anyone's conscience: 'My Mum told me it's a waste of time writing, as you are sure to ignore my request.' Little did his Mum know that Stan's devotion in such matters was unrivalled, and that, during his showbusiness years, the number of letters he wrote and the photographs he signed were to total in the hundreds of thousands. Thus it was that this one request amongst many was fulfilled, and a signed photo, plus the original three-ha'pence, was sent by return.

The presence of the Glasgow City Police Force at that afternoon's visit to the *Scala Cinema* could hardly have been described as subtle. Determined to stop similar scenes to those witnessed at the Central Station, the police escort had swollen to fifty, backed up by six mounted policemen. The foot patrol was employed to link arms along the entire length of Sauchiehall Street, and to stop the crowd of over three thousand from breaking through.

The entrance was designated a no-go area by the ominous presence of two large police horses which, to assert their authority further, were actively prancing up and down on the spot. The stamping hooves must have conveyed the message to the crowd not to enter the reception area, as nothing so much as a toe came near. Laurel and Hardy also benefited from the presence of four of these magnificent creatures flanking their Daimler car, when, on their arrival at 4 p.m., twenty or thirty of the more foolhardy members of the gathering slipped through the police cordon and rushed the car. Determined to stand no such nonsense, the police brusquely swept the offenders back into the ranks. Other members of the crowd were now left in no doubt as to the treatment they could expect if they tried a similar manoeuvre.

With only a brief wave, Stan and Ollie stepped from the car and disappeared into the foyer, where the mood changed rapidly to one of decorum. After the Boys had been welcomed, and Myrtle, Venetia, and Mrs Falconer had been presented with bouquets, an attempt was made to sneak the party through the auditorium and into the board room. The ploy failing, and the comedians being recognised, resulted in some comedy by-play. Ollie, of the screen character, berated Stan for allowing them to be spotted, and Stan duly responded by pretending to burst into tears. The tears soon became real, though, when the film was stopped and the comedy couple addressed the packed auditorium:

> 'We have never experienced a reception like this, and we are feeling ...,' said Hardy. Stan interjected. 'Let me speak too,' he said. 'We want to thank you for this wonderful reception, I only wish my dad were here to see.'

Laurel then told the audience, in a emotionally choked voice, of the wonderful feelings he had on being back in Glasgow. He went on to relate his early experiences in entertainment in Glasgow, and his association with the *Metropole Theatre*. On attempting to close, choking on his sobs, he just managed to utter 'thank you,' before having to turn away. The audience, though, had noticed the tears, and there was an audible gulp in response. Rallying to his partner's aid, Hardy declared 'I'll cheer him up,' and the spell was broken by a fit of laughter from both sides. After a presentation of bottles of whisky to both comedians, Laurel broke down again when the vast audience sang the traditional Scottish song, 'Will Ye No' Come Back Again'. This is considered a huge compliment in Scotland, and, when Stan eventually came off stage, it was quite a while before he could recover.

That evening, the Laurel and Hardy party went on a 'mystery tour' with some of their friends. Although now free from official appearances, they had decided to stay over for one more day so that Babe could play golf on the highest-rated of the Scottish courses, Gleneagles. The following morning, determined to honour the saying 'When in Scotland, do as the Scots do', Hardy duly turned up bedecked from head to toe in tartan golf togs. To compliment the attire, he was given a tartan umbrella by Alex King, who was out to win back his half-a-crown. (Babe was soon to learn that Scottish people don't give up money easily.)

The gift was well received as, after Babe had tempted fate by saying, 'It will probably never be opened as it seldom rains in California', the heavens divided, and the brolly was in use throughout the game. The rain could not spoil Babe's enjoyment, though. He was living out one of his ambitions and, back in Hollywood, would be the envy of his golfing partners. Hardy's day was made even more memorable when a local golf-club-maker, George Nicoll, offered to make him a personalised set of clubs, with his features embossed on each one.

Stan, meanwhile, was back at the hotel chatting to James Reed, whom he first got to know back in 1912 when the two were in The Eight Comics. The company had been run by Jim's father, Bob 'Tubby' Reed, who had been a well-known British comedian. At the reunion, Reed informed Stan that Ted Leo, Stan's old partner from *The Rum 'Uns from Rome*, was now leader of a jazz band at the *Palais-de Danse*, in the city. When another venue, the *Britannia Theatre*, was mentioned, Stan's eyes filled with tears, and he recounted:

> My dad didn't suspect I had a hankering after the stage. He allowed me to go on occasionally as a newsboy or other small character, at the *Metropole*, but I used to slip along to the *Britannia* when those try-out nights were on. Mr Pickard[11] was the man who really gave me my chance on the stage, and I'll never forget him for it.

Monday morning found Laurel and Hardy on Glasgow Central Station, awaiting the train which would take them to Preston on the first leg of their journey to Blackpool. Concerning the crowds that were bound to be awaiting them, a tearful Laurel confessed, 'I'm scared to death.' Hardy was less pessimistic and, smiling confidently, said, 'We've had plenty of practice with crowds here. We'll just have to wait and see.' The scene that morning gave them no cause for concern. In contrast to Friday night's madness the cold light of day revealed the crowds to be politely reserved, and, as Stan and Babe walked across the platform, there were only polite comments such as 'There's Laurel and Hardy.'

In fact the cause of most of the gathering wasn't Laurel and Hardy, at all, but was the usual huge number of travellers prevalent on a bank holiday, plus train-spotters attracted by the Royal Scot on the line opposite. There were, however, some ardent fans around their reserved compartment, for whom Stan and Babe spent fifteen minutes signing autographs. On a happy

---

11   Stan once said that every time he visited Britain he contacted A. E. Pickard. If so, then Sunday evening would have been the most likely occasion, on this visit.

note, Stan got back his watch, after a girl had found it on the platform on Friday night and handed it in to the police. As soon as the guard's whistle blew, there was a rush of people to the comedians' open window to say farewells. With a station policeman running alongside the train to stop any further contact, one young wag shouted, 'Hey, Mr Laurel, where's your buzzing tooth?' (A reference to the recently released Laurel and Hardy film *Pardon Us*.) 'I guess I had that taken out long ago,' was the last thing anyone heard as the train pulled away.

Again, Laurel and Hardy's fate was about to be placed in the lap of the gods, and soon they would find themselves once more in the lion's den.

Chapter Six

The Prodigal Son Returns

To safeguard them from stepping once again into the snapping jaws of a giant crowd, it was decided to transfer the celebrities from the train to a car, at Preston railway station, sixteen miles outside of Blackpool. The first part of the plan went well and, on their arrival, Laurel and Hardy went unaccosted. Posing for photographs on the station's five-barred gate the two comedians told the pressmen they were having a great time, but hadn't seen much. The Boys were then presented with a huge cheese. This was an 'in joke' taken from the 1930 film *The Rogue Song*, in which Stan swallows a fly when taking a bite from a large cheese, thus emitting a buzzing sound every time he opens his mouth. Looking nervous, when a crowd began to gather, Stan made for the car and soon the motorcade of limousines set off for Blackpool.

Passing virtually unnoticed along the south promenade, the car then hit trouble, for the crowds which awaited its passengers extended from Central Beach right up to, and past, the North Pier. So many were gathered at the front of the *Metropole Hotel* that the manager requested police reinforcements. Some of these mounted the car running-boards but, even so, the drivers could not get into the hotel car park, so drove on and dropped off their charges at a side entrance. Once inside, the celebrities went straight to their rooms, where it was made clear to all guests that they were to be allowed to rest. The fans outside had other ideas, though, and, making their presence known, forced Stan and Babe into showing themselves on the front balcony. The huge cheers which followed attracted the attention of those on the nearby beach and promenade, who then joined the happy band. 'See you tonight,' Hardy informed the crowd. Stan nodded in agreement, and the two returned inside for a belated sleep, while police remained on guard around the hotel, to ensure that their peace wasn't broken further.

Of their thoughts on Blackpool, Hardy later informed an *Evening Gazette* reporter:

> This is my first visit to England, and believe me, I've had such a wonderful reception, I wouldn't mind living here always.

Stan said:

> I have never been to Blackpool before, though I have always wanted to. We [Laurel and Hardy] came here on vacation, but it's turned out to be the hardest work we've ever had in our lives. But we don't mind that. We are so overwhelmed by our reception that we'd do anything to show our gratitude to film-goers over here.

Hardy added:

> We never expected all this enthusiasm. It's a thousand per cent more than we ever dreamed of.

In a rare interview, Myrtle Hardy said of her partner:

> My husband is just a big, shy boy. He would like to spend his holiday taking quiet rides into the country. I am afraid we shall all get back home again needing another holiday to get over the effects of this one. But we won't get it. They start work again the minute they get back.

Laurel, feeling he had in some way cheated the fans by not allowing them personal contact, explained to a *Lancashire Daily Post* reporter:

> We appreciate the honour of their welcome, but we simply could not face it. In Glasgow, it was terrible. We were mobbed by thousands of people, and honestly, we only escaped with our lives by a miracle. We could not face any more. When we saw the crowd this afternoon, it made us nervous.

Little did Laurel know that the size of the crowds that evening was to be increased many-fold, and considerably more subterfuge would be called for to gain the two celebrities safe passage.

First port of call was the *Winter Gardens* complex. From the *Metropole* this would normally be only a two-minute car ride but, between the point of departure and the point of arrival, there were around ten thousand people all determined to see and touch their heroes. The crowds were so dense that the journey lasted twenty minutes, and the resultant traffic chaos throughout Blackpool took some thirty minutes to clear. After fighting their way inside the *Winter Gardens*, the two comedians were able to sit down to a belated dinner in the mediaeval-style *Baronial Hall*. The mayor, Councillor L. Newsome JP, welcomed the Boys to Blackpool, and Alderman Tom Bickerstaffe JP, chairman of the Tower and Winter Gardens' board, proposed the toast.

If the numbers in the street had seemed unbelievable, the after-dinner scene in the adjacent *Empress Ballroom* was staggering. There, nine thousand people had crammed into what was supposedly a three-thousand-capacity room. Laurel and Hardy walked on stage to a deafening roar and, awaiting a lull, Hardy asked, 'Can you hear me?', to which nine thousand voices bellowed out a deafening 'Yes!' Stan, who appeared fit to burst into tears, teased 'I can't hear you.' The crowd bellowed again, at which the comedy couple went into a knockabout routine. Having appeased the crowd, the Boys went backstage and were led outside through a back exit.

Over at the nearby *Palace* building the combined audiences in the *Palace Variety Theatre* and *Picture Palace* totalled three thousand. Those in the cinema were having a foretaste of what was to come, with the showing of the Laurel and Hardy film *Helpmates*. Again, the reception when the Boys walked on stage was tumultuous. Having satisfied both houses with the same formula of interchange, the duo popped next door into the world-famous *Tower Ballroom* to repeat the performance for the six thousand fans awaiting them there. By staying on afterwards to shake hands and sign autographs, Laurel and Hardy thought the crowds outside would have dissipated; but once again the tenacity of the people in just wanting to cast eyes on the two of them had been grossly misjudged, for the route back to the hotel was filled with almost as many people as when they had first ventured out. It was gone midnight before the crowd finally relinquished its hold and allowed the two battle-weary stars to get back to their hotel rooms.

Having been seen by just about everybody in Blackpool, but having savoured none of the sea-side atmosphere, Laurel took a very chancy

Blackpool Tower, Central Beach, Blackpool and, to the left, the Palace Theatre (identified by the twin peaks). Although not taken at the time of Laurel and Hardy's visit, the photograph gives one an idea of the vast numbers of holidaymakers who confronted the comedians during the 1932 August Bank Holiday weekend.
(By kind permission of the Blackpool Evening Gazette.)

gamble and, around 1.30 a.m., slipped out past the police escort. He must have felt he had been transported to the moon, for the seafront was almost deserted, and he was able to walk the full length of the promenade to the Pleasure Beach, and back again, without once being challenged. With two sticks of Blackpool rock to show for his adventure, and without being ungrateful for the earlier welcome, the Lancashire lad was to regard this as the highlight of his Blackpool stay.

The Tuesday morning departure time had been kept secret but, still, thousands of people were awaiting Stan and Ollie as they emerged from the hotel and scrambled into their car. With fans climbing on the running-boards, and autograph books being thrust through the windows, the car made slow progress out of the forecourt through the narrow gap made by the police. The fans waving and cheering at the departing car thought it was going to travel along the seafront and on to Preston, but it made a diversionary turn and headed for the North Station, where it dropped off its valuable fares. Here, with only minutes to spare before the train arrived, there was no time for a sizeable crowd to gather, but this did not stop those who were already on the platform from burying the Boys under a deluge of autograph and hand-shaking requests. Viewing his right hand, still sore from the same treatment the night before, Stan remarked to a *Daily Post* reporter:

> If this goes on much longer I shall have to use my left hand. I must have shaken hands ten thousand times since I arrived in England, and my partner has an even greater record. But Blackpool has been wonderful. The crowds were twice as big as those at Glasgow, but they gave us a chance to breathe.
>
> Now we are looking forward to going back to work, for a rest. Honestly, we came here for a holiday, but up to now we have not been able to pay a single visit to our friends.

Hardy added:

> Before leaving America, I had never even heard of Blackpool, but after seeing it, I am surprised that more isn't done to make it known to the Americans.

The last word on the Blackpool visit must, however, go to the writer of the following article from the *Blackpool Gazette*, which serves as a fitting epilogue to the whole British tour. It ran:

At Blackpool we get many notable visitors, and if this week more people have been interested in the two film comedians, Laurel and Hardy, than in the eminent divine, the Archbishop of York, it is merely a reflection of the times. If the leading statesmen of the world, headed by President Hoover and Mr Ramsay McDonald, had walked in procession through Blackpool they would not have excited more interest than these two comedians. Intellectuals may come and go almost unnoticed. Laurel and Hardy are mobbed with friendliness and cheers where'er they show their familiar faces.

Can you wonder that in these hard and serious times we welcome people who make us laugh? Laurel and Hardy's humour is broad, but it is clean. Therefore, they are public benefactors, and this is why Blackpool's visitors this week cheered them with a heartiness which surprised these two modest and simple fellows. Yes, quite simple and modest fellows who, if they were not victims of a whirlwind publicity campaign organised by the film company which employs them, would be contentedly touring the British countryside, unnoticed.

Laurel and Hardy clown with zest for the money it brings. They are under no delusions as to their importance in the world, or to what awaits them. They know that their day as film favourites is a short one. [Slight misjudgement, there!]. So they are frankly opportunists, glad to take the public's smiles and dollars, and ready for the next phase when it comes – supersession by new idols bringing new ideas.

If only the visit had been a few days earlier, or a few days later, the Boys would have been able to savour more of the solitude they so desired for, by an extreme case of bad luck on their behalf, they had arrived in Blackpool on its busiest bank holiday to date. Whatever followed could only be an anti-climax.

On the journey to Manchester, Stan and Babe received no peace whatsoever. Every time the train stopped at a station there was a mad scramble of autograph-hunters clawing at their window. One elderly gentlemen deserves a mention for his enterprise in obtaining the individual autographs of both Stan Laurel *and* Oliver Hardy. He procured Laurel's signature at Blackpool's North Station, but was unable to get Hardy's. Undaunted, he boarded the train and awaited the next stop, at Preston. Here, he jumped from his third-class carriage and ran the length of the train to Hardy's first-class compartment. His efforts were blocked by a horde of people who had been waiting on the platform with a similar aim. Realising the train would be pulling out before his turn came, he sped back to his carriage. At Chorley and Bolton he repeated this procedure, only to be stymied at each attempt. Finally his tenacity paid off, at Salford, and he departed, happily clutching his hard-earned reward.

These scenes were a minor inconvenience compared with the terrible sense of foreboding that Stan and Babe had that there would be yet another mob awaiting them at Manchester Victoria Station. Their fears weren't totally unfounded but, because most people had returned to work that day, the fans numbered only three or four hundred. Hardy, stepping out from the shelter of the station, gained a laugh from the crowd when he opened his famed umbrella and remarked to Stan, 'They say it rains in this locality, Stanley,' and glanced heavenward as if expecting an instant response.

After being subjected to the customary mobbing, albeit on a much smaller scale, the party was driven to the *Midland Hotel* in the city centre. A small press reception had been set up, at which the duo were anxious to impress that they were 'dead tired'. Stan reiterated that they had come to see England, but so far had managed to see only 'people, hotels, more people, theatres, and yet more people.' He demonstrated, by opening one of his travelling trunks, that, even when they left England, he would still have to spend many an hour in dealing with the demands of their English admirers, for he had amassed hundreds of fan letters.

'There are thousands more in London,' he added, 'plus the ones I've already sent on to Hollywood. I should hate to disappoint anybody if we did not answer those letters. The writers would think we were high hat, and that's not so. All these letters will be answered, but goodness knows when. I shall take them all back to Hollywood and answer them as best I can.'

The Boys must have been thankful that not all fans made demands on them, and were especially grateful to those who actually went as far as to bring them gifts. On this occasion they were delighted to receive an extract of their film *Hats Off*, a silent film they had made some five years previously. How ironic that *Hats Off* and *The Rogue Song* (the film which prompted the presentation at Preston) are the only two, out of the one-hundred-plus Laurel and Hardy films, of which there are no known prints.

At the start of the proceedings Hardy had retired to a corner, away from the line of questioning. When approached he would murmur only that he was tired and hungry, and after a while succumbed to his hunger pangs and drifted off in search of food. Stan felt genuine guilt that he had brought Babe to England with the promise of sightseeing and playing golf. He explained to an *Evening News* reporter:

'Poor old Hardy, he's even more tired than I am. Everybody recognises him – he just can't escape.' He continued, '"There's Hardy", they all shout, and make a dash for him. But me – well I'm not so conspicuous. I just look an ordinary sort of fellow. Poor Hardy's big and bulky and you can't miss him. When were together there's no escaping the crowd. England is a wonderful place and the crowds are marvellous but they won't give us a rest. We have wandered through London, Newcastle, Glasgow, and Blackpool, and now we are in Manchester and feel numb.' He added, 'I want this afternoon to myself to gather my thoughts. When working for films, we keep regular hours – going to bed at 9.30 p.m. and getting up at 6.30 a.m. – but the crowds here won't let us rest.'

With that, everyone got the message and left. At 6.30 p.m. the two comedians made their scheduled arrival at the *New Oxford Picture Theatre*, where the police were having difficulty in restraining a large crowd. The roadway was clear of cars as, even in those early days, parking was banned. It was decided to use this in their favour. Instead of riding in one of the limousines normally made available to them, the Boys took a taxi. As taxis picking up and dropping off fares was a common sight, Laurel and Hardy's was ignored, and the pair were able to sprint from the cab to the entrance before the crowd had time to act. They still had problems inside the theatre, though, as the whole audience tried to waylay them.

Meanwhile, feeling cheated, the crowd outside hung on. A waiting car signalled that Stan and Ollie were about to emerge and, as they did so, the two were precipitated into the grasping hands of what had now become a mob. Following a struggle lasting some minutes, the car pulled away and proceeded to Bert Tracey's home in Victoria Park. After the promised cup of tea with Tracey's mother, the party left for the *Manchester Opera House*, where they were sneaked in and ensconced in a private box. Catching only the last act of the production *The Night of the Garter*, the Boys were led backstage and introduced to Leslie Henson, the producer at whose invitation they were in attendance. (For those readers experiencing *déjà vu*, Leslie Henson proferred the same hospitality the previous Wednesday, on their visit to the *Strand Theatre* in London.) Henson was himself half of a double-act, and his partner, Sydney Howard, was performing in the current production. The courtesy call having been honoured, Stan and Babe retired to the *Midland Hotel* to prepare for the following day's trip to Leeds.

By 3 August the Leeds newspapers had been advertising Laurel and Hardy's visit for over a week, prompting two thousand people to turn up for their arrival at the New Station. Stepping from the train the celebrities were met by a wall of pressmen, sandwiched in between which were Stan's Uncle John, Aunty Nant, and their daughter Mary. Introducing the threesome Stan said jokingly to a reporter, 'They come from the Heavy Woollen District "Crackenridge".' (A reference to the family's latest address in Crackenridge Lane, Dewsbury.) Barriers kept the crowds away from the platform, so the Boys were able to walk freely to the station exit. Consequently, for the first time on the tour, it was the comedians themselves who made the headlines, and not the crowd. Standing in the back of an open-topped car, moving at a snail's pace, Stan and Ollie waved and bowed to the cheering masses until they reached the neighbouring *Queen's Hotel*. Hardy later commented, 'We've just got to smile – it's all so darned wonderful.'

Safely inside the hotel, the comedy duo stuck to the formula which had served them best over the past few visits: hold a press conference; shake hands with civic dignitaries; get rid of everyone except friends; have a chat; go and rest. On retiring, the party stepped into the lift to go to their rooms, with Hardy last to enter. As the lift doors closed and the attendant pressed the button the lift gave a resounding shudder and, at half its usual pace, struggled gamely upwards. During the laboured ascent, Babe stood with that look of pained determination normally given by the 'screen' Ollie when things just won't go right. Hardy wasn't at his lifetime's heaviest, but eighteen stone is still a lot for man or machine to contend with.

In the early evening Stan and Ollie were driven the short distance from the *Queen's Hotel* to the *Majestic Cinema*, where thousands awaited them, inside and out. Thanks to the efficiency of the police escort, they gained access to the cinema without too much of a struggle. Their appearance on stage was greeted with rapturous applause, and it took several attempts to break the laughing mood before they were able to get into their 'serious speech'. Having thanked the people for the magnificent welcome, the pair closed with the sincere words, 'Thank you all, and God bless you'. Stepping outside onto the cinema's balcony the Boys found the City Square, down below, black with people. Waving to the fans, and their party at a window in the *Queen's*, they ad-libbed some business wherein Laurel, pretending to lose his balance and almost fall off the balcony, is rescued by Hardy. After the speech, which Hardy opened with 'I would like to ask you all round for a cup of tea,' the two retired inside.

The day after Laurel and Hardy's appearance, *The Leeds Mercury* printed an article which tried to analyse why some people gained so much joy from turning out to see the two film stars, and why others frowned on such behaviour. Those against, questioned the mentality of people who had nothing better to do than 'gape at a couple of clowns going from a train to their hotel'. Some of the critics declared it was 'all vamped-up publicity', whilst others stated, 'the papers ought to have more sense than to encourage a fuss like this'. One veteran posed the question, 'Don't you think this shows how neurotic people are becoming, getting into a fever over nothing?' Mentioning two former stars of the legitimate theatre, the veteran went on to say:

> When *they* appeared, people didn't crush each other's toes to get near them. They didn't have to be rescued by the police from their own admirers. There was more sense in those days. We were level headed then.

The article defended the fans by saying:

> Laurel and Hardy are two very likeable artistes, and it would be very surprising indeed if filmgoers did not want to see them in the flesh. For this sad old world always wants laughter. It wants it more than ever just now, and these two gentlemen cause more laughter than any other laughter-makers in the world. 'What are they really like?' is a natural question.

And went on:

> Chaplin is still the master genius of films, but already his early films seem historical, and whilst we wait for his infrequent pictures, Laurel and Hardy are making new friends every week. In Leeds there is probably not a day goes by without half a dozen cinemas showing their comedies.
>
> The star-building policy in the film world means that when a company gets hold of a really attractive player, his or her [or their] fame is magnified and megaphoned to the ends of the earth. The

comedians are sure to come off best. Their mimicry speaks a language understood from Iceland to the Fiji Islands, and the reputations of Laurel and Hardy leap lightly across all frontiers.

The article finished:

Indignant non-filmgoers may grumble at Leeds for giving such a princely reception to a couple of laughter-makers, but that is nothing to what we shall see in time. Whether we like it or not we have got to get used to all this in our brave new world. For the first time in history, the clown will have an audience of millions, representing every race and language.

The protests did not noticeably put off anyone, for the following morning there was a large contingent of fans awaiting the two stars outside the *Queen's Hotel* as they left. The crowd were, however, very restrained, and their idols were able to walk across the station yard and mount the platform unhindered. For this, the on-lookers were rewarded by the spectacle of the two comedians switching into their screen characters, and going through a whole string of familiar gestures, some of which were captured on cine film by an enterprising amateur film-maker.

Boarding the train, Laurel and Hardy disappeared into a carriage, only for their heads to reappear immediately through the open window; the resulting clash of heads gaining further laughter from the gleeful on-lookers. Hardy then played his *pièce de résistance* and convulsed the crowd by producing his own cine camera and putting the film-maker through the same indignities he had earlier been made to suffer. With that, the train pulled out, and the view of one straw boater and one cap were the last signs that the bright presence of Stan Laurel and Oliver Hardy had withdrawn from the drab Leeds morning.

One hour later the intrepid travellers were thirty-three miles further south, in the city of Sheffield. Following a tumultuous welcome, they rested at the *Grand Hotel*. After lunch both Stan and Babe slipped out to purchase some of Sheffield's famous silverware then, later in the afternoon, entertained friends in the hotel lounge. There, Hardy was delighted to receive the golf clubs promised him by George Nicoll on the Gleneagles Golf Course. In the evening the duo made appearances in front of the 6.30 p.m. and 9.00 p.m. houses at the *Cinema House*, Fargate, and entertained the audiences with their usual party pieces.

Around noon the following day, ten thousand people were awaiting Laurel and Hardy's imminent arrival in Birmingham. The New Street Station was guarded by railway officials and police, and entry was permitted to bona fide travellers only. At 1.26 p.m. the train carrying the two stars duly deposited them on the platform, where they were met by the customary welcoming committee and a throng of pressmen. Accompanied by great rousing cheers, the party jumped into a taxi and took off. Although their hotel, the *Queen's*, was very near, it was hardly possible to take a direct route because of the mass of people. The taxi therefore took the long way round, and as soon as it stopped at its destination the two dashed inside. But the crowd stayed on, baying for attention, and the Boys had to make an appearance from the safety of an upper-floor balcony before retiring inside to rest.

Their rest didn't last long, as the reception committee rounded them up and shepherded them over to the ambiguously named Council House – a civic centre of vast proportion. Inside, they were officially welcomed to Birmingham by the mayor, Alderman W. W. Saunders, while, outside, three hundred fans cheered them on. The evening appearance was at the *Gaumont Cinema* where the comedy duo performed their usual stage routine. Taking Afterwards, taking refuge in the manager's office, they waited until the huge crowd outside had dispersed before sneaking back to the hotel for a good night's rest. (A second visit, to the *West End Dance Hall*, had been planned but it is thought this was cancelled.)

On the following morning, 6 August, the two travel-dizzy film stars boarded the train to London where, upon arrival, they re-booked into the *Savoy Hotel*. Having now fulfilled all the enforced MGM press engagements, Laurel and Hardy were effectively able to disappear for a while from the eye of the national press. It was only one local paper which caught their next appearance – a private one, arranged by Laurel's father.

Arthur Jefferson had by now retired, his last years in active service having been at the *Eden Theatre*, Bishop Auckland, where twice between 1921 and 1927 he had made unsuccessful attempts to revive business. Prior to this he had completed thirteen years' service at the *Metropole Theatre*, Glasgow. It was to his latest address, Drayton House, 49 Colebrook Avenue, Ealing, where he lived with his wife Venetia, that on Monday 8 August Stan Laurel and Oliver Hardy were driven. Here, in the doorway and also on the garden path, some amateur footage[12] was shot of Laurel trying to encourage his stone-faced father to loosen up and play to the camera.

With Stan's promise to visit his father's home having been honoured, all four left to go to the *Walpole Cinema* in Ealing. This was A. J.'s local, and the previous November he had given himself the pleasure of mounting the stage, prior to a screening of *Jailbirds* (the English release of the Laurel and Hardy film *Pardon Us*), to inform the patrons that the thin one in the film was his son and added that, if ever Laurel and Hardy visited England, he would endeavour to make it possible for them to be received on that very stage. Nine months later the wish became a reality. By request there had been no publicity, but word of mouth had ensured a good turn-out. The atmosphere was very homely, and Laurel was touched by the sentimental reception afforded him by the audience, and by his father. Hardy, after expressing appreciation at being received like this, 'a stranger in a strange country', was quoted by the *West Middlesex Gazette* as saying of his partner:

> I have never had a more marvellous friendship or feeling for anybody in my life. He has been a great pal. I had never met his father until I came over, but I knew I should meet just such a man, one of the finest men I have had the pleasure of meeting.

In his reply Stan said:

> You can never realise what a wonderful feeling it is to be received in the way in which we have been received all over the country. When we go back to America we will carry back memories which will live with us during the rest of our lives.

Hardy having left the stage, A. J. stood alone with Stan and said:

> So alive to do honour where honour is due, the British public have lavished their kindness and their affection on my dear boy and his partner. Realise your own feelings under these circumstances and my own poorness of speech in trying adequately to thank you.

With that, a renewed burst of cheering broke out and the guests left to go next door to the *Walpole Hall* and be entertained in private. The audience, meanwhile, were able to compare real-life with screen image, when the film *Chickens Come Home* was shown.

---

12   By some strange means, this short clip comes to be on the end of the footage taken in Tynemouth eleven days earlier, and some three hundred miles away (see pages 54 and 302).

The Boys travelling British Rail 'Economy Class' at the start of a short visit to France. Victoria Station, *London, 10 August 1932.*

Two days later, A. J., Venetia, and Stan's sister Olga waved the two comedians off at Victoria Station on the first leg of their journey to Paris. Hardy, assuring those present that he was going to rest when they left England, expounded: 'We shall stay in Paris for ten days, and hide from everyone.' It was not to be! Once in Paris, no less than the President of France sent his car and had them driven like national heroes down the Champs Elysées. *Claridge's Hotel* gained a great deal of publicity by letting it be known that Laurel and Hardy were staying as their honoured guests, free of charge. But it was publicity like this that Stan and Babe wished to avoid. Now that everyone knew they were in Paris, and exactly where they were staying, they could find no peace. Reluctantly, after only one week, they gave up and, also cancelling their planned sightseeing tour of Deauville, Berlin, Antwerp, Brussels and Madrid, returned to London.

The day the Boys arrived back, 18 August, was the hottest day in England for two years, but they took no advantage of this, and spent the day in the Columbia Gramophone Recording Studios making a commercial recording entitled *Laurel and Hardy in London* (see page 303, and *The Comedy World of Stan Laurel*). Over the next six days, other than Stan's being caught on a reconnaissance mission to the Elstree Film Studios, Laurel and Hardy pretty well achieved their objective in remaining free from unwanted attention, and on 24 August sailed for New York on the *SS Paris*.

Within a few weeks of arriving home, Laurel and Hardy were back doing what they did best – making two-reelers. Having made three by the end of the year, the next project was their first venture into the world of comic opera, *Fra Diavolo*. This necessitated dropping the now-familiar garb of the characters of Laurel and Hardy, and dressing in period costume. Later, both comedians looked back on *Fra Diavolo* as one of their favourite feature films, and dressed similarly for two others, *Bohemian Girl* and *Babes in Toyland*.

Come the making of two more shorts in 1933, there was no doubt in anyone's mind that Laurel and Hardy were box-office stars in their own right: but it was their private lives which were grabbing the headlines. In May Lois filed for divorce from Stan, and, one month later, Babe filed for divorce from Myrtle. A few two-reelers later, during which time the Boys were temporarily reconciled with their wives, they were taken out of their favourite medium and set to work on another full-length feature, *Sons of the Desert*. This was to prove one of their most popular and enduring films, and, against their inner desire, ensured that more features would be forthcoming. By August 1935 they had made their last two-reeler.

Sons of the Desert marked the end of Stan's marriage to Lois and saw him accompanying a fresh partner, Virginia Ruth Rogers, whom he married in 1935. They were divorced on 31 December 1937. Hardy's final split with Myrtle had come earlier that year. On 1 January 1938 Laurel took a new wife, Vera 'Illeanna' Shuvalova, a Russian singer and dancer; he divorced her just seventeen months later. The next move in the marriage market came in March 1940, when Babe Hardy married script-girl Virginia Lucille Jones, some eight months after meeting her during the making of *Flying Deuces*. Also on the set of *Flying Deuces*, the seed was planted for a plan which was to germinate much later. In his book *Laurel and Hardy – The Magic Behind the Movies*, Randy Skretvedt tells of Stan's admiration for the work of film cameraman Art Lloyd, and quotes Lloyd's wife Venice on an offer Stan made to Art: 'We were going to go to Europe for a three-year deal with Stan and Babe – they were going to make films at Elstree Studios in England; they were also going to make stage appearances there and in France'.

This statement is pretty revelational as, up to that time, Laurel and Hardy had never worked together in the medium of live stage. Stan, though, must have harboured thoughts of using Britain as a backup, should Laurel and Hardy's American film career falter, ever since his visit to the Elstree Studios in 1932. Plans for transferring their allegiances to Britain, though, had to be dramatically shelved when an event happened which was to have effects, literally, throughout the world: on 3 September 1939 Britain and France declared war on Germany. Colossal as the repercussions of war were to be, however, it was a separate event, closer to home, which temporarily curtailed Laurel and Hardy's film career, for, on 5 April 1940, when their contracts with Hal Roach expired, no attempt was made by either side to renew them. Roach wasn't prepared to continue with what he considered to be excessive demands from Laurel, whereas Laurel thought that, by leaving Roach, he could gain full artistic expression with another studio. Both producer and star were soon to find out to their cost that their hey-day was over.

Enjoying their newly-found freedom, the Boys accepted an invitation to attend a Red Cross benefit at the Golden Gate International Exposition on Treasure Island, in San Francisco Bay. They decided to do more than just make a personal appearance and, on 22 August 1940, the sketch *How to Get a Driver's Licence*, written by Stan, was performed for the first time. Encouraged by good response from the 25,000-strong audience, the two comedians decided to sample the delights of more live shows, and joined forces with the company of *Thirty Madcap Merrymakers*, which was then renamed *The Laurel & Hardy Revue*. A twelve-city tour began on 27 September 1940 in Omaha, and ended in mid-December in Buffalo. Audiences were enthusiastic and the Boys played to packed houses at every engagement. Their popularity was placed beyond doubt when in mid-April 1941 they appeared to great acclaim at the Mexico City Motion Picture Industry Festival as guests of President Avila Camacho.

Stan and Babe probably believed that, whilst doing these shows, they were allowing time for more lucrative offers of work to pour in. But what they had failed to observe when jumping off the Roach train, was that theirs was the last wagon. All the other comedians from the same era had reached the end of the line before them. Consequently, when it came to hitching a ride with someone else, nobody was going their way. The chances of getting a lift were made even slimmer by Laurel wanting to dictate *his* terms to the driver, which wasn't feasible in the circumstances. Thus, when 20th Century

Fox offered to take on Laurel and Hardy, it was either to be under the studio's terms, or else they find another vehicle.

The agreement, made in April 1941, was to make one picture, with the option of a further nine over the next five years. The Boys would be free during this term to make films with other companies, and to do stage and radio appearances. The offer was too good to refuse, especially as both comedians had just been hit by further claims for alimony *and* back-taxes. Stan had temporarily stopped one of his alimony claims when, on 11 January 1941, he re-married Ruth, but before filming commenced in July he was a single man again.

During the making of the first film with Fox, Stan and Babe soon learned, to their extreme consternation, that they had no control whatsoever over the scripts, editing, lighting, make-up, or the preservation of the characters of Laurel and Hardy. Even worse, the production team was incapable of producing good comedy. This didn't worry the studio heads, as Fox had five hundred theatres at which its films would be shown, regardless of the quality, and the bosses weren't too particular about how much they abused their position. Consequently, the film, *Great Guns*, fired only blanks.

In November 1941 Stan and Ollie were able to get back into their true characters when they embarked on a tour of Caribbean army bases. Over a period of two weeks they visited defence bases in Antigua, St Lucia, Trinidad and British Guiana with a company calling itself *The Flying Showboat*. (Post-war publicity proclaimed Laurel and Hardy to have been the first American artistes to have toured army camps, during which time they had clocked up an amazing fourteen thousand miles of travel.) Other notables on the tour were Ray Bolger and Chico Marx.

The following month, December 1941, the Japanese bombed Pearl Harbor and provoked the Americans into joining the war. In Britain, at the outset of war, all forms of sporting events and theatrical entertainment had been phased out, but it was soon realised that both were necessary to raise morale, enlighten the gloom and, ultimately, to maintain the war effort. Thus, sport and entertainment were encouraged on a wide scale, both at home and abroad.

In January 1942 Laurel and Hardy went on a tour of American army camps with a new company known as *The Hell-a-Belloo*. Performing the now trusty *Driver's Licence* sketch, the Boys played Chicago, Detroit, Fort Wayne, Cleveland and Pittsburgh. On arriving in Boston in late February, Hardy contracted acute laryngitis and the tour had to be cancelled. He recovered in time to start work on their new 'disaster movie' with Fox, *A-Haunting We Will Go*. Laurel firmly believed that this time he would be given some form of directorial control, but his wishes went unheeded and, again, he and his partner were forced to play uncharacteristic roles and to speak unfunny lines.

In order to forget the pain of *Haunting*, the Boys joined *The Hollywood Victory Caravan*. After lunching with Eleanor Roosevelt at the White House, the distinguished company – including Cary Grant, Charles Boyer, Desi Arnaz and Joan Blondell – set off on a tour of major cities[13] in the East and mid-West. This took from 29 March to mid-May 1942, and ended in San Francisco. Over these weeks, other stars to take part were Bob Hope, James Cagney, Claudette Colbert, Eleanor Powell, Charlotte Greenwood, Olivia DeHavilland, Joan Bennett, Pat O'Brien, Bert Lahr and Groucho Marx. The latter was to relate of the tour:

> I shared a dressing room with Laurel and Hardy. I've never drunk so much alcohol, but these two were pleasantly sloshed all the time I was with them. This, I thought, would be the leg-up I needed to outshine them. No way!

With the Roach Lot leased to the US Government, and having no urge to run back to 20th Century Fox, Laurel and Hardy decided to see how green the grass was elsewhere, and signed to make two features with MGM. *Air Raid Wardens*, the first of these – shot in December 1942 – also suffered from bad direction, scripting, editing, and the suppression of the Laurel and Hardy characters. Continuing up to December 1944 Stan and Ollie made five more films, all of which are candidates for the Golden Turkey Awards. With the MGM contract at an end, and realising that to negotiate any form of extension would be assigning themselves to a life of purgatory, Laurel and Hardy gave a sour goodbye kiss to the world of films.

Things were happier on the war front: 5 May 1945 witnessed the unconditional surrender of the Germans, and signalled the end of the war in Europe. The Japanese capitulated on 14 August after the American bombings of Hiroshima and Nagasaki.

With hostilities over, the Boys had nowhere to go. Filming was obviously a closed door, and visiting army bases was too uncomfortable, too

---

13   At the *Convention Hall*, Philadelphia, on 2 May, Laurel and Hardy were caught on film doing their pre-sketch, introductory stage act. The extant colour footage is believed to be unique.

exhausting, and not exactly what one could term a future. They had enjoyed their entry into stage-work, but to do this on a permanent basis, in America, was not an easy prospect. Vaudeville boasted only about a dozen theatres, so artistes had to be prepared to work night clubs, cabaret, and in cinemas, to keep in full-time employment. The cinemas were of gigantic proportions, seating between three and six thousand people, with the usual presentation being a forty-five-minute variety bill sandwiched between two feature films. Somehow, none of these options was the right medium for Laurel and Hardy's soft-approach humour.

As the Boys floundered, a life-line appeared from an unexpected source: over in England a young entrepreneur, Bernard Delfont, was starting to make a name for himself. In just a few years, Delfont had broken the monopoly of the major chain of theatrical agents and become sole-booker in seven venues. Taking advantage of the de-restrictions on sailing across the Atlantic, he decided to emblazon his name on the map by placing it alongside that of 'Laurel & Hardy'. Delfont's first idea was to invite them over to play in pantomime but, on being informed that they had a well-established stage act, changed his *modus operandi* and booked them on a provisional twelve-week engagement of British theatres.

For Stan Laurel it was the begining of a whole new life. The war was over and, just one week after his divorce from Ruth had been finalised (30 April 1946), he had a new wife – Ida Kitaeva Raphael (his second Russian wife). Lucille was unable to join Babe, Stan and Ida for the trip, due to hospitalisation for a minor operation, but would be travelling across at a later date. With the sailing of the *Queen Elizabeth* from New York, it is ironic to reflect that, thirty-five years after deserting the British stage to go and seek a new life in America, Stan Laurel was returning in the hope of mending the pieces of his broken fortunes. The prodigal son was returning.

Chapter Seven

And So to Battle

IN a sense, the war years preserved Laurel and Hardy. The British had been more concerned about their battles with the Germans than with Laurel and Hardy's battles with Fox and MGM, and were unaware of the comedians' decline. After the declaration of peace, it was as if a pause button had been released; and to find that, out of the recent darkness, this glowing light was about to appear in their midst was more than their excitement could contain. Just the thought of the two funny men instantaneously reminded everyone of happy days, and actually to see their faces would complete the illusion. Thus, on 10 February 1947, as the *Queen Elizabeth* sailed in to Southampton Docks, Laurel and Hardy, looking down from one of the decks, may well have been forgiven for saying, 'Oh no! – not again'; for the scene which greeted them was almost exactly as it had been in 1932.

Because their popularity had faded over in America, the two ageing comedians were absolutely amazed at the great love and loyalty which the people of England had retained for them. The press, too, never foresaw this *arrivada*, and were not on hand to record it. The only saviour was Pathé Newsreel, who filmed a short interview, during which Laurel and Hardy announced intentions of also making a film whilst over in England; a skit on Robin Hood, in which Ollie was to play 'Friar Hardy', and Stan, 'Little John Laurel'. Missing from the welcoming party were Stan's father and sister, who were now both living in Lincolnshire. Their village was snowed under, with no chance of anyone getting in or out, so Stan phoned and sent his regards.

'Look who's here,' says Stan Laurel to the awaiting press on board the
Queen Elizabeth.
(by kind permission of Associated Press)

The party then boarded the train to London where, at Waterloo Station, several thousand more fans were waiting to welcome them. The crush was so great that Laurel and Hardy were again split up. In 1932 Babe had found himself alone in a taxi. This time, desperately unnerved in the centre of the crush, he sought refuge on a bus. After showing extreme surprise as to his passenger, the driver asked where Hardy wanted to go. 'Anywhere, as long as it's away from here,' Babe informed him; then added, 'and on to the *Savoy.*'

The following morning Babe, Stan and Ida went along to Caxton Hall, Westminster, to collect their ration cards, for many items were still rationed. Outside in the cold, the visitors happily stood in line with the rest of the people in the queue. Inside, a power-cut led to their registering by candle-light. This was no isolated incident, for electricity cuts extended throughout Britain, and domestic switch-offs were enforced twice daily. As if post-war conditions and shortages weren't bad enough, the weather decided to add to the misery, to such an extent that 1947 is still the worst winter on record.

At the cocktail party given that evening at the *Savoy Hotel*, Bernard Delfont had made sure to invite along the right people, for if the tour were to become successful he would either have to persuade the management of a particular theatre to keep the show on for an extended run, or get other theatres to book it. Amongst those present were Lew Grade (Delfont's brother) from the prestigious Lew & Leslie Grade Agency; Harry Foster, Laurel and Hardy's British agent; Val Parnell, managing director of the *London Palladium*; and Hannen Swaffer and Patrick Campbell, prominent journalists. Acting as hostess was Rosa Heppner from the Association of London Theatre Press Representatives.

The following day, at the *London Casino*, Laurel and Hardy began rehearsals of *The Driver's Licence* sketch with Australian comedy actor Harry Moreny, who was to play 'the cop'. Stan and Babe would have liked to have broken up their work schedule by going to see friends and places they had missed on their last visit, but were hampered by continual snowfalls. So, after twelve days of non-stop rehearsing, Sunday 23 February found them on their way to Newcastle, with Stan, in the words of Hannen Swaffer, 'scared to death' about the act's English debut on Tyneside.

Laurel's nervous energy was totally wasted on the reviewer from the *Evening Chronicle* who submitted only the following observations:

> Those two droles [sic], Laurel and Hardy, ruling an empire as wide as films can travel, hold court amid the acclamation of thousands of their delighted subjects at the *Newcastle Empire* this week. Here they are in the flesh, looking just as they do on the screen, with the benefit of depth as well as width. Their act, a cameo of their characteristic screen life is one of an interesting variety programme.

Whether this reviewer had bothered to go to the show, along with the 'thousands of their delighted subjects', is open to speculation. Considering that a press-party had been given, as well as free access to the show, the coverage is an insult. Bernard Delfont was, however, present on the opening night, and saw nothing to cause him concern. On the contrary, the reception the packed auditorium gave the two comedians far exceeded what either he, or anyone else, had anticipated.

The treacherous route the tour members had taken to get into Newcastle was worsening by the day, and there were fears that, come the end of the

Royal Station Hotel, *Neville Street, Newcastle.*
(Photocrom Company Ltd.)

week, they weren't going to be able to get out. The snows had blocked most major roads, and smaller roads were totally impassable. The London and North Eastern Railway line was also completely blocked, but snow-ploughs were being sent to clear it. Coal had become a very precious commodity, as colliery workers were unable to get to work, and during the night temperatures of –13°C were recorded.

In these arctic conditions Babe, Stan and Ida had to while away the days in the *Royal Station Hotel*. After their opening night success, the Boys took Bernard Delfont and his partner Billy Marsh back there for a celebration. Babe phoned Lucille to give her the good news and, during the conversation, he was informed that the temperature in California was 27°C. Going back to Stan and Ida's room, where he found the company huddled around a meagre fire, he relayed the Californian weather situation. With perfect timing, Stan picked up the last piece of coal and, throwing it on the fire, declared, 'Ah well, there'll always be an England.' With that, the five of them 'broke up', the room shook with laughter, and the tears cascading down their cheeks warmed their faces.

Just before the photograph was taken, Hardy pulled the Mayor's chain to see if he would flush.
Mayor's Parlour, *Tynemouth, 26 February 1947.*
(Kindly loaned by Francis J. Mavin – pictured.)

But things weren't all bad. On Wednesday they were guests of the Mayor of Tynemouth, Councillor Francis J. Mavin, who firstly had them chauffeured to Laurel's former home in Dockwray Square, North Shields. At his last attempt, in 1932, Stan was unable to get near owing to the mass of fans, but this time, having the whole week in which to choose his moment, he found the square relatively empty. Hardy was to say that Laurel was so excited as he neared his home that 'He almost jumped out of the car.' After a short look around, though, Stan confessed, 'It's very distressing to see how the place has been knocked about during the war.' After also calling round to view the *Boro' Theatre* and the *Theatre Royal*, the party adjourned to a civic reception at the *Grand Hotel*, Tynemouth, followed by tea in the mayor's parlour. As a return compliment the civic party was invited to Laurel and Hardy's show that night at the *Newcastle Empire*.

The following day Stan and Babe were guests at a luncheon given at their hotel by the Railway Electrical Engineers then, later in the week, they visited local celebrity Marie Lamb to wish her a happy one hundredth birthday. Having a telegram from the king is one honour – having Laurel and Hardy to tea is another.

Leaving the frostbitten city of Newcastle and travelling far inland to the city of Birmingham might well have made the touring party think they were moving to a more temperate climate. The weathermen appeared to bear this out by forecasting a thaw within forty-eight hours; but the 'thaw' turned out to be the heaviest snowfall of the winter, and was accompanied by gusts of wind up to forty miles per hour. As fast as man and machine were moving the snow, mother nature was putting it back. Olga Varona, one of the acts from the show, has vivid memories of the conditions:

> I will never forget that Winter of '47 in Birmingham, with roads blocked and buses out of action all over the country. On arriving at the *Birmingham Hippodrome*, on the opening night, the queue of people standing in snow piled several feet high, proved how wonderful the British people were in their spirit and love of the theatre. I thought 'Bless you all, you are the salt of the earth.'

Olga was an Australian gymnast whose act consisted of aerial acrobatics on trapeze and vertical rope, in which she was assisted by her husband, Archie Collins. Birmingham was to be her first engagement on the tour, and having the unenviable task of closing the show added to her nervousness. On the first night, half expecting to be playing to a rapidly-emptying house, Olga got on with her act as best she knew. On finishing, she expected the polite applause of the few people who might have stayed on to watch. Imagine her amazement when she received rapturous applause from a full house. Thoughts were now going through Olga's mind that Laurel and Hardy would not appreciate a support act receiving such acclamation. Some stars could not take this, and would have acts transferred to other shows. But, as Olga was to find out, Stan and Babe weren't like that. On future shows, when they'd finished their act, they would cut short the applause and invite the audience to save it for the next act. Then Hardy, in order to persuade the audience to stay on, would introduce Olga with the words, 'she is a great artiste, and something special to watch'. The subsequent weeks when she toured with these two most unselfish of professionals turned out to be a big turn around in Olga's career, and within eight months led to an appearance on the *Royal Variety Performance*. Not bad for a complete unknown.

Left, Olga Varona demonstrating her skill and grace as Australia's 'Queen of the Air', and right, showing her glamour on terra firma.
(Courtesy of Archie Collins.)

Of the opening night at Birmingham, the *Evening Despatch* said:

The appeal of Laurel and Hardy's act is its simplicity and good nature. Hardy bullies Laurel. Laurel takes it on the chin. And finally Laurel, having mopped up all the sympathy delivers the last blow and gets the last laugh. The triumph of the little chap – you can't beat it for a punch line. Thus with a little chat and a snatch of a song, is composed a charming and disarming act, worthily supported by a first-rate bill, in which chief honours go to Olga Varona for the grace and daring of her aerial acrobatics.

The *Birmingham Post* offered:

In 1932 when Laurel and Hardy were in Birmingham last, we were trying to climb out of the depression. Today, things are not much different in point of mood. Now, as then, Laurel and Hardy make us forget that life is real and more than somewhat earnest. Their drollery, buffoonery and small-boy prankishness is achieved with consummate artistry.

The *Birmingham Mail* gave a more profound opinion:

> The great majority of their audience last night having fallen under the persistent influence of their pictorial personalities, were prepared at all costs, rapturously to acclaim, and heartily to laugh. But the few who came to scoff must have remained to laugh and even to praise. The act is perfectly rehearsed and perfectly timed. Their material is not brilliant or even outstandingly good of its kind. In script it would scarcely yield a smile, yet they cause it to become grotesquely funny, and their good natured stupidity shines through.

The script for *The Driver's Licence* is printed in its American format in the book *The Comedy World of Stan Laurel*. In its British format it was presented in three parts, the act being extended by a further eight minutes of business split either side of the twelve-minute sketch:

> The Boys make their entrance to the accompaniment of the 'Cuckoo Song'. Whilst Ollie is addressing the audience, Stan continually interrupts him – the pay off being that Ollie is standing on his foot.[14] A link is then inserted whereby they have to go and renew Ollie's driving licence. As they walk off stage, the curtain lifts to reveal a police officer seated at a station desk. The Boys re-enter and Hardy informs the officer that he wishes to renew his licence. Asked to fill in a form, Hardy is unable to write as his arm is in a sling. Laurel can't help as he 'can write, but can't read'.
>
> The policeman volunteers to fill in the form, but is sorely vexed, firstly by Stan and Ollie's answers to his questions, and then by the discovery that Hardy's existing licence was left to him by his grandfather. The cop next gives them an initiative test, in the form of a hypothetical set of driving conditions. The way the Boys react to his questioning leads to his chasing them out of his office, and firing a shotgun at their retreating figures. A stagehand then runs on, with the seat of his pants on fire, and there is a blackout.
>
> The Boys re-emerge front of tabs. Hardy addresses the audience with the words, 'We hoped you enjoyed our bit of nonsense,' and then

14 This same routine had been in constant use by Laurel and Hardy almost since their partnership began, and was trotted out at most public events, including the appearances in Britain in 1932, and the later 1952 tour.

Left, the Boys doing their introductory act, prior to performing the Driver's Licence sketch.
(Courtesy of Billy Barron.)

And below, Stan annoying 'cop' Harry Moreny as Ollie looks on.
(Courtesy of John McCabe.)

croons 'Shine on Harvest Moon', to which Laurel does a soft-shoe-shuffle [a routine taken from the Laurel and Hardy film *The Flying Deuces*]. Stan follows with the song 'I'm a Lonely Little Petunia in an Onion Patch', to which Hardy does an eccentric little dance. The Boys then close by wishing everyone 'God bless', and Hardy introduces the last act on the bill.

The newspapers for the Birmingham week contained little or nothing else of the exploits of Laurel and Hardy, although, to be fair, perhaps there was nothing to tell. The *Evening Despatch* displayed a photograph of the two comedians having a cup of tea at the *Midland Hotel*, and added a few points of interest on the structure of Laurel and Hardy's comedy, wherein Laurel declared:

'Making comedies is the most serious business in the world.' Oliver nodded in agreement and they both shook their heads rather sadly. Of

To aid rationing, Stan pours Ollie a cup of tea from an empty pot.
Midland Hotel, *Birmingham, 3 March 1947.*
(By kind permission of the *Birmingham Post & Mail.*)

their temporary lapse into music hall, Hardy said: 'I love it. It's far more exciting than making films.'

And Laurel added: 'On the stage you get an immediate reaction and know whether the audience likes you or not. Anything we do in the comedy line has a definite reason – you can't go and fall over and make funny faces without a reason.'

The *Birmingham News*, too, was affected by the inactivity of its subjects:

> What Laurel and Hardy think about Birmingham must remain a mystery, for they were much too concerned with the weather to talk about impressions of anything – but the weather. It is a tribute to our English climate that it has so 'tamed' them that after one month's stay their approach to it already has a native enthusiasm, and huddled over a tiny fire of cinders with two small sullen logs atop, they spoke as wistfully and with as wry a smile of sunny skies and the 28° they left in Hollywood, as might any Englishman.

Having digested all this information, one can only presume that Laurel and Hardy spent the rest of the week drinking cups of tea round a meagre log fire. The important issue, though, is that they had had two weeks preparing their act away from the prying eyes of the London critics, and were now ready to rise up and take London by storm.

Chapter Eight

To Catch a Rat

THE *London Palladium* is now the most prestigious variety theatre in the world, but in the 'thirties and 'forties it played almost exclusively revue shows, with such stars as The Crazy Gang, and Tommy Trinder. When variety started to come to the fore, American acts – such as Chico Marx, Danny Kaye, Jack Benny, Abbott & Costello, Bob Hope, and Bing Crosby – were invited over. Laurel and Hardy, though, were the first of the big American post-war stars to play the *Palladium*, and helped more than anyone to re-establish it on the map to audiences outside of Britain. It needed a large figurehead to do this, and none of the American imports came any bigger than Laurel and Hardy.

Being two old screen comedians trying to establish themselves in variety, though, may possibly have given them doubts as to whether they really had a place on this stage. Len Lowe, who was on the bill, well remembers Babe's show of nerves, and revealed, 'Hardy was in his stage costume, and full make-up, *two hours* before the start of the show. He spent the whole time pacing up and down backstage – sweating profusely.' Hardy need not have worried. *The Performer* said of their first show in front of a London audience:

> It is rarely that Variety top-liners get so uproarious a reception on their first appearance at any particular theatre as that accorded the film couple, Stan Laurel and Oliver Hardy at this house, and it was some time before the pair could even begin to get under way.

The pair have material of no particular strength. Indeed, the script can have caused no wet towels and sleepless nights – but what they do have is the benefit of considerable film following, and in this they score heavily by exploiting to the full the various comedy mannerisms that have endeared them to so many. At the finale of this episode, the duo sang a little, Laurel danced a little, and both seemed not a little overwhelmed at the warmth of their reception.

The *Daily Mail* reviewer saw the show in similar light:

Laurel and Hardy making their West End bow, had the audience laughing as soon as the orchestra struck up their signature tune. They play a sketch about getting a driving licence, which ends surprisingly in a little song and dance.

Their comedy is neat and amiable; all the old film tricks abound. The 'stage' Laurel and Hardy are somehow more like their film equivalent than one could imagine.

Meanwhile, outside the theatre, the bad weather was still raging, and in the next few weeks the populace were to suffer blizzards, floods and a hurricane. During the height of the thaw the Thames rose nine feet. Many homes were flooded, and the telephone lines were dead. The floods weren't just confined to London, but affected thirty counties in all, with roads impassable almost everywhere. The *Palladium*, however, stayed open and the crowds kept pouring in. As a result, Laurel and Hardy's run was extended from two weeks to three.

On the eve of their London debut (Sunday 9 March), Stan and Babe were invited to the *Savoy Hotel* as guests of the Grand Order of Water Rats (see page 104). Part of the cabaret was an adaptation of the popular radio series *The Brains Trust*, with Tommy Trinder acting as the question master and Sid Field, Nat Mills, Billy Butlin and Laurel and Hardy providing the 'brains'. As can be imagined, the item turned out to be a riot of laughs. Two people whom Stan would have particularly enjoyed meeting that night were Lupino Lane, who had been a boy-comedian at the same time as himself, and George Jackley, who had lent Stan the money to get home from Belgium after his disastrous days with The Eight Comics (see page 34). Other top comedians of the day who were present at the House Dinner were Arthur Prince, Fred Russell, Albert Whelan and Will Hay, to name but a few.

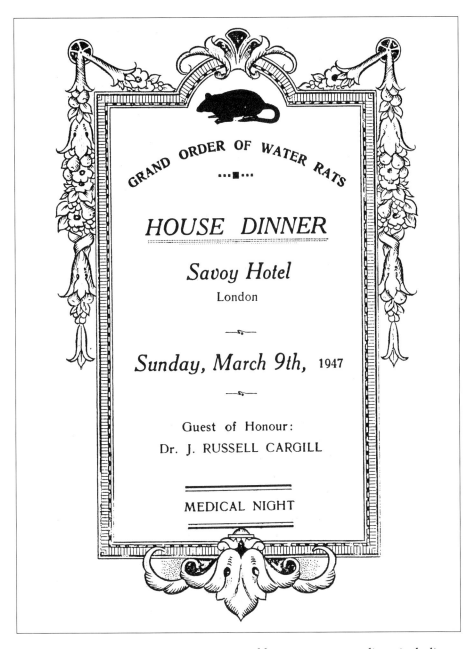

GRAND ORDER OF WATER RATS

...■...

HOUSE DINNER

Savoy Hotel

London

Sunday, March 9th, 1947

Guest of Honour:
Dr. J. RUSSELL CARGILL

MEDICAL NIGHT

'Water Rats – House Dinner' menu, signed by numerous comedians, including:
Lupino Lane, Will Hay, Tommy Trinder, Nat Jackley,
George Jackley, Albert Whelan, Sid Field, Fred Russell,
Stan Laurel and Oliver Hardy.
(Author's collection.)

Autographed pages of the 'Water Rats – House Dinner' menu.

While at the Ideal Home Exhibition, Stan and Babe received a 'Surran' bedwarmer – a device for which, a few weeks earlier, they would have given a gold brick and a bag of nuts.
(By kind permission of Sid A. Singleton.)

During their run at the *Palladium* the Boys found time, and enough clothing coupons, to have suits made at Simpson's of Piccadilly. On the tourist front, they had a look around Madame Tussaud's waxworks, and on 16 March visited the Daily Mail Ideal Home Exhibition, where Babe was filmed hamming-it-up with entertainer Tessie O'Shea sitting on one knee and actress Vera Pearce on the other (see page 302).

An event which received more publicity took place on Friday 21 March, when the comedy couple were invited to partake in the celebrations for the twenty-first anniversary of the Romney, Hythe & Dymchurch Railway, and to open the new section of track between Romney and Dungeness. Immediately after breakfast, Stan, Babe and Ida boarded a train bound for Ashford in Kent, from where a car took them to Hythe Railway Station. They were greeted by the Mayor of Folkestone, Alderman H. Hughes, and the general manager of the railway, Major J. T. Holder, who accompanied them on the train to New Romney. There, despite a constant drizzle, thousands of people had turned out, headed by the mayor, Alderman J. A. Wiles, and the owners of the railway, Mr and Mrs J. E. P. Howey.

With a wave of Laurel's hands, Hardy is turned into a leprechaun.
Hall of Mirrors, Madame Tussaud's.
(Keystone.)

Laurel attempting to make Henry VIII jealous, by flirting with
one of his wives. Hardy fears they will be beheaded.
Madame Tussaud's.
(Keystone.)

Mrs Howey handed the Boys a key which looked as though it belonged to a giant clockwork train set, and directed them towards the tunnel in which the engine was awaiting its unveiling. This afforded the couple ample opportunity to improvise a comedy routine centred around the unlocking of the fake set of doors which had been placed on one end of the tunnel. Once the engine had been brought out onto the main line, raucous laughter accompanied the testing of the controls by Stan and Ollie, followed by further hilarity when Stan and Teddy Smith, son of the Dymchurch station master, tried to push Hardy's enormous frame into one of the new Pullman cars. Fortunately, two camera teams were on hand to capture most of the action.

With everyone aboard, the new line was declared officially open and the train burst through the fake brickwork at the other end of the tunnel, on its way to Dungeness. Hot toddies served on the train were followed by lunch at the *Jolly Fisherman* pub in Greatstone; then it was off to the turn-around point at Dungeness Lighthouse, and back to Hythe for tea at the Light Railway Restaurant. On the following Monday, as a 'thank you' to Laurel and Hardy for giving up their day, Messrs Holder and Howey turned up at the stage door of the *Palladium* and left no less than four hundred photographs for them to autograph. How thoughtful!

Fellow-professionals were also apt to drop in backstage. One was Dump Harris, a comedian and xylophonist who did his act in the guise of 'Ollie'. Another visitor was sketch artiste Louis Valentine who was invited to come round a second time and bring with him his baby daughter, with the strange proviso that he also brought an empty suitcase. During the second meeting, after making a big fuss of baby Susan, Stan asked Louis to make a sketch of him drinking coffee and Babe drinking tea. It always amused Stan that the Englishman was the coffee drinker, and the American the tea drinker. The sketch was much appreciated, and taken back to America where Stan proudly put it on display.

Meanwhile, payment had to be made, so Stan told Louis to open his suitcase. He then proceeded to fill it with all kinds of goodies for Susan, as well as tea, coffee, sugar and so on for Louis and his wife Peggy. Most of the items had been brought with them from America, but the provisions – not readily available during rationing – had been sent backstage by fans. There was so much, that Stan and Babe couldn't possibly consume it all themselves. The only trouble now, was that Louis had to get home carrying a suitcase full of contraband. Needless to say, the journey was fraught with

Mrs Howey hands over the key to Oliver Hardy at the opening ceremony of the Romney, Hythe & Dymchurch Railway. *Romney Station, Kent 21 March 1947.*
(Raphael Studios.)

Hardy is puzzled by the inability of the key to open the train-shed doors. Laurel, meanwhile, opens it by hand.
(Raphael Studios.)

When the track is finally declared 'open', Hardy takes over the role of engine driver from Tony Baker.
('Topical'.)

Laurel, Hardy, and Harry Moreny (stalwart assistant in the Driver's Licence *sketch), with proof that policemen are getting younger every day.*
London Palladium, *March 1947.*
('Topical'.)

panic, and, had Louis been caught and asked, 'Where did you get all this stuff from?' it is doubtful if the reply, 'From Laurel and Hardy' would have produced a favourable reaction from the law.

Another of Stan's friends was less fortunate where the law was concerned. Jimmy Murphy, originally of Newton-le-Willows, Lancashire, first met Laurel in 1938 when working as a pool-cleaner at the World's Fair in New York, where he accepted the offer to become Stan's valet, a position he held for a few years. Now back in England after serving in the army, Jimmy contacted Stan at the *London Palladium* and got his job back. His return was short-lived. Home Office officials knocked at his dressing room door with an order to leave the country: he had become an American citizen and had no work permit.

Having lost their tea-boy almost as fast as they had found him, Stan and Babe were invited to take tea with journalist Hannen Swaffer, 'the Dean of Fleet Street', at his tiny flat in Charing Cross Road. Swaffer was an eccentric person, to say the least, and his appearance gave one the impression he had just dug his way out of a grave using his finger nails. It was not always a pleasure to be a guest of his but, as with Dorothy Parker and Hedda Hopper in America, to decline was to incur the wrath of a powerful enemy.

Stan was quite at ease in Swaffer's company, and able to discuss at length the merits of music-hall stars, past and present. Babe was lost in the conversation, having come from an entirely different background, but, being the polite gentleman he was, remained an attentive listener throughout. After a few hours of their company, during which Swaffer had constantly addressed Stan as 'Ollie', and Ollie as 'Stan', he bid the two farewell: in the words of Billy Marsh, who was present, 'He didn't know the one from the other.'

The Boys' next social meeting was the Vaudeville Golfing Society Dinner,[15] on Sunday 23 March, at the *Savoy Hotel*. Amongst those present were Terry Thomas, Bud Flanagan, Nat Jackley, Donald Peers, Bob & Alf Pearson, Sid Field and Gerry Desmonde. On such occasions as these a kind of inverted snobbery occurs whereby protocol demands that, no matter how big the star guest is, he or she is treated as an ordinary person. The heady reaction which occurred upon Laurel and Hardy's entrance shows the ultra-high esteem in which these two gentlemen were regarded. Arriving late, and trying to sneak quietly to their seats, Stan and Babe were immediately converged upon by a swarm of people. Abandoning all decorum, men and women in evening dress hurriedly snatched menus from tables, and pushed and jostled each other to get them autographed. Pleas were made to allow the honoured guests to enjoy the evening in common with the rest, but it was forty minutes after the Boys had made their entry before the deluge stopped.

The Boys were also greatly admired by the Grand Order of Water Rats (a fund-raising organisation made up of members solely from the entertainment profession), and were asked if they would consider joining the Order. Laurel was proposed by Fred Russell and seconded by Talbot O'Farrell, whilst Hardy was proposed by Will Hay and seconded by Bud Flanagan.

---

15   The society consists of showbusiness personalities who raise money for charity by playing in sponsored golf tournaments.

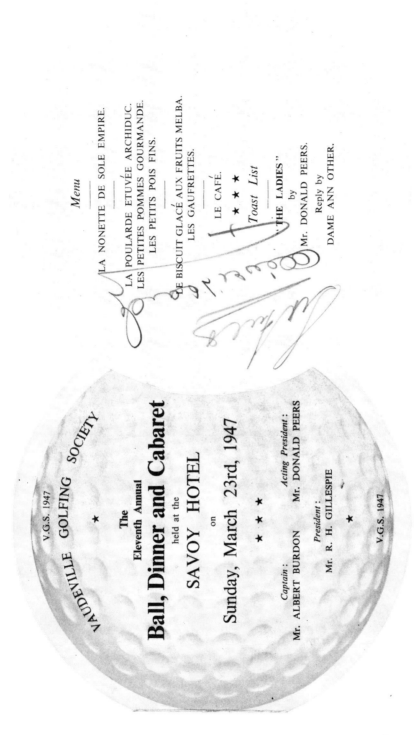

Menu

LA NONETTE DE SOLE EMPIRE.

LA POULARDE ETUVÉE ARCHIDUC.
LES PETITES POMMES GOURMANDE.
LES PETITS POIS FINS.

LE BISCUIT GLACÉ AUX FRUITS MELBA.
LES GAUFRETTES.

LE CAFÉ.

★ ★ ★
Toast List

"THE LADIES"
by
Mr. DONALD PEERS.

Reply by
DAME ANN OTHER.

V.G.S. 1947

VAUDEVILLE GOLFING SOCIETY

★

The
Eleventh Annual

Ball, Dinner and Cabaret

held at the

SAVOY HOTEL

on

Sunday, March 23rd, 1947

★ ★
★

Captain :
Mr. ALBERT BURDON

Acting President :
Mr. DONALD PEERS

President :
Mr. R. H. GILLESPIE

★

V.G.S. 1947

Just one of the many menus which were thrust at Laurel and/or Hardy during the 'Vaudeville Golfing Society Dinner'. Also signed by Sid Field.
(Author's collection.)

The Boys accepted, and on 30 March went along to the home of the Rats, the Eccentric Club in Rhyder Street, London, for the secret ceremony. Will Hay presided in the absence of King Rat Rob Wilton, and Fred Russell was Preceptor. Present at the meeting were Peter Brough, Sid Field, Ted Ray, Albert Whelan, Nat Mills, Harry Tate Jnr, Johnnie Riscoe and Harry Moreny.

When Laurel and Hardy's run at the *Palladium* ended on 29 March, Bernard Delfont, who had so successfully made the switch, there, from revue to variety, repeated the format at one of his own venues, the *Wimbledon Theatre*, of which the *Boro' News* wrote:

> Following their great success at the *Palladium*, Laurel and Hardy come to the *Wimbledon Theatre*. Their sketch has been described as 'boisterously gay' and the comedians at their best. The London critics were unanimous not only in praise, but in the opinion that whereas most film artistes were disappointing on the living stage, Laurel and Hardy were even more riotously funny.

Just whether Laurel and Hardy were able to follow this build-up wasn't revealed by the local newspapers, who totally ignored the two mega-stars. The Wimbledon appearance was followed by another week of packed houses, this time at the *Lewisham Hippodrome*. Here the *Borough News* thought the only interest lay in pianist Charlie Kunz being present at one of the shows. Why the press failed to react to Laurel and Hardy's being in Britain, and attracting enormous business wherever they went, defies logic. On the 1932 tour the press coverage had been blamed for whipping up a wave of hysteria, but in 1947 it didn't have the impetus to whip up a lather in a washing-up bowl. But 'still they came', and the crowds never dwindled.

Whilst at Lewisham the Boys, taking a personal tip from a local greyhound owner, made a large wager on his dog. Norman Munro who, with his wife Vonnie, did a brilliant balancing act in the show, was sent along to watch the race. He reported back that the dog had set off at a fantastic pace, but on coming to the first bend ran headlong into the fence and was killed. The death of the poor animal upset the Boys enough to cure them of making further flutters.

On the Sunday following the week at Lewisham (13 April), Stan and Babe were back at the Eccentric Club to attend their first meeting as Honorary Water Rats. Stan must have been in his element here, talking to Fred Kitchen, who for so long had been a principal comedian with the

Karno Company. Then, along with fellow comedians Sid Field, Tommy Trinder, George Robey and The Crazy Gang, the Boys swopped their tuxedos for farmers' smocks and and popped round to a farmers' charity function at the *Apollo Theatre*, where they confronted the arriving guests with buckets into which they were encouraged to throw money.

Next on the tour came a run at the *London Coliseum*. As at the *Wimbledon Theatre* this was again a gamble, as variety hadn't been staged there for nine years. In fact, there were no other variety shows then running in the West End. The show having to run for four weeks added to the risk, so, for insurance, a strong support bill was put together. This included Elsie & Doris Waters, highly popular theatre, film, and radio personalities, in their guise of 'Gert & Daisy'; and Rawicz & Landauer, world-acclaimed piano duettists.

Hardy was bemoaning his bad luck in having to attend first-day rehearsals, necessary for the stage crew to become familiarised with the artistes' acts, as, that day, his wife Lucille was arriving from America. Her travelling companions on board the *Queen Elizabeth* were Russian-born Hollywood film producer Boris Morros and his wife, Catherine. Lucille, it may be remembered, had worked as script-clerk on Morros' film, *The Flying Deuces*, on the set of which she first met Babe. This time, the two eventually met up at the *Savoy*, and one of the first things that Lucille did was to present Babe with a set of thick underwear that he had left behind in America. At the time of his leaving it had been too tight, but now he thought it might fit him again.

The show at the *Coliseum* became a smash hit, and *The Performer* noted:

> The Laurel and Hardy sketch now has additional gags and is much stronger than when they played the *Palladium*.

In 1983 journalist Derek Malcolm wrote a story of Laurel and Hardy's appearance, which shows that special affinity which the two stars had with their fans – especially children. The show played to full houses throughout its run, but the matinée described below was obviously an exception.

> My mother took me, trembling with excitement to the *Coliseum*, but alas I went to a half-empty matinée. The audience sipped cups of tea, talked amongst themselves, and showed about as much enthusiasm for real artistry as a kipper for being breakfasted upon. I was very sad, and my mother knew it.

(Roy Sims Collection.)

Accordingly, she sent a note round backstage, asking Stan and Oliver whether she could take me to see them. I could scarcely believe it at the end of the show when an usherette walked up to her and said: 'Mr Laurel and Mr Hardy would be delighted to see you and your son now.'

I was ushered into the not very plush dressing room in a state bordering on panic, to find Stan sitting at the mirror taking his make-up off, and Oliver in his shirt sleeves making a strenuous effort to bend down far enough to remove one of his boots. 'Oh hello,' said Stan, 'Did you enjoy the show? Do you know I always watch Elsie and Doris from the wings. They're so good, aren't they?'

'Yes, and so are you,' I mumbled, 'I'm sorry there weren't more in to see you.'

'Oh well,' said Stan, '*You* came, didn't you? How about a cup of tea and a bun? Would you like that?'

'Now then,' said Oliver, having finally got his boots off, 'I've got some sweets somewhere, unless Stanley's eaten them.'

Malcolm goes on to describe numerous bits of business which the two comedians performed for him, and concludes:

The point was, that after a tiring and, for them, disappointing show, they had bothered to entertain one small boy for half an hour before going on again for the evening show. Most stars, I've learnt to my cost, would only do that sort of thing in front of cameras to show how charming they are. With Laurel and Hardy it seemed a perfectly natural act.

On Tuesday 22 April Stan and Babe paid a visit to Scotland Yard's Black Museum, where the exhibits from infamous trials are housed. The following week they were guests of honour at the *Daily Mail* Film Awards at the *Dorchester Hotel*, where they themselves were filmed turning up late and interrupting Lady Rothermere presenting an award to Margaret Lockwood (see page 302). Hardy tried to make amends by pinching roses from a floral display, and handing them around. The night before (Sunday 27 April), the Water Rats staged a charity show, the *Rats' Revel*, at the *Victoria Palace*. One unknown comedian, after finishing his act on this show, didn't remain unknown much longer. The reaction he received was ecstatic. His name – Norman Wisdom. Norman takes up the story:

I was in a show at the *Hackney Empire*. The producer asked me if I would do a charity concert on the forthcoming Sunday. I immediately said 'yes', as at that time I would have done anything to get on stage. I would have made the tea, if they'd asked me.

On Sunday morning, I turned up for rehearsals, and there were all these big stars: George Doonan, Vera Lynn, Will Fyffe, and Laurel and Hardy. I did my rehearsal on about two foot of stage, and nobody took a blind bit of notice. Amongst all these stars, I wasn't known from Adam. In the evening, though – if I say so myself – I went extremely well, and had to take several bows.

The reviews certainly bear out Norman's recollections. *The Performer* said:

Then came one of the outstanding hits of the evening, young Norman Wisdom, who bounced himself up one more rung of the ladder towards stardom with yet another exhibition of uproarious foolishness.

Said *The Stage*:

Vera Lynn, Laurel and Hardy, and Will Fyffe all provided of their best in this half of the show, but it was newcomer, Norman Wisdom, who took the house by storm with some of the funniest business possible.

It was at this show that Norman first gained credibility as a brilliant performer with some of the higher members of the profession. Laurel and Hardy were certainly impressed, for on two future occasions it was *they* who went to watch *him* perform. Stan's immediate response was to approach Billy Marsh and say 'You want to sign this man up. He's a great clown.' Billy Marsh took his advice and, over forty years later, is still Norman's manager.

While Norman Wisdom was trying to establish *his* character, R. B. Marriott of *The Stage* had been asking Stan Laurel the reasons for the longevity of the characters of Laurel and Hardy. What emerged was a fascinating piece of original writing. The article stated that Stan had found after lengthy experiment, thought and practice that:

The basis of lasting success in team-comedy, no matter what the particular appeal of the comedians may be, must be built on always having a strong framework for individual gags, expressions and gestures. In other words, on a story or 'situation'. I do not think a pair of comedians can get very far and become popular over many years if they rely entirely on gags and mannerisms.

Even during the average time on the stage of the star variety-turn, let alone in a full-length film, jokes and gags alone become tedious. But with a story or, if you like, with comedians in a 'situation', such as the one Hardy and I find ourselves in, there is every chance of not only from time to time relaxing from gags and vocal and physical mannerisms associated in the public mind with the comedian's success, but also of enriching the act by 'business' that would otherwise be impossible.

Marriott and Laurel agreed that the idiosyncrasies for which a comedian had become known and loved, must always play a big part. Said Stan,

It amazes me how much the public remember of apparently trivial things – a certain finger movement, a fleeting facial expression, and the like. Hardy and I noticed this especially since our return to variety here after many films. We have frequently been surprised at the response given to odd bits of 'business' that we thought would have impressed only when seen in an actual film. Naturally, this sort of thing going on over the years enables us to build our act more and more securely, in detail as well as in its main structure. But again the value of a story or situation appears. In no other way can the act as liked by the public be kept fresh and varied.

Speaking of the format of their act Stan said he believed that, with its pathos and human touch, its effectiveness remained undiminished.

The sympathy for the little fellow who is knocked about and kicked around is as strong as ever. In my opinion it will always be one of the best liked things in comedy, simply because in the heart of so many of us, there is something of the little fellow himself.

Having read the above, one must now be more able to judge exactly why Stan Laurel and Oliver Hardy chose, as they did, to retain the format of their act. Changing to 'fast-patter merchants', or trying to reshape themselves into a more modern image, would have been denying the public what the public expected to see. By sticking with the old image, Laurel and Hardy may have incurred the wrath of some critics, but they certainly kept the love of the public.

Chapter Nine

Stannie, Where's Ye' Troosers?

THE twelve weeks for which Laurel and Hardy had been booked were now completed, but ecstatic reports caused a wave of demand from many provincial theatre managers. The first to secure a booking were brothers Robert and Maurice Kennedy, who ran the *Dudley Hippodrome*. The appearance of Laurel and Hardy in this West Midlands town was considered a great coup, and served to put not only the theatre on the map, but Dudley as a whole. Tickets were sold out well in advance, and all box-office records broken. The *Birmingham Post* missed the sense of occasion:

> The audience saw and loved, in reality, what it had so often seen at the cinema. Hardy administered rebukes to his partner, both by word and deed, and Laurel accepted them with the familiar tearful mien and much ruffling of the hair. The sketch gave them the fullest scope for their slapstick antics.

Mary Crettol, who worked at the *Station Hotel*, has fond memories of the Boys:

> The *Hippodrome* was adjacent to the hotel and huge crowds would gather to see them. When Laurel and Hardy had finished their performance they would return to the hotel and after a few drinks, entertain the residents.
>
> They both liked English food, especially steak and kidney pie. After the war, when meat was rationed, we served pigeon pie. This was a

favourite of Ollie's. Hardy was a man with a great thirst. He drank large jugs of water with his meals and always ordered pots and pots of tea. He was always the perfect gentleman, speaking almost in a whisper. We had difficulty accommodating him on a dining room chair. He seemed to find the ones we had uncomfortably small for his large frame. Laurel never ate breakfast in the dining room, preferring to eat in his bedroom with his wife. We were young girls, and found it a great privilege to look after them.

After a fabulous week, during which Stan and Babe visited the Cape Hill Brewery, at Smethwick, the company took the train to Liverpool. Harry Moreny got aboard carrying a large parcel, which he took with him into the compartment he was sharing with Olga Varona and her husband Archie. In the next compartment were the Laurels and the Hardys. When the attendant came to ask what time they would like to book their meal in the dining car, Harry opened his parcel and said, 'Can you do anything with this?' The attendant's mouth dropped open when he saw a whole cooked leg of lamb, which a grateful theatregoer had donated to the party. 'Don't move from there,' said the attendant, 'you have more food here than we have in the dining car.' He promptly returned with cutlery, condiments, and tea, bread and butter, and the seven of them tucked into a very unexpected, and delicious, clandestine meal.

John Jones will never forget the week that followed in Liverpool, for he had the delightful daily job of chauffeuring Laurel and Hardy from the *Adelphi Hotel*, along Lime Street, to the *Empire Theatre*. On the Monday morning John duly picked them up and took them to rehearsals. In the evening there was one amazing difference: Lime Street was so jammed with people that mounted police had to be brought in to control them. Billy Marsh said, 'It was an unbelievable sight. Why! I'd never even seen a mounted policeman before.' Inside the *Liverpool Empire* the seats and aisles too were packed, and remained so for the week's duration, with hundreds still left outside each night. The *Daily Post* revealed none of this:

The stage act of Laurel and Hardy is cunningly simple – an introduction, a sketch, and a song and dance with some patter. But from the first note of the famous 'Cuckoo Song' until they were reluctantly allowed to go, the pair kept the packed house in an uproar of merriment with all the tricks and antics that have won them a place amongst the world's great comedians.

In his memoirs in a 1962 edition of the *Liverpool Echo*, TV comedy writer Eddie Braben, best known for his Morecambe and Wise scripts, wrote a far more sentimental account of Stan and Ollie's appearance; an event which, he said, was to play an important part in his later years.

> The lights dimmed and a spotlight lit one corner of the stage; just five notes of a signature tune; the top of the bill act hadn't yet appeared but the ovation was thunderous. Then THEY walked onto the stage and the theatre trembled with clapping and cheering. The ovation lasted for fully two minutes. Now I saw 'Them'. It really was 'Them' – Laurel and Hardy. Stan smiled and scratched his head. Oliver wiggled his tie – they could have finished on that. Never before or since have I seen an audience show such love and affection. It was too much for Ollie, because he cried.

In the time he spent as their chauffeur, John Jones got to know Stan and Babe quite well. He reflected:

> I was an employee, but was not treated as such. I was often invited into their company, in the hotel. There they would buy me a half of beer, and a drop of dry whisky for themselves. They were clean living, definitely not boozers, and I never heard a swear word out of them in all the time I spent with them. They were kindness itself.

At the end of each evening's performance, it was not a simple matter of the comedy duo putting on their coats and strolling out of the stage door, for outside would be hundreds of autograph hounds. The crowds that week had been exceptionally physical and, as a result, the Boys came to dread their nightly confrontation. On the third night, they were delaying as long as possible when Babe suddenly pointed to the door and said 'Well! who's going first?', which 'broke up' the whole company. The next night it was Stan who got the big laugh when he announced, 'I'll just pop outside to see what's happening.' Everyone knew that if he *had* ventured outside the crowd would have 'torn him to pieces'.

On Sunday morning John went along to the hotel to pick up the Laurel and Hardy 'family' and take them to the next stop-over. The police had cordoned off the area to keep back the vast crowd so, getting into character, Stan and Ollie were able to pause for a moment on the hotel steps. Standing there in their raglan overcoats, Stan took off his trilby and scratched his head, and Ollie twiddled his tie. A roar went up, as if the Liverpool football team had scored a goal, and the crowd surged forward. John quickly ushered them into the waiting Rolls Royce, for fear they would be mobbed. What happened next was witnessed by no-one else but him.

> As we pulled away, Oliver Hardy asked me if I wouldn't mind driving them around Liverpool a little. He particularly wanted to be shown some of the bombed areas. I drove them around the worst of these: Church Street, Whitechapel, Vauxhall Road, Derby Road, and up the Dock Road, where many buildings were now just rubble. After a time I happened to glance at Ollie, who was sitting beside me in the passenger seat, and saw that tears were rolling down his cheeks. Ollie said he would never know how the poor British had put up with this.
>
> Laurel, who was sitting in the back of the car, slid back the window and said to me, 'This is one of the things we wanted to see for ourselves. Otherwise, living in America, we couldn't have known what it must have been like.'

John certainly wasn't exaggerating when he later said, 'They had an awful lot of feeling for the British people.'

The journey was continuing along the country roads towards Preston when, at Longton, Stan asked if they could stop at the village pub. John advised the Boys, 'Keep your heads down, and whatever you do, don't speak.' The pub was practically empty but, while pouring the beers, the landlord asked who the VIPs were. 'Just some people I'm taking to More-cambe,' replied John. 'They don't half look like Laurel and Hardy,' said the landlord, who insisted on taking the drinks to the table so that he could have another look. But as he entered the back bar, Stan and Babe turned away, and so he left still uncertain. Next minute his wife entered with a tray of bread and cheese. 'Excuse me, but we haven't ordered that,' Babe politely pointed out. 'It's free,' said the landlady. 'Gee thanks,' responded Stan. At which the landlady, unable to withhold her feelings any longer, enquired 'You *are* Laurel and Hardy, aren't you?' With that, the pub magically filled with people, and they ended up getting a huge send-off from the whole village. So much for a quiet drink! John felt very sad as he dropped them off for the last time. Understandably, he had grown very fond of them.

> Stan seemed really pleased to be home, and I found him such a nice guy to be with. Off stage they were like brothers, often asking each other questions, and were all the time concerned about each other. For

example, Stan would offer Ollie the front seat of the car, as he felt Ollie would be more comfortable there. I never once heard a sharp word, never mind a cross word, between them.

Of the Boys' humour away from the public, John said:

They couldn't help but be funny off-stage as well – it came so naturally to them. It was just the little things. They only needed to look at one another and everyone would laugh. I'm sure they could read each other's minds. They knew exactly what the other one was doing, and what they were going to do next. They were so close.

And of the tour he said: 'Their lives were not their own. It was as if the whole of Britain just wanted to get to know them, to meet them'. Possessed as they were of the characteristics that John described, is it any wonder? John's last memory of them was an emotionally charged farewell, as he shook their hands outside the *Elms Hotel* in Bare, Morecambe.

Later that day the Boys decided to go for a stroll. Instantly, they were surrounded by a crowd of onlookers. After a while the situation became hopeless. Those who had been given attention wouldn't leave, whilst others kept joining the mélange. Eventually the two comedians realised the futility of their efforts and retreated to the sanctuary of their hotel.

On Tuesday Stan took Ida and the Hardys to Ulverston, to see the house and places where he was born and brought up over fifty years ago. After a look around, the party left in time to make the evening shows. Once safely in his dressing room at the *Pavilion Theatre*, in the *Winter Gardens* complex, Stan wrote in a letter to his cousin Mary:

Dear Mary, – Delighted to receive your sweet letter. Funny you should mention Ulverston, just back from visiting there today – quite a turn out. I was presented to the folks at the Coronation Hall and was given a copy of my birth certificate on the balcony outside. Then went over to 3, Argyle Street, went through the old house, brought back many memories. Had lunch with the officials at the golf club, a wonderful time, was thrilled to death.

Stan also wrote a thank you letter to Councillor Simpson, which read:

Just a line to express my deep appreciation for the wonderful reception accorded me on my return to 'Lile Oostan' ['Little Ulverston']. The sincere kindness of you all will never be forgotten.

Ollie tests out the balcony of the Coronation Hall, *prior to introducing hometown boy Arthur Stanley Jefferson to the masses below.*
County Square, Ulverston, *27 May 1947.*

Stan Laurel beaming with delight, after having just shown his comedy partner around the house he was born in:
3 Argyle Street, Ulverston.
(By kind permission of the *North West Evening Mail.*)

Please accept my humble 'Thank you' also to all concerned for bestowing upon me the biggest thrill of my life in the true Lancashire spirit.

My love and fondest thoughts always – Stan Laurel.

On Wednesday afternoon the pair judged a bathing beauty competition at Morecambe's open-air swimming stadium. Caught out by an unusual British temperature of 29°C, they had to endure the heat dressed in suit and tie while most of the 4,500 spectators relaxed in swimwear. Among the dignitaries in attendance were the Mayor of Morecambe, Herbert Willacy MBE, the Earl of Sefton and Lady Sefton, and the Mayor of Lancaster. Popular as the comedy duo were, the crowd were quick to show dissent when they felt that the girl in second place ought to have won.

On Thursday evening Stan and Babe were interviewed backstage at the theatre for a live-on-air broadcast during the BBC radio programme *Morecambe Night Out*. Unfortunately, no transcript has survived. On Sunday the Laurels and the Hardys checked out of the *Elms Hotel*, and made the short journey southwards for a week's engagement at the *Palace Theatre*, Blackpool. On Monday morning, after rehearsals, the Boys stepped out onto the balcony overlooking the seafront and gained an instant response from passers-by. Hats, caps and handkerchiefs were waved, and the familiar shouts of 'Good old Stan – hi-ya Ollie' were heard above the passing traffic.

'Stanley,' said Ollie, twiddling his tie, 'we are in Blackpool.'

'Don't lean on the railing, Ollie,' said Stan, 'we have a show to do tonight.' 'Don't be facetious, Stanley,' said Oliver, his chubby cheeks wreathed in smiles, his eyes twinkling. 'Give the folks a big hand. Remember the siege of '32?' continued Babe.

'Do I?' says Stan.

'I like Blackpool,' says Hardy.

'Me too,' says Laurel, and the two retired inside with the crowd still cheering and waving.

The Blackpool press certainly weren't going to be blamed for instigating another 'siege'; only the *Evening Gazette* gave them coverage:

If you are a Laurel and Hardy picture fan you will get full value for money at the *Palace Theatre*, Blackpool, this week, where the famous Hollywood comedians are making their second appearance in fifteen years.

You will laugh, as packed houses did last night, not so much at the words of the script as at the stars themselves. Ollie calls their sketch a 'spot of nonsense'. It is just that, with a dialogue that is always wholesome and in line with the Laurel and Hardy tradition of uncoloured fun.

The latter point stood out so strongly in the reviewer's mind, that a few days later he took it up again.

Why are Laurel and Hardy so triumphant on their tour? The answer is surely because their humour is simple, unsophisticated, and clean. People like it. At a time when the dirty joke, the sly innuendo, the double meaning, are far too prevalent, these two veterans show that mirth does not solely depend on references to sexual aberration, procreation, or the lavatory. It is comforting to find that comedians like these two can be so successful and so clean.

On Thursday Stan and Babe were invited to a luncheon given by the Water Rats. After cocktails at the *Fleece Hotel* they adjourned to Hill's Restaurant, where most of the leading entertainers in Blackpool had turned up, including Josef Locke and Nat Jackley. After a few 'shandies', lovable maniac Frank Randle felt sufficiently courageous to go to George Formby's house and tackle his wife Beryl, who had forbidden George to keep company in 'a room-full of drunken men'. An inebriated Frank Randle turning up on his doorstep was the last person Formby wanted to fight his case but, somehow, he was reprieved and allowed out of the house. Under strict instructions not to enter the premises, Formby had to stay by his car and Stan and Babe were brought out to meet him. After exchanging pleasantries, he returned home; otherwise he would have had to face from Beryl an onslaught bigger than the one Laurel and Hardy were to receive on their return to Glasgow.

On Sunday, heading north on the train from Blackpool, Stan spent his time gazing out of the window as the train passed through the Lake District. Later, nearing Glasgow, he went into the corridor to obtain a better view and was joined by Archie Collins, a now familiar travelling companion. Although Archie's wife Olga was Australian, he himself was from Pollokshaws, near Cathcart, where Stan's mother was buried. The train went on through Rutherglen and, knowing the area well, Archie said casually to Stan, 'That's Rutherglen.' 'Archie, you have gone quite up-stage,' replied

Stan, 'it is Ru'glen. I went to school there.' This astounded Archie, as he had no previous knowledge of Stan's Scottish background. Needless to say, the two of them were later to spend many happy hours comparing notes.

Laurel and Hardy must have had a forewarning of the huge reception they were about to receive for, miles out from Glasgow, children had turned out in their hundreds to wave flags as the train sped by. To see the look of sincere glee on the children's faces had the Boys almost fit to burst into tears before they even reached Glasgow. When they did arrive it was like another step back in time for there, at the Central Station, was pretty well the same scene they had witnessed fifteen years earlier. Although the crowd of five thousand was considerably smaller than that of 1932, the station area was still crammed tight, and the returning heroes were given the most enthusiastic welcome of the tour so far. The *Evening Citizen* had had more than a little to do with the turn-out, as two days earlier they had advertised:

> Laurel and Hardy are due to arrive in Glasgow on Sunday. Their train from Blackpool gets in at 4.15 p.m. A hint for the fans: watch the first-class carriage nearest the engine.

Railway police and civil police, backed up by mounted policemen, had turned out in force, and all were needed to escort the two idols from the platform to the *Central Hotel*. Even so, the events of 1932 were almost repeated when an ugly scene began to develop. As the party made headway the crowd closed in behind them, shunting them forward like a human train, until eventually the duo were shoved through the hotel doors. People then began to congregate by the front entrance in such great numbers that mounted police were needed to clear them; but even then the crowd did not disperse until Stan and Ollie had made an appearance on the hotel balcony.

To cater for expected audience demand the Glasgow engagement was for two weeks, with several visits, both official and private, also having been planned. The first approach was by Sir A. B. King who challenged Hardy to a game of golf. Sir Alex was still the proud owner of the half-a-crown he had won from Babe in the 1932 re-match (when he was plain A. B. King), and Babe was still the proud owner of the tartan umbrella. Asked if his handicap was still four [sic] Babe replied, 'My handicap is twenty-one stone, and about seventeen, I should imagine.'

In mentioning his weight Babe had forgotten that, since being in Britain, he had actually lost forty-three pounds, making him a much slimmer eighteen stone. (Or was he originally twenty-four stone? – It's hard to tell.)

This he put down to the physical effort required in doing thirteen shows per week. When asked about the food situation by an *Evening News* reporter, Hardy revealed he was feeling much better for his weight loss. Laurel added, tactfully:

> I know it's tough to have such rationing after all that Britain has gone through, but people can still laugh, and it amazes us to hear their capacity for enjoyment. Many of them must have lost everything they had during the war and be starting from scratch again, but still they can laugh. It shows they have a lot of guts.

Of their plans for the near future, Laurel admitted that the prospects of making a film were remote. The bookings for their world tour had piled up at such a rate that he didn't even know when they would be returning to America. The proposed visits were to Scandanavia, Belgium, France and Switzerland. After this would come visits to South Africa and Australia. They would then be back in England in time to do *Babes in the Wood* for the Christmas season of 1948–49, at the *Saville Theatre* in London. (As it turned out, the latter three places were never visited, and the pantomime was never played.)

Eddie Campbell of the *Daily Record*, wrote of his personal feelings towards the two comedians:

> Stars of the cinema make frequent stage appearances these days. All too often the reception they get for their boosted 'personal appearances' springs less from appreciation than from an audience's charity. And what a relief to find two screen performers who are not less worth looking at on the stage, but more. Meeting Laurel and Hardy on Sunday and watching five thousand people milling and crushing round Central Station for a glimpse of them, I felt that no stage artiste deserved such adulation. Watching them on stage, I had to agree that there was at least something to be said for it. For these two are master dispensers of the world's most precious commodity – laughter. They really are genuinely and truly funny. Behind the make-up you get a glimpse of two blokes genuinely embarrassed at the warmth of public approval.

The critic from the *Evening Times* was obviously fond of the Boys, but did not go overboard:

Every seat was occupied for the triumphant appearance of Laurel and Hardy. In their sketch, one realises that their jokes and dialogue are not so very funny at all – it's the actions that count. Papers are thrown in the air, shoulders are pushed, lapels brushed, faces made, and all the other known tricks of the comic pair are produced one after another. There is only one complaint – we could have done with a lot more of their happy clowning.

As artistes in the show, Archie Collins and Olga Varona felt more cause to celebrate than did the newspaper critics.

Never to this day, in any theatre in the world we have played, have we heard anything like the reception given to Laurel and Hardy on their entrance. We thought that the whole of Hampden Park [football crowd] had come to the *Empire*.

Considering the waves of euphoria which had greeted Laurel and Hardy from the children by the railside, the thousands at the station and the packed audiences at the theatre, it is hard to comprehend how blasé the critics remained. As the *Glasgow Empire* held the most dreaded reputation of *all* British theatres for giving the cold shoulder to comedians – especially non-Scottish comedians – one would have thought that such an amazing success story deserved some critical acclaim. It was only the *Evening Citizen* which conveyed some of the hysteria with which their stage appearance was received:

No wonder Oliver Hardy blew most of his 'Thank you' kisses to the gallery at the *Glasgow Empire* last night. The whistles, yells, and cheers of welcome were loud enough to be heard at Charing Cross [London], and the audience just wouldn't let them go. Taken critically, the sketch is quite ordinary and some of the jokes are very familiar. But who wants to be critical with old friends like Laurel and Hardy?

Once again, the public's enthusiasm outshone that of the critics and the 'No seats available' sign was up for the entire fortnight. Robert Hewitt of the *Evening Citizen* added the following personal observations:

If there's one thing I dislike it's snobbishness. And I'm sorry to say I've seen it shown by quite a few stars, some of whom refuse to mix with other artistes on the bill, and walk past stage crews as if they didn't exist. It is an attitude I have always deplored. Let me therefore tell you what a pleasure it is to meet Laurel and Hardy. Backstage I've found them to be probably the most unassuming, modest and friendliest top o' the bill stars who ever walked through the stage door. For them the stagehands would do anything. Every evening before they go on, the Hollywood pair wander around at the back of the stage chatting to the lads. As one stagehand says: 'They're just a couple of regular guys.'

On Tuesday, Sir Hector McNeil, the Lord Provost of Glasgow, invited the Boys to the Glasgow City Chambers. There he presented them both with a copy of C. A. Oakley's book, *The Second City*, in which Laurel is mentioned in the section which deals with Glasgow-born celebrities. This was meant as a tribute to Stan but may well have turned out to be an embarrassment, since he was neither Glaswegian, nor even Scottish. Present also, and undisputedly Scottish, was Harry Lauder, accompanied by his niece, Greta Lauder. Lauder watched the Boys' show that evening, then went backstage to pay his respects and, after spending an hour chatting, left them with an invitation to visit him at his home.

For Laurel, the undisputed highlight of the stay in Glasgow was Thursday's visit to his beloved *Metropole Theatre*, where he was welcomed by the owner Alec Frutin, and the manager Peter Hart. In his haste to re-acquaint himself with his boyhood haunt Stan raced through the building, giving a non-stop commentary as he went: 'There used to be a wide pend[16] there, and the paybox is still the same . . ., and the staircase is still the same . . ., and that's the office . . .,' he announced to his breathless followers.

In the office he recalled where the safe was, then sat down at the desk and reminisced about the times he had sat there as a boy whilst his dad was 'out front'. Leaving the office, he ran up the staircase to the gallery and, going into the paybox, re-enacted his role as ticket boy. From there he went to the circle, then wound his way backstage via the maze of passages in this near-century-old theatre. Having been in every dressing room, he walked out onto the stage and recounted the story of the morning he had stood in that very spot and decided to become a comedian. When Stan finally left the *Metropole*, the tears in his eyes betrayed that he had been through a very emotional experience.

---

16   A colloquial Scottish term referring to the arched entrance to a corridor, alleyway, or staircase.

Following Harry Lauder's efforts with a spray can, Hardy swots an escaped greenfly on Laurel's neck.
Lauder Ha', Strathaven, Scotland. 24 June 1947.
(By courtesy of John McCabe.)

On Friday the Laurels and the Hardys were guests at a luncheon given by the Glasgow Cinema Club. At the end of the dinner all three hundred guests stood up and sang 'Will Ye No' Come Back Again', and this time both comedians were moved to tears. Babe jollied things up by sitting at the piano and leading everyone in a sing-song.

At the end of the first week, Stan, Babe, Ida and Lucille, acting on Harry Lauder's invitation, drove over to Strathaven. At his beautiful residence, Lauder Ha', they found Sir Harry dressed in full Scottish regalia; the best the visitors could manage was diced-balmoral hats. After a stroll through the grounds the party retired inside for a typical Scottish tea (3s. 6d. per head). Stan *and* Babe were thrilled to be in Lauder's company, as every American artiste knew of him through his having played over twenty tours in America. Laurel's conversation was of the *Glasgow Metropole*, which both had played in their earliest days; and the British Karno productions, which Lauder had often watched. Hardy could not resist requesting Lauder to sing the songs which had kept him as a major music-hall star for over thirty years[17] – a request to which Lauder readily acceded, and the Boys were only too happy to join in.

The following evening, during the *The Driver's Licence* sketch, Laurel was puzzled when MacKenzie Reid, one of the support acts, walked on stage playing his accordion. It was only when Stan recognised the tune that he realised this was the company's way of getting the audience to sing

17   Lauder played his last official performance, in Glasgow, in 1947. He died in February 1950.

Stan McLaurel and Oliver McHardy as they appeared on stage in Bonnie
Scotland *at the* Glasgow Empire, *18 June 1947.*
(John McLean.)

The two comic legends addressing the crowd at the opening of a Gymkhana in Eastwood Park. *Lady Weir claps in appreciation. 21 June 1947.*
(Glasgow Herald.)

'Happy Birthday' to him. The following night it was the audience who were given the surprise, when Laurel and Hardy made a sincere attempt to show how much they loved Scotland, and respected Scottish tradition, by performing their act in kilts. The Scottish audiences loved them, in return, as they had done when the Boys wore kilts in their film *Bonnie Scotland* (a film – perhaps not so co-incidentally – being shown that week at one of the local cinemas).

On the final Saturday of their stay the two comedians opened the Eastwood Gymkhana on Lord and Lady Weir's estate at Giffnock, before rushing away to get to the 4 o'clock matinée at the *Empire*. I can think of no other stars, past or present, who, having three shows to do in one day, would put themselves out to make an unpaid guest appearance. But from Stan Laurel and Oliver Hardy, these gestures to their public were frequent.

Having missed seeing at close quarters the beautiful lakes, mountains and greenery Scottish on their previous visit, Stan and Babe had made sure that, this time, they saw as much as they could. During a couple of free days they and their wives had been on guided tours of the Five Lochs, with Sir Alex acting as host to the Hardys in his car and Alec Frutin looking after the Laurels in his. Calling in for some liquid refreshment at the *Inversnaid Hotel* at Loch Lomond, Hardy again treated the company to a sing-song at the piano. A drop of the amber nectar was also enjoyed when the two parties retired to Sir Alex King's beautiful residence *Ta-Na-Righ* (House-of-Kings), after one of their days out. Lucille and Ida were to say of the trips, 'We'd looked forward to seeing Scotland, but it surpassed all our expectations.'

So, having gasped with awe at the beautiful scenery, and cried at the sentiment expressed by the Scots, and with the sounds of 'Will Ye No Come Back Again' forever etched in their memories, the 'McLaurels and the McHardys' bid a very sad farewell to the city and the people of Glasgow.

Chapter Ten

Tripe, and More Tripe

T HE Butlin's Holiday Camp at Skegness in Lincolnshire (opened in 1936) was the first of many similar camps. Among the wooden chalets and steel-and-plaster entertainment centres it houses the brick-built *Gaiety Theatre*, and here the show played twice-nightly to residents and day visitors alike. The critic for the *Skegness Standard* enthused:

> The cheering and applause started even before Laurel and Hardy appeared, for it commenced when the orchestra played the first bars of their signature tune. And as the curtain parted to reveal the two inimitable figures, the cheering changed to laughter, which continued almost uninterrupted throughout their side-shaking act. The pair manage to get into – and out of – every conceivable tangle and, at the end, the audience is near to hysteria!

During their Skegness engagement, Stan and Babe were cajoled into participating in the daytime entertainments programme. In the *Empress Ballroom* they judged the Holiday Princess competition and, while the Boys were keeping their eyes on the girls, Lucille and Ida were keeping their eyes on the Boys, by making up the rest of the judging panel. The four of them then moved out on to the sports field to judge the rather less-glamorous contestants in the Knobbly Knees competition. After these two visual tests, Stan and Babe were called upon to show more of an intellectual aptitude when Billy Butlin himself invited them to join Clay Keyes, Professor Joad and Commander Campbell for an edition of *The Brains Trust*. The Boys

Laurel and Hardy – with stage crew and management – auditioning for the
Butlin's Redcoat Show.
Gaiety Theatre, *Skegness.*
Week commencing 23 June 1947.
(By courtesy of Ron Kerr.) (Author's collection.)

Judging the
'Lady-who's-
been-in-the-
bath-too-long'
competition.
Empress
Ballroom.
(By courtesy of
Steve Bolton.)

*Above: Ida, Stan, Babe and Lucille on the sportsfield, signing the
Anglo-American pact atop the Stars & Stripes and the Union Jack.*
(By kind permission of Dave Bradshaw.)

*Below: 'Putting their heads together' with Billy Butlin and three regular
panellists from the long-running radio show* The Brains Trust.
*Left to right, Clay Keyes, Professor Joad, Billy Butlin,
and Commander Campbell.*
(By kind permission of John Cooper.)

had played this game before with Billy Butlin, back in March at a Water Rats' dinner (see page 96), but not with such a distinguished panel of 'brains'.

On their way through from Glasgow to Skegness the previous Sunday, the celebrities had stopped off at Grantham to meet up with Stan's sister, Olga, and his brother-in-law, William Henry Healey, for a drink and a quick chat in the *Red Lion Hotel*. On leaving Skegness, they had a little more time to spare and called in at Barkston, near Grantham, where Olga and Bill ran the *Plough Inn*. Just after the First World War, Bill Healey had been in the orchestra at the *Theatre Royal*, Grantham and, after seeing Olga on stage, approached her at his aunt's theatrical digs. Following a short undistinguished career in acting, Olga retired from the stage and the two lived together for a while, before marrying and taking over the *Plough*.

Arthur Jefferson, too, was now living at the *Plough*, following the death of Venetia. In 1940, fearing that a German bomb might finish him off, he had moved from London to live with his daughter in the safety of the Lincolnshire countryside. Stan had been to see them on his way to London from Birmingham, back in March, when they had enjoyed a happy reunion.

On this latest occasion the party stayed until late on Sunday afternoon, before catching a train from Grantham, and alighting at Edinburgh's Waverley Bridge Station shortly after 8 p.m. The doors to the station were locked to keep out the fans, and only the official reception party had been allowed onto the platform. The Laurels were dressed for the occasion, with Stan looking dapper in a diced-balmoral hat and Ida sporting a glengarry bonnet. Knowing what to expect, and seeing no point in avoiding the confrontation, Hardy said impatiently, 'What are we waiting for? – Let's get going.' With that, a squad of twelve policemen ringed the party and shepherded them into the street. The ensuing scene resembled Harrod's department store at the opening of the January sales. Thousands of people rushed forward, jostling for leader position. Those who reached the target first were easily able to slip under the linked arms of the police cordon and come face to face with their idols, and so it took several minutes for the foursome to travel the few yards from the station doorway to their waiting car.

The sanctuary of the car was limited, for they now had to manoeuvre it through the ten thousand people congregated on Waverley Bridge itself. The idea had been for the onlookers to line up on the pavement, with the children nearest to the roadside, and wave to the celebrities as they went by. Less-caring adults, though, entered the roadway and, as well as totally obscuring the view of the stars, impeded the car's progress. Taking a firm hand, the police tried to clear a way through and shoved the offenders back towards the pavement. This had the disastrous effect of forcing the people in the roadside onto the children who were lining the pavement. Many of the children were bowled over, and the crowd found themselves playing a dangerous game of hopscotch to avoid stepping on them. Fortunately, no hospital cases were recorded but, for some of the children, what should have been a happy encounter with the two funny men ended in tears.

Ten minutes later the car pulled up outside the *Caledonian Hotel*, and the strong police escort saw the Boys safely inside, after which the vast crowd soon dispersed upon being informed that Laurel and Hardy would not be making an appearance. The following night an equally large gathering awaited the comedy stars outside the *Empire Theatre*. Inside, the show was summed up by the *Evening News* as follows:

> The moment the orchestra struck up their signature tune and Laurel and Hardy strode on to the stage, each arrayed in a kilt of startling hue, they were welcomed by a gust of laughter from the packed audience. It was a fine tribute to two great comedians, and for the next half hour they fanned this favourable breeze into a veritable gale of merriment by an exhibition of supreme artistry. The very contrast in styles is sufficient to make an audience laugh without a word being spoken. And when they speak and clown together the appeal is irresistible. It was pantomime at its best, for which they earned and received a great ovation.

Off stage, the Boys and their wives had to go to the museum in Chambers Street to re-stock their ration vouchers, and on another occasion visited the Enterprise Scotland Exhibition at the Dryden Street store. There, the manager found himself being entertained by two Scottish pipers who looked suspiciously like Laurel and Hardy. With six thousand props to choose from, it was a certainty that the comedy couple would find something amusing to play with.

During his stay in Edinburgh Hardy tried hard to trace the Scottish part of his ancestry. His maternal grandmother was Irish, but his grandfather, Thomas Edward Norvell (from whom he took his middle name) was Scottish, and Hardy was convinced he had been a graduate of Edinburgh University in the 1840s.[18] When asked by a reporter about the name Norvell, Hardy replied:

Stan and Babe wrestle with a couple of octopuses, whilst Lucille and Ida protect their ears from the screams. 3 July 1947. (By kind permission of the *Glasgow Herald*.)

I quote the lines in 'Douglas': 'My name is Norval [sic], on the Grampian Hills my father feeds his flocks', and everyone says the Grampian Hills are not in Scotland. But they are. I have dozens of maps.

After yet another sell-out week, the Boys moved down the north-east coast to the fishing port of Hull, on the River Humber. Here, their appearance was almost totally overlooked, as, out of four local papers, only the *Hull Daily Mail* gave them a mention, and even that was the tiniest of entries:

Few film stars will achieve such success with a personal appearance as Laurel and Hardy at the *New Theatre* this week. They are everything their public hoped for, natural buffoons and as lovable as ever. Children shrieked and adults roared, yet it wasn't the slick wisecrack, just The Thin One and The Fat One happily awkward. The twiddle of a finger from Oliver, the chalky smile of Stan in his endearing simplicity and their battered bowlers were enough. After twenty minutes, which included a typical sketch, and a song from each they left to terrific applause.

On Wednesday the Laurels and Hardys attended a luncheon at the *Royal Station Hotel* given by the local cinema managers. Other than that, nothing else was forthcoming from the people of Hull.

---

18   Leo Brook's research in 1988 revealed that Hardy's grandfather was actually a tenant farmer in Georgia, of very low social and educational status. Babe never found this out.

Any semblance of a pattern in their travel plans was well and truly broken when, from Hull, the company had to make a journey of over two hundred miles to the city of Bristol, on the south-west coast. Coming in to Bristol by train, Hardy remarked how magnificent the English countryside was, and how proud it made him feel to be of British heritage. Both he and Stan made a note to tour the surrounding countryside and visit some of Bristol's historic buildings. Tragically, Bristol had been badly bombed during the war, and several buildings of note had been damaged or destroyed.

The people of Bristol knew exactly when to expect Laurel and Hardy as the *Evening World* had announced: 'Fans please note: Stan and Ollie arrive at Temple Mead Station from York, at 6.26 on Sunday evening.' Consequently, they were met by an estimated one thousand people, whom Stan described as being 'good humoured, but a bit boisterous.' This number may seem rather small after some of the crowds the Boys had encountered, but one thousand people can do an awful lot of damage to two men. In fact, *one* person can do an awful lot of damage, as was proved when Hardy got a very painful dig in the back from someone's umbrella. The incident was passed off with good humour at the time but, once in the hotel, Babe began to feel the effects. Apparently, the metal ferrule on the brolly had poked him in the exact spot where, earlier in his life, he had had two ribs removed. After minor treatment from a doctor and a hot bath at the *Royal Hotel*, he felt a little better.

The farcical claim about Laurel and Hardy making a film had now been dropped. The reason for this was given as 'due to weather uncertainty and Continental commitments'. This leaves one wondering if a film crew, plus producer, actors, costumes, millionaire-backer and a finished film script, would suddenly have materialised if the sun had chosen to shine.

Regarding Laurel and Hardy's current theatre tour, John Coe of the *Evening Post* said of the opening night at the *Bristol Hippodrome*:

> Come the sketch in which Mr Hardy wants to obtain a driving licence. How do they handle it? By provoking the traffic officer into a paroxysm of rage with their misunderstandings of his simple purpose and intent. Mr Hardy puts on the bold front, while Mr Laurel meekly sits back and blows up a balloon, plays with a fingerstall, oblivious of the situation which is about to explode.
>
> Their technique is of course, superb. The timing to the split second of the hilarious gag is as good as the economy of their script and patter.

And the sketch builds up into a wildly funny climax which is in the best slapstick tradition.

John Bennett of the *Evening World* was also very complimentary.

Laurel and Hardy's perky signature tune was the signal for a full minute's applause. It was three minutes before Ollie spoke his first words: those minutes were packed with miming fun that convulsed the huge audience. Their opening minutes on the stage are a gem of the generous helping of comedy they give, though their little sketch is typical of their grotesque [sic] humour. If, as they say, it cost £1,000 to bring them to Bristol for a week, Bristol is having its money's worth . . . with even some elephantine dancing from Ollie and some 'Sinatra-like crooning' from Stan, to the end of the show.

Earlier that day Stan and Babe had sat backstage bemoaning their fate: desperately wanting to see the sights of Bristol, they knew from previous experience that they wouldn't get ten yards. Hardy, especially, couldn't go anywhere without being recognised. He was so big, and stood out so much in a crowd, that he simply had nowhere to hide, and nearly always ended up having to stay in the hotel. Laurel was luckier; if he wasn't actually with Hardy, he could sometimes escape notice. Taking advantage of this, Laurel changed partners and ventured out with Archie Collins to find a theatre he had appeared at in the early 1900s. With collar pulled up, and hat pulled down, Stan wound his way unerringly to where he remembered it to be.

Although his memory was faithful to him, the years weren't, for the theatre[19] was now used as an engineering workshop. Stan still wanted to look around, but he was spotted. Within five minutes the whole of the labour force had turned out, and were fussing around him as if he were an old mate. He was shown over the premises, and after much hand-shaking finally allowed to leave, with promises from all present to attend the show.

On Thursday both Laurel *and* Hardy and their wives were driven from Bristol to Weston-super-Mare, twenty-two miles away. When the car arrived on Weston promenade, a tussle ensued during which the police cordon failed to keep back the very large and enthusiastic crowd. Eventually, the VIPs were led through three huge queues of people outside the open-air swimming stadium, to be officially welcomed at the entrance by the mayor

---

19   The Broadweir Hall, at 7 Broad Weir – now demolished.

and mayoress, Alderman G. E. Bosley and his wife. Inside the pool area, a further six thousand people gave them a rousing welcome.

After the foursome had judged the Modern Venus beauty competition, Lucille and Ida were presented with bouquets by the mayoress; then, thanks to a number of fans who had generously donated sweets coupons, Stan and Babe received a one-pound box of chocolates. If this weren't enough, an anonymous donor, who had heard of Hardy's weight loss, tried to make up for it all in one go by having the mayor present him with a four-pound juicy steak ('smothered in onions', no doubt). Having used up Glasgow's supply of clothing coupons to purchase kilts, it appeared that Laurel and Hardy had now exhausted Weston-super-Mare's supply of food coupons.

In conversation with Laurel in the early part of the week, Archie Collins had described the beautiful cottage he and Olga were renting while in Bristol. Stan liked what he heard and suggested that Archie invite over the Laurel and Hardy 'family' (as Stan called them). A few days later the invitation was taken up, and the party was driven to the Marlborough Hill district and dropped off at the gate of Kozy Kot Cottage – a beautiful two-storey building with a lovely view over the Bristol Channel.

During afternoon tea Stan returned the invitation, asking Archie and Olga to have tea with the Laurels and the Hardys at the *Royal Hotel*. When he subsequently saw the starch and starkness of the hotel, Archie said, 'If this is what you get for being top of the bill, I'm glad were only a support act.' This was taken in the humorous spirit in which it was meant, and all enjoyed fond memories of Bristol, and especially Kozy Kot Cottage.

One would have thought, after Laurel's several solo appearances in and around Manchester (see pages 269–279), and his 1932 visit with Hardy, that the Manchester press might have made something of Laurel and Hardy's two week run at the *Palace Theatre*. Amazingly, the *Evening Chronicle* offered only a critique, and even that was short in the extreme:

> Beyond applying unavailingly for a driving licence, Laurel and Hardy do nothing in particular. But they do it so well that a co-operative audience end by being surprised at the passage of time and asking for more. The screen is the famous pair's best medium, but it is a pleasure to see at close quarters Stan Laurel back in the city where he first joined Karno's show to understudy Chaplin. Apprehensive, self-deprecatory, able to hold an audience by the movement of a finger, he is, in his own way, a consummate actor.

The *Evening News* also went in for paper rationing:

> Laurel & Hardy – like Marks & Spencer's and fish & chips – are a natural pair. Straight from stage to screen they bring the familiar trappings of the elfish and elephantine buffoonery. When not tormenting each other, they combine forces to torment a hapless police officer. Last night's packed audience enjoyed every minute.

Fortunately, one particular member of that audience found the experience totally unforgettable. Then, he was a young boy, but during the 'sixties he became a household name himself, and star of countless radio and TV series – ace impressionist, Peter Goodwright. Peter recalled:

> I remember the almost tangible murmur of anticipatory whispers which filled the auditorium as the first few notes of 'The Cuckoo Song' were played. They walked onto the stage and the supressed excitement and pleasure at their appearance erupted into a never-to-be-forgotten roar of welcome. The applause was deafening as the audience rose to its feet to greet the two men. They stood centre-stage – Ollie twiddling his tie, and Stan removing his hat and scratching his head.
>
> In the evening of their career in America – having been ousted out of position by Abbott and Costello – here they were being afforded the honours usually only conferred on heroes. Still the ovation continued, and so great was it, that it became very emotional to realise what high esteem these two comedians commanded. In retrospect, I think the audience were saying: 'Thank you for making us laugh during the dark days of the war. And thank you for coming to England to see us. And thank you for being Laurel and Hardy.' Whatever it was, the approbation afforded to these two men – containing as it did, a mixture of love; admiration; delight; and laughter – was one I had never experienced before – nor heard of since.
>
> Eventually the audience subsided into their seats, with men and women alike, wiping away tears of emotion. During the sketch, laughter and applause rang constantly around the theatre, and at the end of the show I remember feeling very privileged to have been there to see these two gentlemen perform.

Alma McKay ran theatrical digs in Longsight (a suburb of Manchester), and was looking after some of the support acts in the show. Apparently, Stan and Babe weren't too happy with the food at the *Grand Hotel*, and wangled an invitation over to Alma's, at Astra House. Although she, too, was feeling the pinch, she treated them to cakes and sandwiches, after which they were quite happy to stay on a while, merrily chatting. The food at the *Grand* probably also prompted the following amusing incident: One evening when Hardy fancied some 'good old fish and chips', Laurel decided to have tripe and onions – a traditional Lancashire dish he hadn't had for years. Popping out of the theatre, Stan gave the order to the girl in the shop and waited at the counter. On bringing out the order, the girl chanced to give him a second glance and, with dawning recognition, said, 'Oh no!', to which Stan said, 'Oh yes', and she promptly dropped the lot on the floor.

On the middle Sunday of the two-week engagement, Stan took advantage of not having to pack up and move on and attended a long-awaited family reunion with a party of close relatives, most of whom were living in close proximity to each other in Yorkshire. These were his cousin Jack from Leeds Road, Woodkirk, who had spent four days with Stan during Laurel and Hardy's recent stay in Blackpool; cousin Mary (Jennings) of East Street, Batley; cousin Nellie (Beaumont) of Newsome Street, Dewsbury; and cousin Charlie (Shaw) of Mount Pleasant, Batley; plus their spouses and children. John Shaw reported:

> We all had a great time together. Stan has a serious outlook on life – he couldn't have got where he is if he hadn't. He knows showbusiness inside out, but we don't talk shop with him.

And Nancy Wardell, daughter of Laurel's cousin Mary, who had first met her world-famous uncle during his engagement in Morecambe, further revealed that

> Stan's cousin Jack met Stan and Ida at the *Dewsbury Empire* and took them back to his home. After an early lunch they went on to cousin Nellie's house, where his cousin Mary (my mother) and the rest of the family welcomed him. He was totally at ease and fell in with all the family's fun-and-games. It was hard to realise he was so famous. Sadly the time passed all too quickly, and though at the time everyone promised to have another get-together, it never happened.

Dates were still being added to Laurel and Hardy's tour without the luxury of being able to choose the venues in order of location. From Manchester in the north west, the tourers had to make make yet another two-hundred-mile-plus journey for their next engagement. In Southsea, near Portsmouth, the press was again in a coma, and reported nothing whatsoever of the celebrities' stay there. Nevertheless, the public were well aware, and the box office at the *King's Theatre* did great business.

A rather touching event happened that week, which the participants' modesty forbade being made public. Olga Varona related the circumstances of her husband Archie's chance meeting as follows:

> Laurel and Hardy's driver for that week, asked Archie if he knew his brother, Hector St Clair, who was in showbusiness. It turned out that Archie had known him very well, right up to the time of his death. The driver then asked Archie if he wouldn't mind visiting his sister, who lived near the theatre but was bed-ridden. Archie gladly obliged, and entertained the lady with tales of her late brother, and some of his songs. This made her very happy, but later she was even happier when, having been told of her plight, Laurel, Hardy, and Harry Moreny paid her a visit.

The bad weather which had plagued the company earlier on, was now well and truly behind them, and they enjoyed another week of glorious sunshine, during which Stan took a look over *HMS Dolphin*, a submarine base in Gosport.

On Sunday morning the touring party had a most pleasant drive through the New Forest on their way through to Boscombe, near Bournemouth.

Stan Laurel dressed to do some decorating, but the liquid in the can is not paint, but the King's rum. HMS Dolphin.
(By kind permission of Lt Cdr R. Swift, Rtd.)

The press made nothing of their presence, except for a review in the *Bournemouth Daily Echo*:

> Those first class slapstick comedians, Laurel and Hardy, had the large audience at the *Boscombe Hippodrome* rocking with laughter from the time they made their appearance until their exit. For the majority of people it was the first time they had seen those popular screen comedians in person, and the event was regarded with some importance by both young and old. For nearly half an hour Stan and Oliver delighted the audience with their simple but cleverly timed actions.

The Boys spent most of the week in the *Chine Hotel*, owned by Fred Butterworth, who also owned the the *Boscombe Hippodrome*. (Butterworth proved to be a good contact, for on the 1953–54 tour Laurel and Hardy played a further six of his theatres.) Gerald Warr JP visited the hotel that week and recalled:

> Laurel and Hardy seemed to enjoy their own company within the hotel where they kept themselves privately, but separately. I met them both, though not together, and throughout the talks they were most cordial and entertaining. I attended one of their shows, but was a little disappointed, as the stage did not reflect their film performances. The best part was some very memorable singing and some dance steps. The reception given them was very warm, as this was considered a tremendous booking. The audience came from Dorset as well as the greater part of Hampshire, and the theatre was sold out at nearly all performances.

Remaining on stage after their sketch on the Monday night, Stan and Ollie had the pleasure of crowning seventeen-year-old Pauline Ashdown as Carnival Queen. Stan rushed up to Pauline with a hammer, but Ollie got there just in time. Said Stan: 'Well they told me to crown her.' The carnival itself was held mid-week in King's Park, where fifty thousand people turned out to watch. Laurel and Hardy wisely stayed indoors. They might have acted daft, but they weren't stupid!

After travelling along the 'sole and heel' of England, the show members arrived at the Kent holiday resort of Margate for what would be their third week in a row of sunshine and sea air. On booking in at the *St George's Hotel* in Cliftonville, Babe presented his party's ration cards to a surprised and delighted young lady called Dorothea Neal. Each evening, from behind the reception desk, Dorothea would observe the two comedians as they waited in the foyer for their car. Stan struck her as being morose, whereas Babe was always very outgoing and pleasant. What she was probably witnessing in Stan was the nerves which most comedians experience before a show, wherein they totally withdraw and notice little of what is going on around them. Babe's nerves, however, didn't show themselves in the same way. He never classed himself as a comedian, but saw himself only as acting as a foil to Stan. That he was totally wrong in his estimation, is a sign of the man's immeasurable modesty. After the show Laurel would be in a more relaxed mood, and would stay up for a 'nightcap' with the others.

On the Monday evening Bill Evans, reporter for the *East Kent Times*, met the Boys backstage between houses:

> Laurel and Hardy stepped onto the stage at the *Winter Gardens*, and received a great ovation. But what are these two characters like off stage? Very simple and philosophical, and great in the tradition of their calling. It is not often Americans find our weather as hot as of late, and Oliver Hardy, mopping his brow, was in his shirt sleeves. 'It's been 93 where I've just come from,' he said, 'and it seems hotter than California's 105 degrees. It's a different kind of heat.' Oliver used to be a first-rate golfer with a handsome handicap though he has not played for four years.

John Eddols, resident drummer at the *Winter Gardens*, remembers having to make sound effects during Laurel and Hardy's sketch. One particular piece of business required a loud cymbal crash and, one night, as the drumstick hit the cymbal, the head broke off and flew across the stage. Stan observed it, picked it up, leant over the edge of the orchestra pit, and with considerable aplomb said to John, 'Is this what you're looking for?' This may not seem funny in writing, but the audience who were witness to the way in which Stan brought magic to such a simple act, dissolved into paroxysms of laughter.

On 24 August the Laurel and Hardy Company left Margate, by train, to travel to Coventry. This beautiful Midlands city had been badly bombed during the war, but even so the people of Coventry had kept up morale, and life went on as normally as possible. Most theatres and cinemas had stayed open during these troubled years, and did good business, but the shows had started and finished much earlier. One cinema which didn't survive the bombing was the local *Rex* which, legend has it, was blown to pieces during the run of *Gone with the Wind*.

To cater for the demand, it was decided that Laurel and Hardy should play two weeks at Coventry. The decision was well taken, and from the outset one could see that the visit was going to be a success. The crowd waiting to greet them at the station was so great that it was practically impossible for the two comedians to get through the main exit. They were therefore led out of a back exit, which hadn't been used for years, and were able to get into their waiting car with not a fan in sight. The *Evening Telegraph* had had more than a little to do with the turnout.

Hollywood's Greatest Comedy Couple -
STAN LAUREL and OLIVER HARDY
ARE ARRIVING AT COVENTRY STATION
TOMORROW (Aug 24th) AT 6.30 p.m.
WHY NOT BE THERE WITH US TO WELCOME THEM?

What a nice change it was to see the press taking an interest in the Boys, misguided as their efforts were; after previous scares, Laurel and Hardy had had enough of greetings at railway stations. The *Coventry Standard* wrote:

Laurel and Hardy head a tip-top show at *Coventry Hippodrome*, and their buffoonery – simple, but clever – keeps the audiences thoroughly amused. In a short sketch they apply for a driving licence. Hardy explains he cannot read and that Laurel cannot write, and later Laurel says that though he can read he cannot read writing! But even if they remained completely silent their clowning is sufficient to keep folks roaring with laughter.

The *Telegraph* gave only cryptic clues as to the on-stage action:

And so one is drawn to Laurel, the classic clown, and his perfect foil, the amiably pompous Oliver Hardy, upon an irresistible wave of nostalgic reflection. The skit ends characteristically in a riot of knockabout retribution. This is excellent fun, but many will prefer the gentler sequel, when the couple face the audience in an intimate frolic, sometimes at the expense of their Hollywood contemparies. Incidentally, it gives Hardy an opportunity to air a surprisingly well-pitched tenor voice.

What *is* suprising about the last comment is that Babe was suffering from a sore throat that week and, to alleviate the problem, had requested George Cockayne, the sound operator, to lift the sound during his song. Although Babe didn't lose his voice that week he had, since the beginning of his stay in England, lost twenty-three pounds. Of this, he commented,

> I don't blame your Mr Strachey [Minister of Food]. It's all due to hard work. Rationing doesn't worry me. I'm a light eater anyway, and I never touch breakfast or lunch. I brought two small trunk loads of canned food with me from the States, in case of emergency, but I have only dipped into six tins. I intend to give the remainder to a newly-married couple in London.

Considering the amount of dinners to which Hardy was invited, and the contraband gifts of food which were lavished upon him, it's not surprising that he hadn't yet needed to raid his tuck-box. The *Standard* reported that Hardy had lost forty-six pounds since arriving in England which, if both reports are correct, would mean that he had lost twenty-three pounds in five days. Laurel said he knew Hardy's weight very well, 'because he often treads on my foot'. Of their on-stage comedy, Stan said he was convinced that there was still a great future for slapstick comedy, because

> (. . .) it had universal appeal. Peoples of different nations might not understand the finer points of English, American, or French humour, but they shared equally with Europeans in their delight at seeing a man receiving, for instance, a blancmange full in the face.

While in Coventry the Boys, uncharacteristically, stayed at separate hotels – and even in different towns. Stan stayed at the *Abbey Hotel*, Kenilworth, while Babe stayed at the *Clarendon*, Leamington Spa. A *Morning News* reporter on enquiring after Hardy at his hotel, was told: 'He won't see anyone. He was pestered to death – that's why he's here. He really has so many demands on his time, he doesn't take telephone calls, and all arrangements are made through his agent.' Persistency paid off, though, and the reporter secured an interview. Asked about his impressions of Leamington, Hardy replied: 'We [Mr and Mrs Hardy] have only walked a few blocks, but this is one of the cleanest and prettiest towns we have seen.' He went on to tell the reporter how chance had brought him to Leamington – and how glad he was at the outcome:

Harry Moreny (in peak cap) arrests Laurel and Hardy and their wives, Ida and Lucille, for camera hogging.
Coventry Hippodrome, *25 August 1947.*
(By courtesy of George Cockayne – front, right.) (Author's collection.)

In another district, some accommodation difficulty arose and the closest bath was a block away. But here at the *Clarendon*, this is one of the nicest places we have been in. The service and the people have been an absolute revelation. We have been continually on the go since February, but the peace and quiet we found here – that is something.

With memories of the severe winter still fresh in their minds Babe and Lucille were very much surprised that an English summer could follow such weather. The reporter concluded that Mr and Mrs Hardy had decided upon Warwickshire as their favourite part of England. Said Mrs Hardy: 'Your little villages are absolutely fascinating. Anything written, painted, or said about England in the spring is not half enough. It is so entirely different from anything we have.' Asked about sightseeing, Hardy told the reporter they'd been to Stratford-upon-Avon, where he deplored the modernistic appearance of the *Shakespeare Memorial Theatre*:

'It looks so out of place to represent something with so much tradition behind it.' He added that he first saw the theatre after a visit to other places of interest at Stratford which were more in keeping with the Shakespearean setting, and consequently the theatre came as a surprise.

Guests at the hotel saw little of Hardy as he usually remained in his apartment till afternoon. Twice he and Lucille went for a short walk in town where, whilst wearing his horn-rimmed glasses, he was recognised by few people. A shopping trip in Leamington Spa, though, where he met up with Stan, had to be curtailed when a walk around Woolworth's resulted in the shop becoming jammed with sightseers. The Boys did manage to get out to a private dinner, the circumstance of which demonstrates the total openness which Laurel and Hardy afforded their fans. Arthur Brearley, now of Halifax, said

> Instead of dreaming of meeting them, I wrote to them at the theatre and invited them to tea. To my amazement and delight, they came. My children were not old enough to enjoy their company as much as I did, but Laurel and Hardy put themselves out to entertain them. It is something I will always remember and I was the toast of the neighbours for months.

The next visit was to the Triumph Standard Auto Works, in Canley. The day must have started off chilly, as the Laurels and the Hardys were well wrapped up. As the day wore on it got hotter and hotter and, inside the metal building, the party began to cook. Subsequently, they all retired to the canteen, where Babe had two large mugs of tea to 'top himself up'.

A private visit similar to the one in Southsea also occurred in Coventry. It started when a lady sent a letter thanking Laurel and Hardy for the wonderful job they had done in boosting the morale of the British people during the war. She regretted being unable to attend the show and thank them in person, but since the war she had gone blind. The letter closed with her wishing them every success possible. Sincerely touched by this tribute, Stan and Babe sent a car to bring her to the theatre. Given a seat in the front row, she was later led backstage for tea with the Boys themselves, before being driven home. Once again, Stan Laurel and Oliver Hardy had shown utter sincerity and genuine concern for the welfare of their fans.

The company next found itself in the cotton-mill town of Bolton. This Lancashire town had remained untouched by wartime devastation, the nearest bombing having been on Manchester. Nevertheless, many of its cinemas and theatres had closed during the war years. The show was staged at the *Lido*, and though there were more suitable venues in the town, these would have been booked up long before Laurel and Hardy's tour was conceived. One must remember that the tour was originally planned for twelve weeks only, so all the later bookings were being done at short notice. As Billy Marsh admitted, 'Laurel and Hardy were put into theatres which would normally not be considered. There just weren't theatres around to satisfy the demand.' Ida Laurel recollected to John McCabe,

> It was a really dirty, drafty [sic] old theatre. Stan wanted to send out for some fish and chips. Stan adored fish and chips. But the stage-door keeper protested – he said indignantly fish and chips would smell up the place. Stan just looked at the man, and took a deep breath, getting that backstage air in his lungs. 'Bring the fish and chips please,' he told the man politely. 'They'll be like perfume to the air floating around in here now.'

Nora Chadwick, who still lives in Bolton, said of the show:

> I remember the occasion with great happiness at actually seeing Laurel and Hardy in person. I never thought it possible. We had seats on the front row of the stalls, and were amazed at how agile Hardy was able to dance, and so quietly, too – such a big man. I well remember the part of the sketch when Laurel answered the telephone and on Hardy enquiring 'Who was that?', Stan replied, 'Long distance from Glasgow.'[20]

Although there were hotels in Bolton at which Stan and Babe could have stayed, they chose to stay at the *Brooklands Hotel* in Sale, Manchester. The rest of the cast, however, stayed in 'pro digs' in Bolton, run by a Mrs Wotherspoon, who one night cooked tripe and onions for them. This was thoroughly enjoyed by all; so much so, that a full description of it was relayed to Stan. Not being one who could resist the taste of tripe and onions, he charged Jack Whitmore, their tour manager, to coerce the landlady into sending some round to the theatre. The following evening Mrs Wotherspoon duly obliged, and the Boys were able to savour for themselves the

---

20   A reworking of the gag: 'It's a long distance from Atlanta, Georgia' – from the film *The Fixer-Uppers*.

delights which the others had already enjoyed. Every time Stan cooked the dish in future, it was from Mrs Wotherspoon's recipe.

On the last day of their week at Bolton, Saturday 13 September, Laurel and Hardy were also to be seen at the Poolstook Stadium in Wigan, where they were given a rousing welcome by eight thousand people awaiting the start of the speedway racing. The two comedians then had to speed themselves, in order to get to *Bolton Lido* for the show. How they managed to fit in this appearance, plus a matinée, and two evening shows, has not yet been figured out.

Chapter Eleven

The Final Cut

THE Boys and their wives made the two-hundred-mile journey from Bolton to Swindon by road, but sent the company's forty pieces of luggage by rail. As the tour was now taking its toll, they stayed well away from the theatre, at the *Bear Hotel*, Hungerford, where they would not be pestered by over-zealous fans. Of the show at the *Swindon Empire*, the *Evening Advertiser* reported:

> The question that comes to mind is whether Laurel and Hardy live up to their reputations as two of the finest comics the screen has produced. The answer is: 'They do.' Their sketch provides full scope for their mimicry and will even further endear them to their fans.

Stan had played the *Swindon Empire* twice before, in *Sleeping Beauty* (1907) and *The House That Jack Built* (1909), but his only memory of Swindon was that 'it was winter and, as we were kids, we played snowballs'.

The Boys' gambling habit, from which their wives thought they had been cured after the greyhound incident at Lewisham, returned when a tipster put them on to a horse called Stuart. Having been convinced it was a cert, they instructed Billy Marsh to place a considerable bet on it and to keep doing this as long as funds lasted. There then followed an amazing run of wins which extended into the New Year, and the Laurels and the Hardys were actually back in America when Billy Marsh phoned Stan: 'What are you going to do with all this money, Stan?' enquired Billy. 'What money?' puzzled Stan. 'The money from the horse. It kept winning. I got over fifty quid here,' explained Billy. Without a moment's hesitation, Stan said: 'Give it to the Water Rats.'

On 22 September Laurel and Hardy were back in London for the last theatre engagement of the tour. If they'd been hoping for an easy week on which to finish they were soon disappointed, for they ended up working literally twice as hard. The previous week Bernard Delfont had brought over the American singing quartet The Inkspots who, after a wrangle over contracts, had returned to America prematurely, leaving Delfont without a 'name' act at the *Chiswick Empire*. The ever-obliging Stan and Ollie agreed to stand in and, on Monday evening, by changing the running order, played two houses at *Finsbury Park*, and two at the *Chiswick Empire*. If this weren't a big enough labour in itself, Laurel was given a further handicap when a foot-rule used in the sketch flew back off Harry Moreny's desk and struck him on the forehead, causing a cut. After having a stitch inserted, Stan was able to carry on, and the rest of the week went off without further incident. *The Stage* said of the show at *Finsbury Park Empire*:

> Are Laurel and Hardy as funny on stage as in films? Realising how some have sadly failed to adjust themselves, one went prepared for disappointment – and got a surprise. They are funnier. At least, seeing them in the flesh brings home more forcibly than photography the inborn sense of clowning of this most lovable couple. They have the advantage of good material here in their sketch, which with its cinema technique of action going on all the time – knockabout scattering of papers and exchange of hats – gives constant laughter.

Of the same show, *The Performer* observed briefly, 'Young folk more than usual in evidence in big audience this week, with Laurel and Hardy giving the fullest satisfaction. In short they were a riot.' The *Chiswick Times* was equally short: 'What good showmen Laurel and Hardy are! Without doing anything in particular, they can stand in front of a microphone for ten minutes at a time and keep the audience rocking with laughter.'

On the eve of the London appearances Stan and Babe had attended a banquet at the *Savoy Hotel*, given in their honour by the Water Rats. Present amongst the three hundred male guests were Will Hay, Val Parnell, Bernard Delfont, Billy Marsh, Lupino Lane, Louis Valentine, Archie Collins, Hannen Swaffer, Harry Moreny and, rather surprisingly, Ben Shipman (secretary of Laurel & Hardy Feature Productions). Bud Flanagan, in proposing a toast, pointed out: 'One of the guests is English, and one is

American. After seven years of rationing, it's not hard to tell which is which.' This tongue-in-cheek statement was followed by a sincere acknowledgement to the fund-raising, and troop entertainment done by the Boys during the war. He went on to say, 'Laurel and Hardy aren't finished. With their comic abilities they will never be finished as performers.'

Tribute was then paid to the Boys' generosity in presenting the then colossal amount of £1,100 towards the purchasing of new premises for the Rats. (The money raised was from the fees given to Laurel and Hardy for appearances, outside of their theatre work.) Then, as a token of thanks, Stan and Babe were each presented with a leather-bound volume containing the history of the order, and inscribed by all their brother Rats. When the cheering had died down, Laurel was first to stand and reply to the toast:

> I can scarcely find words to express our appreciation of the grand way in which we have been received. Everyone has made us wonderfully happy, and our visit has been made a memorable one. I am particularly grateful to the Water Rats for extending so warm and brotherly a feeling to us, and we are proud to have been admitted into their ranks. The beautiful book I will treasure all my life. Our hearts are full of love and affection for all of you. We hope to return to this country, and when we do, we hope to see the new clubhouse well under way.

Babe then stood up, and replied:

> I don't think I have sufficient words to express my appreciation of the hospitality and friendship extended to Stan and I since our arrival in Britain. I would like to start by thanking Bernard Delfont and Billy Marsh for having the courage to bring us over.

At this, cheering broke out. Babe continued:

> I must also extend thanks to Harry Foster and Leslie MacDonnell; and to Val Parnell for his friendly pat on the back at the start of our tour. We are also very grateful to the people of Scotland for the wonderful receptions they afforded us. We must thank all the theatre managers for the way they have treated us; and most of all we must give a special thank you to Harry Moreny for his assistance in our act.

This well-deserved praise for Moreny was echoed by theatre critics and newspaper reviewers throughout the tour. Archie Collins said of him, 'He was more than just a foil to them – he was a terrific back-stop in every way.'

Babe closed by thanking the Rats themselves, and ended with: 'Please don't ever forget us, for we shall always remember you.' The evening was a fitting tribute to Laurel and Hardy, and the sentiments expressed by all were genuine and heart-felt affection for these two lovable men.

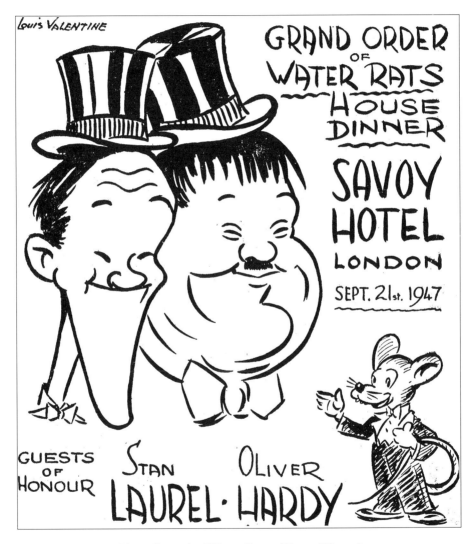

Menu from the 'Water Rats – House Dinner',
held in honour of Laurel and Hardy.
(Artwork by Louis Valentine.)
(By courtesy of Peggy Valentine.)

One week later, on 30 September, the Boys attended their last lodge meeting before leaving Britain. As if they hadn't already given enough, they presented the Water Rats with accessories to a silver desk-set (which is now housed in the Water Rats' museum), and 'the egg'. This is a real egg, diamanté studded and suspended on a ribbon, which is placed around the neck of a Rat as a penance for telling a really awful joke. Stan invented the idea as an addition to the Rats' existing ritual, and the same egg is still in use today.

Oliver Hardy had now used up all his permitted time in Britain, but a Euro-

'Two minds without a single thought'.
Palace Hotel, *Copenhagen.*

pean tour, which the Boys could start on immediately, had been hastily knocked together. So, on 1 October, the *Crown Prince Friedrich* picked up the Laurels and the Hardys from British soil and ferried them to the Danish port of Esbjerg, en route for Copenhagen. Although suffering from a bad case of sea-sickness, the two comedians managed to put on a happy face for the hundreds of fans who turned up to give them a great reception. The smiling had to continue throughout the train journey from Esberg, as crowds were at every stop to wave to them. Using the *Palace Hotel* in Copenhagen as a base, Laurel and Hardy played shows at the *Tivoli Gardens*, Copenhagen (4 October), and others in Aarhus and Odense.

Sweden was next on the tour, with an appearance at the Uppsala University in Stockholm and others in Gothenburg and Malmo. Reception was cool, as the events were poorly advertised and badly organised. The comedians had their bags searched on suspicion of currency smuggling, but nothing was found; an incident which tended to dominate the press cover-

The Godfather makes Laurel and Hardy an offer they can't refuse. (Left to right, actors I.B. Schönberg, Paul Reichardt and Peter Malberg.) Copenhagen, October 1947.

age and spoiled the whole visit. Returning to Copenhagen they made a radio broadcast, then went to dine at the home of Prince Harold, the late king's brother. Next day, 28 October, after keeping his guests up till 2.30 a.m., Prince Harold and his son saw them off at the station.

On their arrival in Paris the screen-turned-stage comedians were given a tremendous welcome at the Gare du Nord Station, but their stay in the capital was not to be a happy one. Booked into the *Lido de Paris*, they were faced with performing to an audience composed of people of several different nationalities,[21] as well as being put in the degrading position of having to do their act in the middle of the revue of nude showgirls.

The run of nightly shows was punctuated by a trip back over to England, where Laurel and Hardy were surprised and delighted to have been selected to appear on the *Royal Variety Performance*. Having had less than ten days' notice, and being allowed no time off from their current engagement to attend, Stan, Babe and their wives had to take a train ride and make a channel ferry crossing, there and back, within twenty-four hours.

Doing the show meant a return to the *London Palladium*, a venue they had conquered earlier in the year. This night, though (Monday 3 November

21   Confusion exists as to whether Stan and Babe did their act in French or English. The French magazine *Image du Monde* printed an abridged version of the script, in French, with the caption 'Laurel and Hardy perform this sketch every night. They don't know what they're saying, because they don't understand a word of French.' As there is no substantiation that the writer of this article saw the show, it could quite easily have been speculation, drawn from a misunderstanding of the publicity sheets.

1947), would prove to be a whole new challenge. Firstly, it was to be in the presence of King George VI and Queen Elizabeth (now the Queen Mother), and their younger daughter, Princess Margaret, and was attended by many dignitaries and showbusiness celebrites. The occasion was further marked by the first public appearance, after the announcement of their engagement, of Lieutenant Philip Mountbatten and Princess Elizabeth (now Prince Philip and Queen Elizabeth II). Secondly, instead of Laurel and Hardy being the star attraction, with hand-picked support acts around them to complement their act, they were to be only one of many top-class acts. Whether or not the audience regarded the show as a competition, there is no doubt that most of the performers did, and each would be striving to achieve the greatest acclaim.

The audience too would not be easy. Because it was a charity show, ticket prices were well up on the usual admission charges. (As a gauge, consider that for the *1992 Royal Variety Performance* tickets were from £35 to £200.) Val Parnell, the show's producer, admitted to *The Stage*:

> The audience at a *Royal Variety Performance* is hard-boiled, and there's nothing worse than for an act to be received in stony silence. I don't say that variety is exactly on trial at this show, but it is a test of performance.

These then, were to be difficult conditions under which the duo were to be tested, and they were going to need the head start given to them by their film status if they were to survive on the London stage amidst its most revered and popular performers, and theatreland's hardest critics.

In a 1957 radio interview, Arthur Friedman asked of Stan, regarding the *Royal Variety Performance*: 'Were you [Laurel and Hardy] the only representative from this country [America]?' to which Stan replied: 'Yes, I believe we were.' As it happens, American acts were well represented with Dolores Gray and Bill Johnson, Jack Durant, Borrah Minevitch's Harmonica Rascals and Wally Boag, to name but four (see page 289). Of the Anglo-American combination, the *Birmingham Mail* had this to say:

> By the interval, it was obvious that British and American acts on the bill were fighting for honours. The English artistes may or may not have been a little hurt at the trans-atlantic emphasis in the programme. But from the moment they came on, they were determined to persuade the Royal Family that music hall is still something we can do better.

The *Evening Standard* believed that England ultimately won in the honours stakes, when they wrote: 'It was the Britons and not the Americans who dominated the show.' Having established that Americans were in proliferation, consider Friedman's next statement: 'According to the information I have, Laurel and Hardy received perhaps the greatest ovation that any act had received.' To this Stan made the irregular reply 'We did – yes, we did.' I say 'irregular' as Stan was not wont to make false claims. In this instance, though, it must be presumed that Stan replied in the affirmative to discourage Friedman from further questions on the subject: for Laurel and Hardy had received, to put it kindly, a rather mixed reception.

The *Birmingham Mail* wrote, 'There was also a failure: Laurel and Hardy in a humourless sketch about motoring.' The *London Evening Standard* was a little kinder: 'Laurel and Hardy struck me as a little over-awed and too subdued.' *The Stage*, noted for being kind to showbusiness artistes, pointed out that 'Their first appearance in front of the curtain was the signal for a burst of cheering, and the Royal party seemed to know their work and worth.' After describing the plot of the sketch, the review finished: 'The two popular comedians kept the house in the merriest of moods.'

John McCabe, Stan's biographer, holds the view given by *The Stage*, and refutes the claim that 'they wouldn't say anything unless they could say something nice.' Although McCabe wasn't present, he has the benefit of testimony from three people who were – Stan, Ida and Lucille. These three were unanimous in declaring Laurel and Hardy a hit. Their opinions were strengthened by Charlie Henry, Chief of Production at the *Palladium*, who told Stan he had observed the king 'laughing long and loud . . . throwing his head back while laughing in great appreciation.' Note, though, that both Henry and *The Stage* credit the laughter as originating from the royal box.

Consider the weight of this evidence alongside that supplied by Billy Marsh and Bernard Delfont who, to date, have produced no fewer than thirty *Royal Variety Performance* shows, as well as booking the three post-war Laurel and Hardy tours. Both were present on the night, and had the comedians' interest totally at heart. Marsh said in a personal interview:

> They were a very tough audience – even infamous for being hard – because they'd paid their money, and said: 'Come on – show us'. They weren't very good audiences at all. The acts only did it for the honour.

Having stated the case for the artistes, Marsh then presented the case for the audience:

You have to bear in mind that Laurel and Hardy weren't a sophisticated act. They couldn't go out and fight an audience, if things weren't going well. They were considered to be only a 'light' act. [Tommy] Trinder could go out there and have a go – but not them. They were successful on their own shows, but that night wasn't one of their best.

And, on Laurel and Hardy's acceptance, Delfont commented only: 'They got by, nicely.' When asked what he meant by that, he again remarked, 'They got by.' Then added, 'They were a hard audience.'

When a despondent Babe Hardy asked backstage the possible reason why they hadn't scored with the audience, Charlie Henry jokingly replied 'Don't worry! They're always hard first house on a Monday.'

A possible answer is that the Boys' mental preparation and, ultimately, their usual faultless timing, were affected by two main factors: firstly, their spot was cut from twenty minutes to just eight; and secondly, the act who were to go on before them, Dolores Gray and Bill Johnson, failed to arrive in time from the *London Coliseum*. This unnerved Stan and Babe who, instead of following a singing act, now had to follow a strong comedy act – ventriloquist, Bobbie Kimber. Billy Marsh puts down this reshuffle as the major contributory factor in the disappointing way their act was received.

The debate over the *Royal Variety Performance* should not be taken too seriously. The only issue at stake is whether the audience were too hard, or Laurel and Hardy too weak. After the comedians' track record earlier in the year at the *Palladium*, it should be obvious to everyone which option is correct. This one-off, egotistical audience, whose main aim on the night is not *to see* but *be seen*, should not be allowed to detract from the fact that Laurel and Hardy were asked to entertain the Royal Family, and can rightly feel the utmost pride for having done just that. Stan and Babe's personal disappointment was not in their performance, but in missing the opportunity to be presented to the Royal Family, for they had to dash from the theatre to make the train connection for the ferry back to France.

From the presence of royalty at the *Palladium*, it was straight back to the peasantry in the *Lido de Paris*. This is not an ungenerous statement as, in wintertime, most of the people who make Paris a cultural meeting place are not present. Stan hated every minute of their stay, and regarded their run there as a flop. Reviews, though, would suggest that the flop was in Stan's eyes only. The bad pervading atmosphere was not just limited to the interior of the *Lido*, though, for by a horrendous stroke of bad luck the visitors had arrived back in Paris at the beginning of the Great Strike. Riots were frequent, and at times they were in fear of being caught up in the violence. The mains services became inoperative, and made their stay at the *George V Hotel* an uncomfortable one. At the end of the painful six-week run the tourers were in a dilemma as to how to get out of the French capital, as the transport system was at a virtual standstill. In the end, a Belgian bus was hired to ship them secretly out of France, in the middle of the night, and into Belgium. On arriving in Brussels, they were rewarded by the luxurious surroundings and first-class service of the *Metropole Hotel*.

Between 10 and 18 December Stan and Babe spent time rehearsing at the *Alhambra Theatre*, where the show commenced on 19 December. It was a variety show, billed as *Hollywood Parade* – even though Laurel and Hardy were the only Hollywood act in it – and once again they did the *Driver's Licence* sketch. The reviews went from good to jubilant in their praise although, rather puzzlingly, one of these billed Jacques Henley as their assistant, and not Harry Moreny. Certain comments found in the French and Belgian reviews suggest that Laurel and Hardy performed their act in French whilst in Paris, but in English when in Belgium. (A third theory, put forward by John McCabe, is that Laurel and Hardy inserted only the odd phrase or two, in French, into the sketch.)

At the end of the two-week run, which took them into the New Year, they embarked on a series of two shows a day around other parts of Belgium, as the following schedule for January 1948 shows:

Date:		Town:	Depart:	Arrive:	1st Show:	2nd Show:
Fri	2	Antwerp	1.15 p.m.	2.00 p.m.	4.00 p.m.	9.00 p.m.
Sat	3	Charleroi	1.00 p.m.	2.00 p.m.	2.45 p.m.	7.30 p.m.
Sun	4	Charleroi	1.00 p.m.	2.00 p.m.	2.45 p.m.	7.30 p.m.
Mon	5	Verviers	9.30 a.m.	noon	3.00 p.m.	8.00 p.m.
Tue	6	Brussels	11.00 a.m.	2.30 p.m.	4.30 p.m.	8.00 p.m.
Wed	7	Liège	10.00 a.m.	noon	3.00 p.m.	8.00 p.m.
Thu	8	Ghent	9.00 a.m.	noon	3.00 p.m.	8.00 p.m.

At Verviers they stayed at the *Grand Hotel* and played at *La Meuse*; in Liège at the *Hotel du Suède* and the *Coliseum*. At the *Sports Palace* in Antwerp their appearance was at a sports gala attended by a crowd of twenty-two

Lucille, Babe, Belgian actress Helene Maréchal and Stan, singing 'Auld Lang Syne' on the very last day of the Boys' European tour.
Termonde Hotel, *Ghent, Belgium, 8 January 1948.*

thousand. The sketch could not be performed, so a more visual presentation was dreamt up. The idea was for Stan and Ollie to improvise a comedy cycling routine around the indoor track; but the whole spectacle fell flat. Knowing of Laurel's perfectionism, it is easy to understand how uncomfortable he was made to feel by this quickly arranged farce. Hardy – a fifty-six-year-old, twenty-one-stone man – was also none too grateful for being subjected to the indignity.

The European engagements were completed on 8 January, which brought to an end more than eleven months of continual touring. Babe and Lucille took a well-earned week's holiday, before leaving Antwerp on 15 January aboard the *MV Bastogne*. Stan, meanwhile, went back over to England, where he stayed until 28 January, before sailing to New York on the *Queen Mary*.

Although glad to be home, Stan Laurel and Oliver Hardy were most concerned that job prospects for the future looked extremely bleak. After their one-year absence, they had to face being treated with indifference by most of the American public, and also come to terms with a younger generation who didn't even know them. With the two comic legends already in danger of sinking into oblivion, worse was to come when, in 1949, Stan was diagnosed as having diabetes. While he fought his way to recovery, Hardy side-tracked his career and toured in a stage play, *What Price Glory?* On completion of its run John Wayne, who was in the company, asked Hardy to appear in his next film, *The Fighting Kentuckian*. The result was a very creditable performance from Babe, in a straight acting role, which led to his being invited to play a cameo role in the Bing Crosby film, *Riding High*. Then, before there were thoughts of a permanent solo career, Laurel and Hardy were offered what seemed a lucrative contract to make a film in France. They grasped it with both hands, and didn't let go until it was far too late and they'd been dragged through twelve months of sheer torture.

Firstly, in June 1950 the Boys were sent on a tour of Italy to promote the film – before they'd even started to make it. They especially loved Rome, and the Italians especially loved them, and mobbed them everywhere they went. At one venue they found their 1933 film *Fra Diavolo* was being re-released for the thirteenth time. Then, the short holiday over, it was back to base at the *George V Hotel* in Paris.

The film itself, *Atoll K*, was ill-fated right from the start. Filming in France, the two comedians found themselves unable to fight back against the insurmountable odds of having actors of several different nationalities in the cast, each speaking their native language, and a production crew which was totally inefficient. Coupled with this, both comedians had serious set-backs to their health. Laurel, laid low by diabetes, had suffering heaped upon suffering when he contracted dysentry. Although hospitalised for a time, he insisted on finishing the picture and can noticeably be observed, on screen, metamorphosing from a body weight of one hundred and sixty-five pounds to just one hundred and fourteen pounds.

Hardy, meanwhile, was having Stan's problem in reverse. By the end of the picture he had put back every pound he'd lost during the gruelling 1947–8 tour. His weight, combined with the intense heat of the French Riviera, caused the development of a heart flutter. After the interminable length of time it took to complete, the film emerged as haggard and sick-looking as its two leading players. Having waited six years to regain credibility as film stars, Stan Laurel and Oliver Hardy had been dealt the cruelest of blows, and in the Spring of 1951 returned home to recover.

Stan Laurel, in going to meet his comedy partner as he arrives from America, is confronted by several bogus Hardys.

When the real one turns up, Hardy gets the girl – and Laurel gets the brush-off. St. Lazare Station, *Paris. 17 June 1950.*

Just when it looked as though they might never work again, fate seemed to relent. Without doing anything whatsoever, Laurel and Hardy were suddenly in demand by everyone. The cause of the about-face was the mushroom-spread of television throughout America. In addition to the

As Hardy appears to be about to sneeze-out the candles on his birthday cake,
Laurel moves the plant to a safe distance.
La Tour d'Argent, Paris, 18 January 1951.
(Stan came out of hospital, that day, just to wish his partner
a 'Happy Birthday'.)

earlier Laurel & Hardy films being shown in the home, they were also being re-issued in cinemas, and old and new audiences alike were able to see the two comedians at their peak. Offers poured in for stage and screen roles, not only from Hollywood, but from Italy and Japan. Sad to say, all Stan and Babe's high hopes were raised for nothing, as every offer fell through.

So, early in 1952, after three years of unemployment and one year of hell, the Boys were more than happy to accept an offer from Bernard Delfont to do a second tour of British theatres. From now on the stage would be the only medium in which they were to work. On the film-making front, Laurel and Hardy had made the final cut.

Chapter Twelve

Where Has All the
Slapstick Gone?

Aｌｔｈｏｕｇｈ 28 January 1952 was the coldest day in Britain for two years, it didn't stop two local girls, Gillian Moore and Barbara Wilding, from dressing in Hawaiian costume and treating Laurel and Hardy to a hula-hula dance as they disembarked from the *Queen Mary* at Southampton. This welcome (re-enacting a scene from their film *Sons of the Desert*) was certainly the most humorous, but the crowd was short by several thousands on the numbers which had greeted them on previous visits.

Again starting off with a stay in London before the tour proper, Stan and Babe decided to enjoy a little socialising. Firstly, they went to the *Wood Green Empire* to watch a pantomime – a medium they had been promising themselves for a long time time to play in; then on 31 January the Variety Club treated them to a luncheon at the *Empress Club* (see page 302). On the 3 and 17 February they also attended lodges with the Water Rats but, apart from these outings, most of the next four weeks was taken up in rehearsing. As Stan said, 'It is one thing to make an audience laugh at a completed sketch, but it takes a lot of hard work to prepare for those laughs.' That they were performing a new sketch added to the necessity for such prolonged rehearsals. The plot for *A Spot of Trouble*[22] was basically as follows:

---

22   Part of the script of *A Spot of Trouble* can be found in the 1990 American reissue of *The Comedy World of Stan Laurel* (Moonstone Press).

162

*Laurel and Hardy racing to beat women and children to the lifeboats,
on board the* Queen Mary.
(Associated Press.)

The Boys arrive separately for a pre-arranged meeting at a railway
station. They go through the business of walking past one another
several times, without one spotting the other, then do a 'take' on
making contact. They wish to take a train, but have neither tickets nor
money. As the next train won't be for a while, anyway, they decide
to get some sleep on the one and only available bench. Lots of
mileage is gained from Hardy's vast bulk taking up almost every inch
of the bench, and Laurel constantly swopping ends and changing
position to try and find a bit of space. (Similar routines can be seen to
good effect in the Laurel and Hardy films *Pardon Us*, and *Berth
Marks*.)

Just as they are settling down, a policeman happens along. To avoid
being arrested as vagrants they agree to aid the policeman with a
scheme to get himself into the police chief's good books. The idea is
for Laurel and Hardy to stage a robbery in the police chief's house, let

Mr Laurel and Mr Hardy with their screen wives in Sons of the Desert *(1933).* (Roach Studios.)

the policeman catch them, then he will let them go without punishment. (This piece of the plot was lifted, directly, from the film *Night Owls*.)

Scene two finds Stan and Ollie outside the window of the police chief's house. They gain entrance, but not before several mix-ups with the opening and closing of the window and door. Once inside, they are indeed caught by the policeman, but his plan backfires when the police chief catches him with the stolen loot and accuses him of being the burglar. The sketch ends with the police chief chasing the policeman around the room, whilst the policeman in turn chases Laurel and Hardy.

Nineteen years later, art imitating life, with their real wives. Washington Hotel, *London, 28 January 1952.* (*Associated Press.*)

For the start of the tour, Stan and Babe travelled by train to Peterborough where, at the North Station, a crowd of about seven hundred gave them such an enthusiastic welcome that the police had to be called in. Admittedly, this was nowhere near the size of the crowds which had greeted them on earlier tours, but as it was now twelve years since Laurel and Hardy had made anything resembling a decent film, and five years since they were last in the country, the number was highly encouraging. Because the sketch they were to perform was not tried and tested, 'insurance' was again taken out by assembling a first-class supporting bill (see page 292). Bernard Delfont need not have worried. Over the two weeks, commencing 25 February, the Boys smashed all box office records for the *Embassy Theatre*. This did not seem to impress the critic from the *Peterborough Standard*, who had rather

Left: Sitting on a railway bench marked 'No Loitering', Stan Laurel pours Oliver Hardy a demi-tasse of coffee (in a big cup) in the opening scene of A Spot of Trouble.
(Rimis – London.)

Right: Scene two finds them gaining entry into the police chief's house.

Left: Once inside, they help themselves to whisky and cigars, before commencing to burgle the house proper.
(Rimis – London.)

fixed ideas of the kind of 'business' Laurel and Hardy's act ought to contain. Under the heading, 'Not the Laurel and Hardy of Custard Pie Fame', he wrote:

> Laurel and Hardy disappointed a section of their admirers. The reason was a matter of style, for they forsook, almost completely, their true 'custard pie' roles. The two presented a new sketch which, although highly amusing, was not typical of the performances which made their reputation. Probably in an effort to modernise the act, the sketch tended to neglect the personalities of Laurel and Hardy and concentrated on witty words and amusing circumstances. That being said it must be stated that many of the audience enjoyed the act. The reputation of the popular comedy team satisfied some, and others, taking the act at face value and ignoring precedent, found in it a welcome relief from the normal round of music hall turns.

In analysing the above, a Laurel and Hardy buff would immediately take exception to the phrase 'of custard pie fame'. In the *Battle of the Century*, one of Laurel and Hardy's earliest films, Stan had tried to bury the custard pie image once and for all. It is therefore hard to comprehend why the reviewer should choose to retain a single image from one of their films from the 'twenties, and relate it to a stage sketch in the 'fifties. One must accept that Laurel and Hardy *did* have a slapstick image, but because they were now elderly, and with Laurel still not over his illness and Hardy at his lifetime's heaviest,

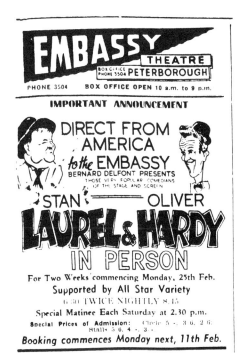

This advert, placed in the Peterborough Standard *on 8 February 1952, weeks before Laurel and Hardy's appearance, certainly bore out the old adage 'it pays to advertise'.*
(By kind permission of the *Peterborough Herald & Post.*)

Hundreds of fans greet Laurel and Hardy outside the Red Lion Hotel,
Grantham *on 28 February 1952. (Margaret Roberts was not amongst them.)*
(By courtesy of John Cooper.)

anything too physical was ruled out. Slapstick, though, was still a major
part of the act, as the *The Stage* will testify.

> The sketch is on the lines of the comedians' old comedies, and contains
> many of the hilarious situations associated with them. The setting is
> first a railway station, and then the living-room of a police chief's
> house. At the beginning we are treated to some typical Laurel and
> Hardy patter, and the scene where they both try to sleep on a small
> bench is particularly funny. In the house, where the two comedians
> are supposed to be burglars, the sketch builds up to one of those
> slapstick affairs, in which the police chief chases the police officer
> round the room, while Laurel and Hardy make a quick exit.

From the above account, it can be seen that, with 'the bench' and 'the chase'
scenes, dialogue was limited and slapstick was prevalent.

On Thursday Stan and Ida, and Lucille and Babe were driven from the
Great Northern Hotel, where they were staying, to Grantham, thirty miles
northward. After a civic luncheon at the *Red Lion Hotel* their hosts, the

Stan Laurel signs the register after marrying the Mayoress of Grantham. The best man and bridesmaids look on.
The Guildhall, *Grantham, 28 February 1952.*
(By kind permission of the *Nottingham Evening Post.*)

Mayor and Lady Mayoress of Grantham, Alderman and Lady W. Good-liffe, took them to the Guild Hall. As soon as their car arrived, a crowd of several hundred surrounded it and jostled to see them. On emerging, the two comedians ascended the Guild Hall steps, where they entertained the crowds below before going inside to view the Chamber of Trade Exhibition. Stan's sister Olga, and brother-in-law Bill, took advantage of the visit and popped along to see them.

On the second Monday of their stay in Peterborough the Boys looked round the offices of the *Citizen and Advertiser*, where Hardy revealed that he had worked in a printing office when a small boy. The small boy was brought out in Stan on Sunday 9 March when the Laurels and the Hardys revisited Glasgow. Arriving in late evening, the party was met by several hundred fans at Queen Street Station. After police had forced a way through for the visitors, many of the spectators simply followed them to the *Central Hotel*; but the terrifying scenes of 1932 and 1947 weren't repeated.

In the Scottish accent he had acquired in the early 1900s Stan enquired of the staff, 'Oh aye, how are ye?' To reporters, he hinted that the current seven-month tour might be extended, because of the proposal for them to play the 'robbers' in the London pantomime, *Babes in the Wood* (originally planned for 1948). Hardy offered: 'Or we may go back home and do television work. We'd do complete new shows on film for this medium.'[23] The talk of television was causing a lot of excitement that week, not because the Scots would be able to see Laurel and Hardy on TV, but because they had received their first television transmission. Meanwhile, it was on with the live appearance at the *Glasgow Empire*, the review for which appeared in the *Evening News* under the headline 'The Screen Magic is not there'.

> On what all the best critics call a well-balanced bill, there emerge Laurel and Hardy, two comedians who have made me laugh uproariously on the screen, and made me smile last night. They are a preposterously engaging couple, but they have to struggle with the sort of sketch which is only funny if it's performed in a kirk [church] hall with your cousin in the cast. It just comes to this – that you can't imitate on stage what you do on the screen.

Gordon Irving of the *Daily Record* thought that the appeal of the comedy couple lay with the children.

> Laurel and Hardy offer simple, homely fun. It's the kind of absurd knockabout comedy which made them famous in so many film comedies, and without which, as they say, 'we'd not be Laurel and Hardy.' Their new sketch is 'cops and burglars' stuff, with no subtlety and demanding nothing of intelligence. The fans will relish it as a flashback to happy times spent at film matinées. And the 1952 child who has not come to expect anything too sophisticated will still laugh at this funny pair of opposites. The whole variety bill is ideal kiddies' fare.

Laurel's departure from his beloved Glasgow would not have been as hard to bear as on previous occasions, as his next stop-over was at the place to

---

23   Two years later the Laurel and Hardy television shows became a possibility, but had to be shelved when, just before they were due to go into production, Oliver Hardy was struck down by a heart attack.

which he felt he belonged – Tyneside. Arriving at Tynemouth on Sunday, he was again reminded of his strong ties with the area by the great reception given by the huge crowd. Waving to them, Stan confided, 'I get a great kick out of coming back to Tyneside.' But things got off to a bad start. The party was unable to obtain a reservation at the *Royal Station Hotel* in Newcastle, and as a last option ended up at the *Grand Hotel*, Tynemouth, about which Laurel wrote to a friend:

> We spent a miserable two weeks. The place was so dilapidated & run down & most uncomfortable – was happy to leave the place. I wouldn't have stayed there one night if we could have found other accommodations.

Their first commitment was on Sunday 16 March, the day they arrived, with a guest appearance at the *Gaumont Cinema*, North Shields, where they were immediately mobbed by the hundreds of fans unable to gain admission. Inside, in the manager's office, the Mayor of South Shields, Councillor Oliver, bade them welcome. Out front, twenty-seven-year-old Eric Nicholson was compering a Charity Gala Concert. In 1987 he recalled, very vividly, his feelings at the time:

> I do not think any experience ever brought the drama, immense enchantment, and sheer exhilaration which I felt that night. During one of my long rambling stories, the laughs were coming along nicely, and getting stronger by the second. I was thrilled. Great guffaws were greeting me, and at the end of the story there was rapturous applause. Just then, I saw two very good reasons for all the laughter and applause. There, walking towards me down the centre aisles were Stan Laurel and Oliver Hardy.
>
> The audience was going spare. What was I to do? There was I, a nobody, and bearing down on me were the world's two greatest comedians. Silently, I pleaded for help. The great men were now just a few rows away, and the audience were 'tearing the place apart'. Two spotlights hit them, and I blurted out, 'Just you two wait till I get you up here.' They stopped advancing, paused, then Ollie slowly put his hand up to his bowler hat and wiggled it. His hand descended to his tie which he pulled out and wiggled in turn. Stan's reaction to my 'telling them off' was to burst into tears. At this, I, along with the audience collapsed in total hysteria.

The furore lasted a full five minutes during which they ascended to the stage. The show was now well and truly stopped, and the two stars spent many minutes apologising to me for interrupting my act. I needed no apologies at all. They'd made me that night. I was in ecstasy.

The *Shields Evening News* added:

On stage, Stan and Oliver – accompanied by their wives – were given a civic welcome by the Mayor of Tynemouth, Councillor T. A. M. Hails. Introductions over, Oliver spoke first – 'This is going to be Stan's night. Tonight I'm going to let him be General Buller again.' (The part Stan played in the Relief of Mafeking celebrations in 1900.) To more cheers, Hardy added, 'Your boy and my boy, Stan Laurel.'

Said Stan, 'It will be kinda difficult for me to express my, and our, grateful thanks . . . it really is wonderful to be back in my old home town . . . it brings back memories.' To remind him of the Mafeking celebrations, his old pal Roland Park, who had played Lord Roberts, came forward. Then to the wild cheering and clapping of fourteen hundred people, the local-boy-made-good made his way to the circle, to watch the rest of the show.

During the interval, the Boys went backstage to speak to the acts on the show. Sunderland-born Billy 'Uke' Scott's recollection of his feelings after they'd complimented him on his banjo playing was:

I was surprised how much bigger Ollie was than the impression one got from the films. That might seem surprising as we knew he was big, but when a screen image comes to life, you feel dwarfed. There was a slight unreality about it. I began to wonder if they were there in a real life, or if I was part of one of their films.

Even though Stan had so many people to see, and so many wanted to see him, he made time for everyone. Observing how happy and smiling the two comedians remained under a deluge of autograph-hunters, a reporter asked Hardy, 'Don't you get sick of this continual signing of autographs?' Without hesitation Babe replied, 'I'd get more sick if they didn't ask.' The comedy duo then went off to perform another service – this time to present stars of merit to two of the *Gaumont's* staff.

The next night Laurel and Hardy were to reappear at the venue where, in 1947, they had made their British debut – the *Newcastle Empire*. The press made only two superficial comments: 'Laurel and Hardy have shattered theatre records at Peterborough and Glasgow, and it would not be surprising if they did it here'; and the review of the first night's performance, which stretched to the following: 'In a programme embracing many top-line variety acts, Laurel and Hardy have to be at their best, and they are.' The manager wrote in his notes at the end of the week: 'Both scenes get loud laughter, but lack a good finishing tag.' Emily Hopper, an usherette, related a different side of the story:

> Seeing them on stage was something I thought could never happen, after watching them for years at the local cinema. I thoroughly enjoyed the act, but the theatre was only half full, and they didn't go too well. Each night, because there were so few people in, we would move the ones at the back to the seats near the front, so that from the stage it appeared full.

The Boys' disappointment was later confirmed in a backstage conversation between Mrs Hopper and Babe's wife, Lucille. Trying to ascertain the reason for the decline in the public's interest in Laurel and Hardy would be very difficult; but, sad to relate, they were soon to experience that cold, unwelcoming feeling again.

Be that as it may, there were still old times to talk about and, after visiting his boyhood pal Roland Park, Stan sought out William Henry Harmon, who had worked for his dad at the *Theatre Royal* in North Shields. As the black saloon carrying Stan pulled up outside Mr Harmon's house, Stan was treated to a big cheer from the huge congregation of neighbours. Inside, Stan was told he hadn't changed a bit – William could still picture him standing in the wings of the theatre in his conventional Eton collar. 'How old are you,' enquired Stan. 'Seventy-two' came back the reply. 'Then I'll race you down the street,' said Stan. Asked where Ollie was, Stan said 'The fog has made him lose his voice a bit.' Then he laughed, 'He's not a Geordie, like us.' After meeting William's family, Stan was thoughtful enough to make an offer: 'If any of the neighbours out there have autograph books, just tell them to hand them in.'

That week Stan met his sister Olga's son for the first time. The nephew, professional organist/entertainer Huntley Jefferson Woods, recalled:

> I approached the meeting with 'Uncle Stan' with mixed feelings. After all, I didn't know what the reaction of such a famous star would be –

even to a relation. Especially as he had never seen me, and knew me by name only.

As it turned out, he was pleased to see me, and showed interest in my musical career. I also met his wife, who was equally charming.

All in all, a marvellous night, which I shall always cherish.

Of his overall impression of 'Uncle Stan', Jefferson was to say: 'A great man, with the common touch.'

During the following week, for their appearance at the *Sunderland Empire*, the party would go down to the quayside at North Shields each night, get on the ferry (nicknamed by Stan in his boyhood days, the Happney Dodger), cross the River Tyne to South Shields, then complete the journey by car. After the show they did the journey in reverse. Stan had worked in Sunderland in the early 1900s, and backstage a face from the past appeared to remind him of those days. The face belonged to seventy-year-old Benny Barron who had been in Sleeping Beauty with Stan. Benny's visit came as a pleasant surprise and, whilst waiting for the start of rehearsals, the two old troupers were soon lost in reminiscences of those 'good old days' of music hall. The Sunderland Echo recorded the conversation as follows:

> 'And they were grand times,' said Stan. 'The money wasn't much but we were happy all the same. I remember playing in Sunderland years ago – was it the *Villiers Institute*? Times have changed a lot since then though, but there's one thing that remains the same – Northern audiences. They're wonderful.'

The article continued:

> On one point Stan and Benny agreed: 'You miss all that grand slapstick humour today. The new generation has never even seen that humour of the past.' This week Stan and Ollie bring back to Wearside just that. As they settled down to rehearsal, Benny quietly left by the stage door, still chuckling over the memory when he too was 'one of the gang', and Stan Laurel was a pantomime golliwog.

A little of Stan's and Benny's views on humour of the past was echoed in the review of the opening night, given by the aptly-named *Sunderland Echo*. Under the heading 'Slapstick Humour' it ran:

> Perhaps the finest tribute to Stan and Ollie is that they remain the same on the stage as they do on the screen. For that I am deeply thankful.

To have emulated the style of Danny Kaye, or even the brisker and less ingenuous slapstick of Abbott and Costello, would have been a betrayal of their reputation.

The material they use seems like a chunk of film-script. If today people find it feeble and unfunny, it is only because the funniest things about Laurel and Hardy films have always been Laurel and Hardy. Nobody cared then what their films were about, and those enthusiasts who learnt to recognise and appreciate their particular brand of humour, won't fail to miss it in their stage appearance now.

After the opening show, Benny Barron proudly took his son backstage. Billy Barron, who played trumpet with the Empire Orchestra, found both Stan and Babe to be extremely pleasant. Of Stan's past relationship with his father, Billy wrote

> My dad toured with the 'Levy and Cardwell Company', in a double-act known as 'Graham & Barron'. They were well-established, and Stan saw them perform many times. The facial expressions Stan adopted were exactly the ones my father used in his act, as he was the one who got everything wrong, and used to 'cry' when his partner knocked off his straw-boater.

Graham & Barron, from whom Stan Laurel first learned the art of the comedy double-act.
(By kind permission of Billy Barron.)

Just how Benny managed to be in a juvenile company at the age of twenty-six is rather puzzling, but that he was is beyond doubt. There is also a strong possibility that Billy Barron's version of the origin of Stan's 'cry' is correct. All comedians in their formative years have a tendency to copy those comedians to whom they have regular exposure. Bear in mind, also, that Stan never felt comfortable doing 'the cry', which might imply that it did not come from 'within', and was thus borrowed.

In Hanley, Staffordshire, the following week, the theatre critic for the *Evening Sentinel* wrote of Laurel and Hardy's act:

> The undiminishing popularity of the famous film and stage comedians was clearly demonstrated at the *Theatre Royal*. Their appearance was the signal for roars of anticipatory laughter, and their many smart comedy moves, familiarised by their many successful films, kept the audience highly amused.

The Boys told the reporter they were enjoying the tour, and that British audiences were 'the best in the world'. Of his partner, Hardy revealed, 'When we are rehearsing, he still seems so funny to me that I often burst out laughing.' He described their partnership as not only one of the longest in showbusiness, but 'certainly the happiest'. The article said of Stan:

> He has not been well of late, and, although a variety tour is no rest cure, he is enjoying the change. 'The stage is in my blood,' he said, 'and British audiences are so wonderful to play to. We don't go in for the sophisticated type of thing. It is the real, old-fashioned knock-about stuff, and people seem to like it, for it is the kind of thing they used to love in the old variety halls. Our act is really a pantomime out of season. We both like the provincial theatres. It is here where our act is best appreciated – especially by the children.'

The Laurels and the Hardys stayed the week at the *North Stafford Hotel*, a couple of miles outside Hanley, opposite Stoke railway station. Although the newspapers reported only Laurel as being unwell, others noted Hardy to be constantly breathless, and finding it difficult to rise from his chair once he had sat down. An insider also revealed that Hardy felt it necessary to bathe three times daily, as he was constantly perspiring. Between shows, however, Hardy managed frequent trips to the *Mechanics Inn*, opposite the stage door of the *Theatre Royal*.

Several years after Stan and Babe had left Hanley, Fred Peake, owner of the *Theatre Royal*, was asked why he kept a worn and battered settee in his front room, when he could so easily afford a new one. He replied, 'Laurel and Hardy sat on that settee, and when that goes out of the house – so do I.' Apparently, Fred had loaned the settee as a prop for the second scene of the Boys' sketch.

From Hanley the company made the relatively short journey to Leeds, a place Stan had first worked whilst in his teens, though there is no documentation of this. In 1952 little had changed, and there was no press write-up of Laurel and Hardy's arrival or departure. The review of the first night's performance was also in danger of being overlooked. It read:

> There is no doubting the popularity of the two comedians, Laurel and Hardy, to judge by the packed first house at *Leeds Empire* last night. The two went through their film antics in a comedy sketch and the result was uproarious. If you like Laurel and Hardy then you will not be disappointed in their real selves as compared with their celluloid ones.

The *Yorkshire Evening News* wasn't much better:

> Laurel and Hardy's sketch is amusing without being hilarious – for the obvious reason that they are not backed by all the tricks and paraphernalia of film making. A legitimate complaint will be, that having come all the way from Hollywood, their appearance is all too brief.

After neglecting their stage characters, no less than three journalists sought to find out what Laurel and Hardy were like in private life. Just what caused the sudden fixation remains a mystery, but here are the 'facts' as discovered by Edgar Craven and Con Gordon of the *Yorkshire Evening Post,* and R. C. Scriven from the *Yorkshire Observer*:

> The star dressing room at *Leeds Empire* is small anyway. Occupied by the 6 ft. 1 in., 22 st. presence of Oliver Hardy, duplicated in wall mirrors, it seemed as though I was interviewing the great man in a telephone kiosk. There was an air of unreality about the proceedings. It seemed so improbable that the idol of one's boyhood could be there in the flesh – all 22 st. of him. It seemed even odder that there was no Laurel. Then the door opened a few inches and Stan Laurel managed to enter. At once everything seemed natural. One somehow felt the vague pervading influence of the Mad Hatter, an impression heightened when Hardy boomed, 'Boy,[24] could you find some tea?'
>
> He brought a very English tea tray complete with brown teapot and rich plum cake. 'Stan converted me to English afternoon tea,' said Ollie. He cut the plumcake into enormous slabs and handed them

---

24 The 'Boy' was Bert Tracey, Babe's old friend from his pre-Laurel days (see page 49) who, needing a job, had been appointed as Hardy's dresser.

round. Laurel reached out eagerly. 'Stanley!' said Hardy at his most majesterial, 'Visitors.' Abashed, Laurel fidgeted with his tie. It was rather like the dormouse and the teapot. In fact in real life Laurel and Hardy are each rather the opposite of their screen personalities. Laurel is a quick, lively, facetious talker, always ready to crack a joke at his friends expense.

Con Gordon said of Laurel, 'He's no fool. He has in fact a touch of intellectual acerbity.' And of Hardy:

Hardy is no bulky egotist. He is a big, simple, friendly soul, who every day says his prayers, and reads the Bible. He is proud that their stage act is clean enough to be commended by the clergy and simple enough to be applauded by children.

On the state of British music hall, Stan said:

What I miss, is the sort of comic we had in my early days on the stage – men who played comic characters – George Formby Snr, Harry Weldon, Mark Sheridan, Tom Foy, and a lot more. They didn't just walk out in a dinner suit and reel off gags. They were funny to see, as well. You seem to have only a few of that sort left.

Later in the week the *Evening News* chose to submit yet more trivia:

Quite a few people I know who rarely go to see a variety show have been to *Leeds Empire* this week. They went, I think, not merely because this droll pair epitomise a type of comedy which never palls and, despite modern sophistication, never will. To many they were the first favourites of childhood cinema-going and in twenty-five years of film-making they must have amused several generations of young-sters.

Have they had as much fun out of it as they gave? I put the question to them during a chat this week.

'It used to be fun,' replied Stan Laurel, 'but now it's different. It is all too commercialised, too much production, too many people telling you what to do. Nothing is done spontaneously – and spontaneity is the essence of our work.'

Oliver Hardy put in, 'For eighteen years Stan produced and wrote all our pictures. We made things up as we went along. That was the best time.'

The two are housed in separate dressing rooms – Stan in a large one, Ollie fitting his bulk into about one-third of the space, next door. But Stan needed the larger accommodation. He has been receiving the family between shows. Quite a crowd of them were in the other night – mostly cousins who live in Dewsbury and other parts of the West Riding.

Stan's wife Ida had rather less luck with her one visitor. While she was allowing herself an unaccustomed afternoon away from the theatre, a caller arrived at Stan's dressing room and announced: 'I'm your wife's cousin, from Shanghai.' After enduring dressing rooms full of Stan's visitors, it was just Ida's luck that on the one day someone came to call on her, she wasn't there to meet him. Fortunately, her cousin was resident at Leeds University, so the two were soon reunited. Stan's family reunion, meanwhile, was to continue the following week in Nottingham.

Chapter Thirteen

Highlands, Islands, Ireland

IT was a glorious, hot Easter Sunday and, after signing in at the *County Hotel*, Nottingham, the party were driven on a further fifteen miles, to go and have tea with Stan's sister. Olga and her husband Bill were now at the *Bull Inn*, Bottesford, having moved from nearby Barkston shortly after A. J.'s death on 14 January 1949. Ethel Challands befriended Olga at the *Bull*, and found her to be a total extrovert.

> She was a strict landlady, but fair. Despite her tender years, she was always doing eccentric things to show us how athletic she was. At times, she would swing her leg high in the air and cock it on top of the bar. Other times, she would stand on her head in the corner. Anything for a laugh!

It was gone 2 o'clock when the visitors arrived, by which time the pub had been cleared of patrons. 'Footlight', from the *Nottingham Guardian*, was allowed an interview and found the two comedians to be

> (. . .) good natured, easy and natural. They just can't help making themselves look ridiculous. Their audiences, public or private, have to laugh. Even off duty, they still sparkle. One sets the other off – and that, I think, is the secret of their success. They are natural foils, perfect partners, and true clowns. They make their audiences feel superior. Even the smallest boy thinks to himself when he sees the pair in a spot of bother, 'Gosh, aren't they silly. I could do better than that.' Yet they

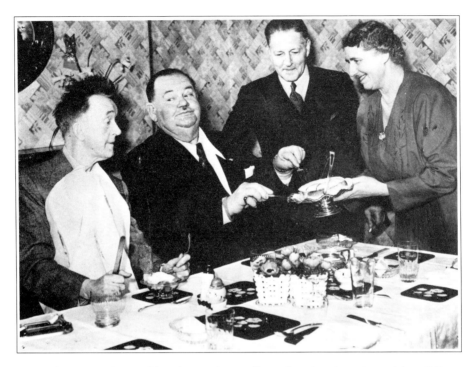

*Laurel's sister Olga and brother-in-law Bill Healey give American visitor Oliver
Hardy preferential treatment with the apple flan.
(Note the salt and pepper pot.)*

*Later that day,
'Bert and Alf'
chat up a
couple of
floozies in
Denker's Beer
Garden.
Bull Inn,
Bottesford,
13 April 1952.*
(By kind
permission of the
*Nottingham
Evening Post.*)

inspire sympathy and affection at the same time. The laughter they inspire knows no boundaries. The situations they meet and create are the things that happen to ordinary people every day all over the world.

I came away impressed that these two professional funny men are warm, genuine human beings, kindly and courteous, and aware of what is going on around them, true artistes in their interpretation of it.

The VIPs were then left alone to enjoy Sunday roast, a few English beers, and five hours of privacy before the pub reopened; after which Olga and Bill bade them farewell, with the promise of coming to the show during the week. If the review in the *Journal* is to be believed, the comedy twosome then magically transported themselves to Nottingham:

Had anyone asked 'Do you believe in fairies?' at the *Nottingham Empire* last night, the whole audience would have roared 'YES'. They could not have helped it. For the fairies were there in person – Laurel and Hardy. There they were, materialised in the flesh, exactly as the screen had always told us. It was a lesson to all unbelief. Their panto on stage seems even more exquisite than it is on the screen.

The comedians next materialised in Shrewsbury, where the press found difficulty in stringing together two sentences regarding their stage appearance:

Laurel and Hardy's names still have the magic to pull in their audiences at the *Granada Cinema*, Shrewsbury, and if their appearance continues on the same lines as Monday's show, then all box office records will be broken. Their act is very much on the lines of their films – two down-and-outs in trouble with authority – and despite their mellow years the comedy couple still invest it with some energy.

The only report outside the theatre was for late Wednesday night, when the Boys and their wives attended a Police Ball at the *Music Hall* where, when pausing to sign one of many autographs, Laurel remarked to the Chief Constable, Douglas Osmond, 'It's a change not to be asked for fingerprints.' It was Lucille's birthday, and she celebrated in the company of scores of policemen. Three days earlier she had had £55 stolen from her room at the *Raven Hotel*. The detectives sent to investigate the theft reported back that Mrs Hardy was an exceedingly difficult person to deal with, whereas Mr Hardy treated the whole incident as a great joke.

At the next destination, Edinburgh – where mass hysteria had accompanied the stars' two previous arrivals – barriers had been erected to keep back the fans. Ironically, they weren't needed as the expected thousands turned out to be just one hundred. Once inside their hotel, Stan and Babe were told of the precautions which had been taken to protect them from being kidnapped. This was only a light-hearted threat made by the students' union, who were holding their annual rag week. Laughing it off, Hardy said of the kidnappers, 'They would have a load on their hands.' Despite the small numbers who turned up at the station, the show itself did good business, as the *Evening News* confirms:

> Laurel and Hardy had no reason to complain of their reception at the *Edinburgh Empire*, a full house giving them a cordial reception both before and after their sketch. It was typical Laurel and Hardy stuff, and if the stage does not give them the elbow-room of the film, the couple put over the laughter raising antics with genuine artistry.

In May newspaper headlines were reserved for Queen Elizabeth II, who was taking up residence at Buckingham Palace, and Laurel and Hardy had to content themselves with being mentioned only in theatrical reviews. In writing of their next show, in Birmingham, Norman Holbrook of the *Evening Despatch* questioned his own merits as a member of the audience:

> Twenty years ago Laurel and Hardy were names to conjure with. If the ecstatic behaviour of last night's near-capacity audience is any criterion, they are still. Which, when you come to think of it, is quite an achievement. The sketch in which they appear is woefully thin, but what of it? The old, odd antics are still there, although perhaps less exuberant than in the old days. As one of their fans of 1932 I was a shade disappointed when I saw my old comical heroes at close quarters. But then I usually am.

Brian Harvey of the *Post & Mail* did not give any quarter. Although his review would send any Laurel and Hardy fan running to find a pair of boxing gloves, a 'buff' would accept most of the sentiments he expressed.

> As you come away from *Birmingham Hippodrome* this week, you can assure yourself that you have seen Laurel and Hardy 'in person', as the posters say. What more? Little, I'm afraid. Last night, at their opening performance, the greeting they received was shrill with de-

lighted anticipation in a way which made the applause at the end of their twenty minute sketch seem tame. The sketch itself is flimsy material; and, to do them credit, they do not waste any exertion in trying to stretch it beyond its somewhat pathetic limits. Frankly, any pantomime producer would be accounted a failure who could not put more pace and more 'gags' into these proceedings. But then, we are seeing Laurel and Hardy – 'in person', and most people will be satisfied to know that Oliver's size is really as massive as it appears on the screen, and that Stanley does scratch his own head.

Harvey's questioning of the 'pace' and the 'gags' seems to be more than a little harsh, considering that the sketch was written by one of the best film gagmen in the business. But then this wasn't film – it was live stage. The rest of the review is simply a statement of the facts as the writer sees them, and his was by no means an isolated opinion, as other reviews show. But no-one was about to tell the old master anything he didn't already know. According to John McCabe, Stan said of the script of *A Spot of Trouble*: 'It worked for us at the time, but I would not like to be remembered for it.'

At their next port of call, Laurel and Hardy were in danger of being forgotten altogether. Although they had landed at Southampton on three different occasions, the local press had allowed their comings and goings to pass almost unnoticed. Now that they were actually about to spend some time here, at the *Polygon Hotel* and the *Gaumont Cinema*, no attempt was made to redress the balance. The *Southern Daily Echo* said only:

Laurel and Hardy – in person – are the big attraction of this week's variety bill at the *Southampton Gaumont*; and let it be said at once that this is probably the best variety programme the *Gaumont* has put on since stage facilities were restored in 1950. Stan and Ollie themselves are a riot; they are just as much at home (and just as funny) before the footlights as before the cameras. None of the old magic has gone, and although the sketch does not, perhaps, do them full justice, Stan can still bring the house down just by looking at his audience (those famous eyebrows!).

They are in every sense of the word, a team; and if your taste in humour is not too rigidly highbrow, you will laugh as much as I did. And what a joy to hear that comic little signature tune; from a real live orchestra; in a real live theatre; to introduce a real live Laurel and Hardy.

In Liverpool the following week, the *Liverpool Echo* was none too complimentary:

> Laurel and Hardy's 'bit of nonsense' – their own description[25] – provides glimpses of this famous comedy team at their best, but suffers from a flimsy plot. The act follows much along the line of their film shorts, and the audience delight in their slapstick, double-takes, and other antics – but even the best of nonsense requires some sense of reality.

On completion of the Liverpool appearances, the touring party had all day Sunday 25 May to rest before catching the overnight ferry to Dublin. The following morning, still very tired from their journey, they missed breakfast, and it was 11.30 a.m. before a reporter from the *Evening Mail* witnessed any indication of life at the *Gresham Hotel*, Dun Laoghaire:

> Stan Laurel was the first on the scene looking every inch like that silly little man who was guaranteed to get his partner into every conceivable mess. Immediately he spoke, however, a big difference was noticeable. Instead of that squeaky high pitched voice which comes from the screen, one listened to a soft, deeper toned voice from a quiet man who had not a great deal to say but a very charming and rather shy way of saying it. Then came Oliver Hardy, looming even larger in life than he does on the screen, and still sporting his tiny moustache. This is their first visit to this country.

That night, the party had more chance to catch up on some well-earned rest, as the show was cancelled because the scenery couldn't be brought over in time. So Laurel and Hardy's first show on Irish soil got under way on Tuesday, and the *Evening Mail* saw it as follows:

> A howl of laughter greeted Laurel and Hardy as they walked on stage at the *Olympia Theatre*, looking exactly as they do in all their films. The laughter came from the adult members of the audience who had been fans for the past twenty-five years and were obviously delighted to see all their old mannerisms and facial expressions brought so wonderfully to life before their eyes. Their act is ideal for children of all ages, containing the maximum of slapstick [a view which contradicts

---

25 Hardy was still using the line from the 1947 tour, 'We hoped you enjoyed our bit of nonsense,' at the end of their act.

that of the *Peterborough Standard*], but it has a very special appeal for those who have been faithful followers and will, therefore, recognise many of the scenes. There is not enough of them, but the time they are with us is filled with laughter.

The *Evening Herald* was also much taken with the Boys:

On to the stage strode a little man wearing a broad benign grin, a pair of big baggy trousers, a battered bowler, and carrying what once upon a time might have been a respectable-looking violin case. The crowd roared with delight, only to break into a howl of mirth a moment later when he was followed by a somewhat large gentleman, with a worried countenance, and a gleam in his eye that spelled trouble for the little man with the benign grin. Yes, it was Dublin's welcome for those famous comedians, Laurel and Hardy. Personally I found them much more entertaining in person than in celluloid. In two short scenes they manage to convey their genius for the trade that has kept them in the forefront for so long.

The *Dublin Times* wasn't going to spoil the party:

What Laurel and Hardy have to say to each other doesn't really matter. They merely have to appear on stage, and the house rocks, shrieks and hoots with laughter. The verbal jokes are good, old music-hall jokes, but the real felicity of the comedy lies in situation, slapstick and facial expression. It's all childishly simple; it's all clean; and it's all uproariously, unanalysably funny. Much of the laughter came from children, but their parents were spellbound, too.

With two shows per night, plus matinées, a guest appearance at the The Crystal Rooms, and nightly cinema showings of their film, *Robinson Crusoeland* (the British release of *Atoll K*), it would appear that every Dubliner had been satisfied; so Laurel and Hardy moved on, a hundred miles due north, to the *Grand Opera House*, Belfast. This magnificent theatre, with its splendid mixture of Baroque, Flemish, and Oriental architecture, holds one thousand people but, even so, it was necessary for Laurel and Hardy to play two weeks there to cater for demand. This is what the *Belfast Telegraph* thought of the show:

The sketch shows much of the hilarious technique so familiar on the screen. Its best moments are when the two comics tie themselves in knots trying to find comfort on a railway waiting room seat. In the second part, a burglary scene, there is less of the knockabout fun that one might have expected, but the drole [sic] appearance of the two loveable characters should satisfy most patrons. A tribute in itself to their skill is that their patter is spotlessly clean.

Being seen in the theatre by two thousand people per night didn't seem to staunch the flow of people who also wanted to see them by day. An article in Saturday's *Belfast Telegraph* ran:

> Laurel and Hardy are 'prisoners' in Belfast.

> In a second-floor apartment of the *Midland Hotel* this afternoon, the two loneliest men in the city sat silently listening to the radio. To the hotel staff they have become known as 'the prisoners of Room 113'. The only contact with the life of the hotel comes when a waiter takes them food. The 'prisoners' would very much like to go out, but that is impossible. Since they arrived their only glimpse of Royal Avenue has been from a speeding car. When they are due to go to the theatre the car draws up at the *Midland*, and a few seconds later they make a dash through the hotel lobby and drive away.

> Reason is that the famous pair are so well known, they attract crowds whenever they appear in public. Oliver Hardy told me: 'We've had a wonderful reception in Belfast – and we'd hate it too if we weren't recognised – but as things are we just have to stay locked up in here.' Then Oliver put the phone down and went back to his easy chair and the radio.

If the above can be taken seriously, one young man must consider himself very fortunate to have met the Boys in the way he did:

> One afternoon, I was passing the *Midland Hotel* when out of the front door came Laurel and Hardy. I couldn't believe my eyes, and immediately smiled at both of them. Then I said: 'Good afternoon Mr Hardy, good afternoon Mr Laurel.' – It was like looking at a movie. I said: 'Thank you for the many hours of happiness you have given me.'

> They both reached out their hands and Ollie pushed Stan's hand away as he had done a thousand times in the movies. – I was convulsed. They got into a taxi, obviously to go to the theatre. The longest day I live I can still see them, as they waved me goodbye.

This lucky youngster is now a popular personality himself; he is Irish comedian, Frank Carson.

After seventeen weeks of working at a high energy level, the Boys were finally forced to take a week off. Babe was in need of a rest and, with Lucille, took a holiday in Dublin. Poor old Stan, though, was in a bad way. He had been suppressing his diabetic condition for a while, but it had now got too much for him, and so he wisely had himself admitted to the Musgrave and Clark Clinic in Belfast. He told a reporter, 'I'm only going in for a check-up. It's nothing serious.' But he was wrong. A fully-trained nurse, Nancy Jane Reid, was assigned to Stan. She remembered him looking like 'a little, lost soul', and added:

He was painfully thin, and the dressing-gown he wore didn't do anything for him – but when he got up and put on his suit, he looked very nice.

I remember a desk was brought up to his room, for he seemed to be always writing. I thought perhaps he was writing a book, or a script for his show. He was a very nice writer.

His room was at the end of the building. It had a big window which looked out onto a nice lawn, and a tall chestnut tree. He used to sit and look out quite a bit, watching the birds. He was quite sneaky, as the following incident will show:

Dr. Smith, who specialised in diabetes, was looking after Mr Laurel. He was very worried that he couldn't get him 'stabilised'. Then one afternoon Mrs Laurel phoned Dr. Smith's office to inquire about Stan's progress. When told he was having trouble getting him stabilised, his wife said: 'Don't say I told you, but Stan has a very sweet tooth, and you might be enlightened if you took a look under his pillow.'

So next morning the doctor came in and Mr Laurel was sitting up in bed – the picture of innocence, and Dr. Smith said: 'How are you this morning, my good man?' Mr Laurel said: 'Fine.' By this time, the doctor had edged up towards the top of the bed and slipped his hand under the pillow, and sure enough, there was a box of chocolates and papers from other candies.

Poor Mr Laurel! What a mess he had got himself into. He wasn't even able to scratch his head. He wouldn't say where he got the chocolates. I think he brought a good supply with him, for when we searched, he had some in his case. After that, his blood checks soon

*'Handout'
signed to Nancy
Jane Reid, who
nursed Stan
Laurel during
his stay at the*
Musgrave
Clinic, *Belfast,
w/c 22 June
1952.*
(By kind
permission of
Nancy Jane Reid.)

became normal, and he was able to be discharged. Before he left he signed autographs for all the domestic staff, from a pile of photographs he brought with him. He was a real gentleman!

The convalescence seemed to do the trick, and Stan was able to complete the rest of the fourteen-week schedule without a break. On hearing that Laurel was fit again, Bernard Delfont informed the Boys there was a distinct possibility he could get them the parts of 'Captain' and 'Mate' in *Dick Whittington* for the forthcoming Christmas season at the *London Palladium* (*Babes in the Wood* had obviously fallen through). Meanwhile, the tour continued.

In 1932, when Boys had visited Sheffield, they had seen little more than the railway station and the inside of the *Grand Hotel*. This time they were able to go wherever they wished. The *Sheffield Telegraph*, however, credited them only with attending the prize-presentation of a competition run by their newspaper, but did get a reporter to interview them:

It must come as a relief to the thousands of Sheffielders who have seen their film comedies, that Laurel and Hardy are just the same off screen as on. In baggy trousers, tattered white shirt with string in place of cuff-links, Stan was sipping pop in his dressing room, at the *Sheffield Empire*. With him was his wife, who was born in Siberia, brought up in China, became a naturalised American, and is now British on Stan's passport. Complete with his doleful expression, Stan butted in, 'But she loves Yorkshire pud.'

Hardy was next door, with his very charming wife who comes from Texas. In terrible French, Hardy shouted 'Entrez-vous' as I knocked on his door, and we immediately got down to the question of bowler hats. With a delicately poised finger and an authoritative air, he took a relic down from the shelf, used his sleeve with mock care to 'dust' it and said: 'This one is over twenty years old. We used to buy them by the dozen until we got hold of some which were practicably indestructible.'

As soon as the signature tune trickled out to a darkened stage, the applause was spontaneous with neither of the team yet in view. Briefly, they break into the house of the chief of police with enough commotion to wake the dead.

The critic from the *Sheffield Star* wasn't very informative, either:

Bereft of many of the mechanical aids to humour with which Hollywood has garnished their films, the pair will have to rely mainly on verbal comedy for their success. Will they make it? Certainly! Both Stan and Ollie are natural comics, and if their scope is limited, their wit will be as crazily fanciful as ever.

After seeing the two in action, the same reviewer followed up with:

CHILDREN'S CORNER

DEAR Boys and Girls.—Here is another chance for you to try your skill in the Laurel and Hardy painting competition.

The most important job is to fill in noses, eyes, and mouths to give the expressions which appeal to you most.

There are four classes: Six to eight years, nine to 11 years, 12 to 14 years, and 15 to 16 years.

Book prizes worth £5 will be given. They will be autographed by Laurel and Hardy and presented on July 5 from the stage of the Sheffield Empire, where Laurel and Hardy are appearing next week.

Fill in the coupon below and send to Uncle Timothy, Laurel and Hardy Competition, "Sheffield Telegraph," Kemsley House, Sheffield, 1.

Entries must reach me by the first post on Tuesday.

Name ....

Address ....

....

Age ...... Ring ....

Your affectionate

UNCLE TIMOTHY.

Many Laurel and Hardy painting competitions were run, by theatres, in local newspapers. This one is from the Sheffield Telegraph, *28 June 1952.*
(By kind permission of
Sheffield Newspapers Limited.)

The genius of Laurel and Hardy is that their comic situations are based firmly on reality. The things that happen to them could happen to anybody – or almost anybody – but their treatment of events is highly individual. In fact, they turn life inside out. On the whole they translate well into the atmosphere of live theatre. The two scenes of the sketch are often very funny, especially in the comedians' attempts at burglary, but the slapstick ending would profit from extension.[26]

The journey from Sheffield, in the north, to Brighton, on the south coast, is not one to relish undertaking with any regularity, and, during their week's stay, Stan and Babe were going to need all the recuperative powers that the resort could offer. Not that this one journey was to blame; the accumulated toll of travelling, twinned with the incredible number of shows performed, was proving to be exhausting, and, again, Laurel had to see a doctor. He mused: 'I'm like a car battery – I need a spot of recharging now and again'. It then leaked out that Stan had been under medical supervision for quite a while, but had refused to miss out any of the dates on their schedule.

Concerning the show, the *Brighton Evening Argus* came up with a personal and affectionate account:

Laurel and Hardy showed us at the *Hippodrome Theatre*, why they are still the most popular film and comic-strip team. After their act had been duly acclaimed by the audience, a smiling Hardy walked up to the microphone to tell us that watching the show in a box was none other than George Robey. Slowly a surprised Mr Robey got to his feet – and lifted those famous eyebrows. Then all three stood in humble acknowledgement of the crowd's expression of gratitude for many an hour of entertainment.

It was a simple, sincere gesture from two grand troupers to the greatest figure in English Music Hall. And that simplicity and sincerity are the secret of the Laurel and Hardy success story. They try no tricks, no subtlety, no sophistication. They know the audience want only to see them as they are on the screen and in the comics. It is the good old slapstick action stuff that first put Hollywood in the money. And the audience love it.

---

26   The sketch suffered from the same syndrome as many Karno sketches in that, although it had many good moments of 'business', the ending was very weak. During a chase around the house by the two policemen, Hardy would sit down, exhausted, and utter the immortal words: 'Here's another nice mess you've gotten me into,' and the curtain would come down.

To meet Robey backstage after the show was a great thrill for Stan, as he had been a fan from before the days he became a comedian himself. Stan loved Robey's 'dame' and also took from him the use of a monologue, compiled from extremely long and over-complicated words. (An example of this is heard in the attic scene of *Sons of the Desert*. It starts: 'For the meticulous care with which you have executed your finely formulated machinations . . .' etc.)

Joan Turner, top female impressionist of her time, was on the bill that week, and gave her personal opinion of Laurel and Hardy as follows:

> After the first show, Stan came to my dressing room to congratulate me on my act, and apologised that they [Laurel and Hardy] 'didn't have better to offer'. Their timing was dreadful. You see, they weren't really a theatre act. They were used only to working on film sets, where – because there is no audience – timing is totally different. Later in the week, when I accepted an invitation to go to Babe's dressing room for coffee, he too apologised for the poor standard of their act, whilst congratulating me on mine with, 'Sure did like your Gracie Fields, Miss Turner.'

Considering the reception Laurel and Hardy had received, and that it was their name, and theirs alone, which filled the theatre, it is hard to understand why they found a need to apologise at all. It was, however, this almost constant awareness of the strength of their act, and the desire continually to improve it, which kept the comedy duo at the top of their profession for so many years, and is one of the reasons why no other act will ever replace them.

One of Stan's visitors that week was local author John Montgomery, whom he had first met at Hannen Swaffer's flat in 1947. Offering his services as a guide, John asked if there was any part of Brighton Stan would particularly like to see. The *Royal Pavilion* having been selected, the two met up the following morning. Babe, meanwhile, was at the West Brighton Golf Course. John recalled:

> Although Stan was now an elderly man, he was immediately recognisable, and people stopped all along the street and in the Pavilion Gardens to shake his hand, ask for his autograph, and grin at him. During the walk, Stan revealed he had played Brighton as a boy, but couldn't remember in which theatre or what production.

The Royal Pavilion, *Brighton.*

John didn't press him to remember, as the idea was for Stan to enjoy a relaxing stroll, and not to be badgered for an interview so, unfortunately, this little piece of information is still unknown. So, after a week during which he re-acquainted himself with the sights of Brighton, Stan headed back up North, to the city he had visited the most during his stage career – Manchester.

Chapter Fourteen

Southend, Southport, South Wales

THE press coverage for Laurel and Hardy's 1947 Manchester visit had been exceedingly poor, and in 1952 showed no improvement. Of the show at the *New Manchester Hippodrome* the *Evening Chronicle* revealed:

> Said the small man to the fat man: 'Are you really all one person?' Said the fat man to the small man: 'Shut up and go to bed.' Laurel and Hardy have been doing this kind of thing for years and years and it is still whole-hearted fun – and clean as a whistle. They have the sense not to stay on the stage too long; nor to attempt anything they can't do. But everything we wanted was there – Oliver wagging his fore finger, Stan bursting into tears and telling the cop: 'I'll sue you for inflammation of character' and remembering, after looking through the wrong end of his field glasses, that he can't read anyway.

A second review, in the *Manchester Guardian*, ran:

> There is no denying those unequalled film clowns Laurel and Hardy are somewhat diminished in a stage appearance. It may be that we have been used for so long to their screen predicaments in close-up form. The enormous time-bomb of Hardy's patience and Laurel's sad but hopeful attempts to do the right thing, like a small boy tinkering with the fuse, seem to need those long excruciating silences that they get on

the screen, but did not get last night. Yet their dramatic sketch had some wonderfully funny moments. Particularly when they were trying to sleep on a bench.

On Wednesday night the Boys were invited by Noel Coward to a party at the *Midland Hotel*, to celebrate the opening of his play, *Quadrille*, at the *Opera House*. Other than that, they appear to have had an uneventful week.

Playing inland theatres during the summer months can be the kiss of death, for the local populace is not wont to sit in a theatre when all outside is bright and sunny. People at seaside resorts, however, go by tradition to theatres. To them, a holiday would not be a holiday without the sun by day and the shows by night. Thus, after having met indifference at some of the places they had played, Laurel and Hardy were heartened by, and genuinely thankful for, the reception they received in the North Wales resort of Rhyl. On the first night, queues outside the *Queen's Theatre* extended along the promenade in both directions, and the police had to be called to control the crowds who had besieged the stage door. The 'House Full' signs stayed in use throughout the week, and potential customers were turned away nightly. The *Rhyl Leader* reported:

> It is saying a lot to say that Stan and Ollie are just as funny on the stage as they are on the screen. In a screamingly funny two-act sketch they prove that they are born comedians, whose popularity will never wane. Their actions in the waiting room at the station[27] are the quintessence of good comedy, and when they 'break in' to the Chief of Police's home, nobody but Laurel and Hardy could possibly concentrate so many laughs into such a brief space of time.

Having had no problems filling the *Queen's Theatre* all week, on Friday morning Stan and Babe were asked if they would go along and do the same for *The Hanroy* cinema in Deinolen. After a warm welcome by the delighted village residents, the comedy couple were invited to watch themselves in one of their classic feature films, *Way Out West*.

At the Saturday afternoon show, in Rhyl, Stan and Ollie met the winners of what had become a regular newspaper item at each stopover – the Laurel

---

27 Local historian Bill Ellis remembers that, in the first scene, the two comedians worked on a bare stage with just a bench borrowed from Rhyl railway station. As the bench was an important prop it follows that a similar arrangement must have been made at every venue, as it is hard to imagine the Boys towing a huge bench around the country.

PRINCE'S International Circus Co
(LONDON & EDINBURGH)

CIRCUS PROPRIETORS & SHOW PRODUCERS

London Address
30 WESTWOOD ROAD
BARNES COMMON
S.W.13
Phone PRO 2051

Touring:
PRINCE'S INTERNATIONAL CIRCUS
PRINCE'S ROYAL CIRCUS

All Communications to:
CAPT. A. PRINCE·COX · F.R.M.S
SUITE 5 WAVERLEY MARKET
EDINBURGH
Phone Edinburgh 1618

Members: CIRCUS PROPRIETORS' ASSOCIATION OF GREAT BRITAIN.
AMUSEMENT CATERERS' ASSOCIATION.

ASSOCIATION OF TOURING AND PRODUCING MANAGERS

July 28th, 1952.
Westminster Hotel. Rhyl.

Dear Friends.

Firstly, may I say how extremely delighted we were to have had the real pleasure of meeting you great folks. It was a most pleasureable week for us I can honestly assure you. I sadly miss you for it is like a "morgue" in the Hotel without your grand presence. I have no boozing pals and all the people staying here are "Tea-Cup" merchants. I think they must have all been weaned on blasted "tea". Oh for a few nights like we had together. I am sure I shall sign the teetotal pledge and go "crackers" fefore the week is over, so do not be surprised if I rush over to Bradford to break it.

May I heartily congratulate you upon a very fine performance, but perhaps only what one expects from two such grand troupers. I suppose we all get a little hard-boiled at times, but I honestly laughed more at your brilliant comedy than anything I have seen for ages, especially after watching our "lousy" clowns doing the best to send the customers to the undertakers to get measured up.

Do trust that you have settled in at Bradford nicely and that The Ladies are happy also your good selves.

Hope Mrs Laurel is feeling better and that the old throat is much easier and that the "Gargle" department is having the desired effect, also hope that you Stan is feeling better and that you will soon be able to join us in a little "Jack the Dandy".

Well old Pals, good luck, good health and God Bless is the sincere wish of the trio with an extra whack from your humble.

All the best.

Laurel & Hardy.
The Alhambra Theatre. Bradford.

Yours.

Prince

WAVERLEY MARKET EDINBURGH	THE PAVILION RHYL	OPEN-AIR SWIMMING POOL RHYL	ALHAMBRA THEATRE MORECAMBE
International Circus & Carnival Winter Season	*Royal International Circus Summer Season*	*Prince's Water Phantasy Summer Season*	*Royal Circus Summer Season*

Each night, after the shows in Rhyl had finished, some of the acts would rendezvous at the Westminster Hotel, *where the Laurels and the Hardys were staying. The above letter, written by 'Prince', proprietor of the circus at the Pavilion Theatre, gives one an illuminating insight into the celebrities' social activities there.*

(By kind permission of John McCabe.)

and Hardy painting competition. On these occasions there was never any attempt by the Boys to fob the children off with a quickly-given prize and a brief handshake; instead, they always went to great lengths to ensure they were truly memorable events. The children would first be taken backstage and shown around, allowed to watch the show for free, and then be invited on stage to receive their prizes. Prize-giving ceremonies in the hands of bad presenters can be dull affairs, but in the hands of these two masters of mirth they became scenes of helpless laughter for participants and on-lookers alike.

In Bradford, next on the tour, the reviewer from the *Yorkshire Observer* would have been better described a 'non-observer'; he wrote only:

Last night at the *Bradford Alhambra*, Laurel and Hardy opened to a capacity house. They brought back to Bradford slapstick comedy which had the entire audience rocking in their seats and one particular sequence when Stan's foot became entangled with Hardy's braces almost stopped the show.

Local boy Joseph Ellis had ensured he didn't miss the show by buying tickets as soon as the advance booking office opened. He recalled:

When Stan and Ollie made their entrance, they stood centre stage for a full five minutes or more, and the audience simply laughed and laughed continuously. Everyone was mesmerised – we just couldn't believe we were actually seeing the lovable pair in the flesh. What followed was just like watching one of their films. They were just as funny on stage – in fact, they could have been filming, their timing was so perfect. But it is the memory of that initial entrance, a magical moment, which will always stay with me.

The two couples stayed at the *Midland Hotel* in Bradford, where the hotel receptionist, Bea Winterburn, thought she was doing the Hardys a favour by booking them into a room with twin beds. The Laurels, she thought, could more easily fit into one double bed. 'Imagine my surprise,' she said, 'when they came downstairs and told me they'd swopped rooms.'

On Sunday 10 August the party arrived in Southend-on-Sea for their one and only appearance in Essex. On Tuesday the *Southend Times and Recorder* recorded their show as follows:

Laurel and Hardy began a week on the stage of the *Southend Odeon*, on Monday. They were given a great reception by a large August Bank

Holiday crowd as the band struck up their familiar signature tune, and all the familiar grimaces with their own brand of droll humour, make the twenty minutes as well worthwhile as any ever spent in the *Odeon.*

As it turned out, spending time inside the *Odeon* was a pretty good idea, as torrential rain the whole weekend made it 'the worst Bank Holiday in years'. Laurel and Hardy stayed at *The Palace* – an enormous hotel built on the seafront, overlooking the Thames estuary – where, on the Friday, a luncheon was laid on for them by Essex Odeon Cinema managers.

Coventry, where Laurel and Hardy had received such an enthusiastic welcome in 1947, was the next stop. Here, the *Evening Telegraph* commented on their performance at *Coventry Hippodrome*:

The fun is as fresh as ever. The pair have lost none of those characteristics so typically 'Laurel and Hardy' – they are all there. The pace of the sketch never flags, the comedy is wholesome, and all together it is no trouble for onlookers to get a good laugh out of Stan and Ollie's latest dilemma.

(Courtesy of L. Crane)

Oliver Hardy pins a 'Courtesy and Service Star' on usherette Eileen Winfield. Odeon Cinema, *Southend, Essex. Week commencing 4 August 1952.* (Roy Sims collection.)

Essex Odeon cinema managers at a luncheon for Laurel and Hardy, getting ready for a chorus of 'We are the Sons of the Desert' at the Palace Hotel, *Southend. 8 August 1952.* (Roy Sims collection.)

The *Coventry Standard* too, waxed lyrical:

Laurel and Hardy do rather more than prove the indestructibility of slapstick as a medium for laughter; they provide an object lesson for all would-be comedians by giving us nearly a half-an-hour of high-pressure, unadulterated nonsense in which there is not a single word out of place, which can be remotely called indelicate.

If ever proof were needed that it is possible to be clever and clean, this is it and for that reason, in these days of innuendo, double-meanings, and blue-edged gags, I salute these masters for reducing their audience to the point of near-hysteria simply by exploiting absurdities; and for leaving us limp with laughter, but refreshed.

Even though the two comedy stars had no background in the area, the people of Coventry had built up a special affinity for them. In an article in the *Evening Telegraph*, Hardy reciprocated the feeling to some extent. Under the heading, 'Ollie may become a Warwickshire man', it ran:

Off-stage, Mr Laurel and Mr Hardy are very modest people. Says Mr Laurel: 'We know what we can do, and we stick to that. Why should we change? Neither of us is a great talking comedian, so we just say enough and carry on as we always have.'

Asked if they were enjoying their second tour of Britain, Hardy gave the very definite answer, 'Yes, my wife and I think the English countryside is beautiful. I like the English provinces – after all, big cities are the same all over the world – and I like the people. I've never seen such hospitality. I like the way people live over here, too.' Then he let me into a little secret: 'Mrs Hardy and I have often thought that when I retire we would like to settle somewhere in Warwickshire, because we both think this is the most beautiful part of England.'

The following week the comedy duo were back amongst the holiday-makers, this time in Southport, a resort situated between Liverpool and Preston. The standing joke about Southport is that the tide there recedes farther than Yul Brynner's hair-line. The day before Stan and Babe arrived, though, the joking had stopped when a thirty-foot high tide damaged the Marina at the north end of town. Mercifully, the storms and flooding did not recur, and 'another fine mess' was averted.

Of Laurel and Hardy's show, the *Southport Visiter* [sic] wrote:

Crowds gathered at the stage door of the *Garrick Theatre* to catch a glimpse of Laurel and Hardy and, inside, the theatre was full to capacity. 'Here in person' announced the placard outside. When I was a small boy, if anyone had offered me £100 or the chance of seeing these screen buffoons in person, I would have refused the money. Accordingly the small boy in me rose in delight to greet Stan and Ollie when they appeared on the stage. They had the audience rocking with laughter, which grew even more uproarious as they blundered about as housebreakers. The old tricks and the familiar mannerisms were present, and it was truly Laurel and Hardy IN PERSON.

The tour had now been running for six months, and both comedians were feeling particularly tired and weak. Stan was receiving constant attention from a doctor, and being given daily injections of drugs flown in specially from America. On their arrival on Sunday both celebrities had been jostled by a crowd of fans, so Hardy requested a police escort for the week. He was reported as saying, 'We don't want to go anywhere except the back of the stage and our hotel.' The *Southport Guardian* added:

> Once their two-hundred-yard car ride to the *Prince of Wales Hotel* is over, Stan Laurel goes to his room on the first floor, and Oliver Hardy to his on the second. Behind the safety of his bedroom door, Laurel can relax, for doctors have told him he must do nothing else but. His twenty-five minute turn on the stage is his only exertion.
>
> Said a friend of Stan's: 'We often wonder how he carries on. He is a very sick man. A special diet has been arranged for him, but he takes his trouble cheerfully.'

At the hotel special instructions were put into force. Neither comic had to be disturbed, and phone calls could not be put through until a certain hour – and even then only friends and managers could be connected. The hotel restaurant and public lounges were not used by the Laurels and the Hardys, who remained in their private suites. During the week, the Boys turned down an invitation to judge a heat of the English Rose (a beauty competition for young ladies), fearing that the strain of facing the crowds would be too much for Laurel.

Having spent three out of the last five weeks at holiday resorts, Laurel and Hardy were next precipitated into the residential atmosphere of the London suburb of Sutton. When they arrived for Monday-morning rehearsals they were besieged by youngsters demanding autographs. A press photographer naively invited the comedians to go to Manor Park to meet some more youngsters.

> 'No thank you – no parks' responded Stan. 'We have tried that before, and had the police on us for causing an obstruction. Hundreds of kids just float in from nowhere.

'It's sort of funny, too, when some old man with a long beard comes up and says that he saw you on the screen when he was a little boy.'

At the *Burford Bridge Hotel*, Box-hill, where Stan and Babe were staying, their meals were being supervised by floor-waiter Claude Johnston, whom they had brought over from the *Palace Hotel*, Southend. Johnston said of Hardy's eating habits, 'He has a big breakfast with plenty of bacon and eggs, but no lunch. Then he has a very big meal at night with plenty of ham and chicken.' Stan, it was revealed, was eating very little since his illness the previous year. Hardy had again brought over lots of tinned food from America, but the food situation had improved so much since 1947 that he found little need of it.

A *Surrey Herald* reporter interviewed the Boys backstage at Monday-morning rehearsals, and wrote:

'It's been tough going,' smiled Ollie, 'Two shows a night, three on Saturday, but we have enjoyed every minute of it.'

The two comedians return to Hollywood next month, but hope to be back before long to make a picture in this country.

Looking very fit after his recent operation in Paris, Stan had plenty of praise for one exclusive English topic – the Weather. 'It's been really grand; almost like dear old sunny California,' he laughed.

While the reporter was talking to them, Bert Tracey, their dresser, brought in a pile of autograph books and enquired, 'There are a lot more people waiting; can I bring their books in?' 'Sure,' said Ollie, 'bring 'em all. If people are kind enough to stand and wait for our signatures, who are we to refuse?' Of their stage work, the *Advertiser* wrote:

Laurel and Hardy at the *Granada*, Sutton, are proving to the audiences that they are still in the first flight of comedy teams. Their comedy is the inimitable fare that they have presented for so long, but their technique and artistry make it evergreen. Their patter and clowning is rich in humour and throughout their act their team work is brilliant. Their timing in everything they do is faultless.

One member of the audience, Kevin Henriques, was less kind, but honest, when he wrote of his memories of the show:

I was seventeen at the time and recall how excited I was to have the chance to actually see on stage two of the funniest men I had ever seen on the screen. Alas, my certain and clear recollection of my visit to the first house, Monday night, is total disappointment. Maybe it was because it was opening night, but the audience was surprisingly small and the two funny film men were decidedly unfunny on stage.

Henrique's opinion of Laurel and Hardy's reception is rather hard to take, especially when one compares it with the glowing press report. That for once the enthusiasm of the press outshone that of the public, however, is confirmed by a letter written by Stan some eight months later, when he still felt embittered enough to write:

> Delfont wants us to do panto at the *London Casino* this year, but am afraid that's out and if we come over in Oct. I don't know where the hell we could play during the Panto Season as all the Variety [venues] change policy for that Period and I certainly don't want to play places like Sutton!

Studying the places played on the tours, one might notice that in 1947 Laurel and Hardy had spent a total of ten weeks in the London area, whereas in 1952 they spent only one – in Sutton! When asked why London didn't figure on the itinerary, Bernard Delfont revealed that this was at Laurel and Hardy's own request. They much preferred the provinces. To repeat what Hardy had said in Hanley, 'We both like the provincial theatres. It is here where our act is best appreciated.' Maybe the reception at the 1947 *Royal Variety Performance* still rankled them as, on all but a couple of occasions after that, Laurel and Hardy gave London a very wide berth.

The picture brightened the following week when the reviewer from the *Bristol Evening World* was prompted to write:

> Laurel and Hardy were cheered and whistled for a whole minute when they walked on stage at the *Bristol Hippodrome*. It seemed as though half the children of Bristol had persuaded their parents to take them along to see this popular screen couple. Or did the parents need persuasion? No, I don't think they did. For Stan and Ollie, who have been amusing us on the screen for more years than we like to remember, have a brand of nonsensical fun that endures because it is so human and so very clean.
>
> Laurel getting pushed off the seat when Hardy wants to curl up and go to sleep, and Ollie trying to saw his way through the window while Stan, having found the door unlocked, watches him with interest from

the inside, are lovely moments of silent burlesque in their act, and although it is nonsense, meant only for broad laughs, it is as refreshing as a cool breeze in a stage world in which the titter too often takes the place of the guffaw. Laurel and Hardy give us plain, hearty guffaws, and it's grand to hear them again.

From the theatre on the Friday night Stan and Babe and their wives were whisked over to the *Grand Spa Hotel*, Clifton[28] as special guests at a ball in aid of the Lynmouth Relief Fund for the victims of the terrible floods which had occured in Lynmouth three weeks earlier. Among those present were the Lady Mayoress, the Duchess of Beaufort, and the Lord Mayor of Bristol, Alderman V. J. Ross. After supper the guests were treated to a cabaret show by various artistes including Laurel and Hardy themselves (see page 296).

At Portsmouth the following week, the *Evening News* came up with a short exclusive:

Double Tax Sends Stan and Ollie Home! – Five years have made a big difference to this country say Laurel and Hardy. 'When we were last here there were so many shortages,' said Stan. 'You couldn't get lemons, grapefruit, or bananas. Vegetables were hard to get, the bread was coarse and dark, and people's clothes looked shabby. Now everything is better.'

He and Ollie have been delighted with the receptions from British audiences. Stan and Ollie were asked to stay to do a pantomime, but if they had done so they would have had to pay tax here as well as in America. As Stan put it, 'We would have owed ourselves money.' But they are coming back next year for a longer visit and hope to do a pantomime then.

Of their theatre work, local writer Tony Wheatley gave the following personal view:

I went to see Laurel and Hardy through utter devotion to their screen personalities, and for the laughter they caused in me through their films. The opportunity to see them personally, so close to home, was too good to miss.

---

28 Not to be confused with the *Grand Hotel*, Bristol, where the Laurels and the Hardys were staying.

Sitting in the *Theatre Royal* awaiting their entrance, I had a sense of disbelief that, within a few minutes, they were actually going to set foot on that stage. All around was a quiet air of expectancy, and a general hum of excitement. As they walked on stage they were given a huge, warm, welcoming reception. They were very, very funny. Their age did not appear to have diminished their skills. Everything anticipated was met and surpassed, their timing superb, their rapport with the audience, perfect.

Les Pudney saw the Boys in an entirely different light:

They were really on their last legs – completely worn out. When they *tottered* on to the stage, we were all pleased to see them, and the theatre was crowded – standing room only. Everyone stood and cheered them for about five minutes, but it was a sad occasion, as they were so obviously tired out. Hardy had to sit down, and said softly: 'Another nice mess' etc. However, they were a delight to see in the flesh, and afterwards went into the lounge, where everyone present shook hands with them.

Les is quite right in saying the Boys were absolutely worn out. After all, here they were, both gone sixty, having done thirteen shows a week for the last twenty-seven weeks. They'd criss-crossed the length and breadth of England, Scotland and Ireland; made numerous public appearances; been to late-night functions; and stayed behind after shows to mingle with their fans. Both, too, had their illnesses, so it's a wonder they were able even to *totter* on stage. The manager of the Portsmouth *Theatre Royal*, however, allowed them no excuses and, after reporting them as being 'very disappointing,' stated he would not have them back.

Each night after finishing at the theatre the only place our subjects could get something to eat was at the *Queen's Hotel* in nearby Southsea. By all accounts, the night porter's attempts at preparing a meal would have been frowned upon by the 'screen' Laurel and Hardy. After a few days of enduring the bad food, the Boys aired their complaint to a contractor, Perce Champin, who was fixing a window sash in their room. Stan also moaned about having to put money into a gas meter, when they were already being charged such high prices for their rooms. He resorted to asking Perce if he knew the address of a local landlady who would give them a fair deal.

A presentation in the hands of Laurel and Hardy was never a quick peck on the cheek and a limp handshake. Here we see the two comedy favourites spending time with the winners of a local newspaper's painting competition.
Dudley Hippodrome, *20 September 1952.*
(By kind permission of Jock M. Whitehouse, pictured left, rear.)

Perce turned the conversation towards local theatres, and thrilled Stan with stories of the acts he had seen: Florrie Ford, Billie Bennet, Old Mother Riley, and Dante (the magician who had appeared with the Boys in their 1942 film *A-Haunting We Will Go*). Feeling considerably cheerier for his chat, Stan invited Perce to be their guest at the theatre. Typically of Laurel, anger had rapidly disappeared, and kindness, rather than wrath, had followed.

Having seen out the week in Portsmouth, the Boys found themselves back at *Dudley Hippodrome*. Bob Kennedy, who was still director, told the following story of one happening that week:

One night I suggested to them that as there was a big crowd outside the stage door, we could get them out of the theatre another way. But Laurel insisted on going out that way, remarking: 'When they are not there, we shall know we are not wanted.'

Doris Payne, who had been working at *Dudley Hippodrome* since its opening night in 1938, gave a very unusual insight into Babe Hardy:

> At the *Hippodrome* we had a clientele of around two thousand, who came every week, regardless of who was appearing. I would put tickets by for these people, and just wait for them to turn up on the evening. Hardy, though, didn't retain my faith. If all the seats weren't taken by fifteen minutes before 'curtain up', he would come round to the box-office, and say things like, 'You'll have to let the tickets go, Mrs Payne, [that is, sell them to the people queueing to buy tickets]. We can't let there be any empty seats.' As it was, the seats were filled all week, but Hardy would not rest until he'd seen it for himself.

From Dudley in the West Midlands, the cast headed south-west to Swansea, a Welsh port in the inlet to the Bristol Channel. There, the *South Wales Evening Post* printed little more than a synopsis of the sketch:

> Adult fans who recall Laurel and Hardy's popular two reelers, and children who know them from comic strips and their full-length films will not be disappointed by Laurel and Hardy at *Swansea Empire* this week. The well loved gestures and fondly remembered expressions of their screen shadows are re-created in substance on the stage. Stan and Ollie make the audience roar without recourse to the frenzied knock-about of modern slapstick comics. They know the value of stillness in their gentle nonsense, and were given a warm ovation, which left Hardy shaking with merriment.

Of their 'welcome in the hillsides' the two comedians later reported:

> 'Welsh audiences,' said Stan, 'are good. You know as well as I do that audiences differ, and in Swansea the people were wonderful. You can feel the warmth, you know.' Ollie nodded. 'Wonderful reception,' he said.

So pleased were Stan and Babe with the warmth of their reception that during the day they were often to be seen on the balcony outside their rooms at the *Mackworth Hotel*, waving to the passers-by below. At the end-of-week prize-giving presentation at the theatre, for the Laurel and Hardy painting competition, one young lady, Carole Anne Williams, distinctly remembers, on being kissed, that Hardy's breath smelled of vinegar. She later came to learn that this smell was something quite different.

Uncle Stan and Uncle 'Babe' with The Lonsdales, who also assisted The Great Cingalee. New Theatre, *Cardiff, 4 October, 1952.*
The captions read:
left, 'Fond thoughts Pauline – you greedy little bug – love Uncle Stan xxx'
right, 'To Pauline, My dear, I will always remember your sweetness to my darling wife and I. God Bless, Uncle "Babe", 1952'.
(By kind permission of Claudie and Charlie Cairoli Jnr.)

Upon leaving Swansea, the company had only a short trip to Cardiff, for what was the last engagement of the tour. Only the *South Wales Echo and Express* bothered to do a story on the two comedians, after sending round a reporter to interview them at rehearsals. Talking on his favourite subject of comedy, Stan said:

People are fed up with looking at stuffed shirts on stage. They like action and human characters. Too many would-be comedians today want to take the easy way. They don't want funny clothes or dirty faces. They want to throw away their tramp's outfit and walk on stage in evening dress . . . and talk.

Words . . . words . . . no action, no characters.

Hardy added:

> There's a careful design behind slapstick stuff. As we talk, we act. You've got an awkward situation and two funny characters who make it laughable. Take out the funny characters and put in straight players and you've got drama. See what I mean?

In all the other local papers, headlines like 'Tea Rationing Ends Today', and 'Chaplin Invited to Appear on *Royal Variety Performance*' took precedence over Laurel and Hardy's appearance, and the tour ended in a total anti-climax. A sour note also hangs over the week, in the form of a story which originated from the hotel where Stan and Babe stayed.

> When that great comedy duo Laurel and Hardy stayed at the *Park Hotel* it posed problems for the staff, as they weren't on speaking terms. They also insisted on taking their breakfast at the nearby *New Theatre*, so that they weren't disturbed by the attentions of their fans. This curious arrangement meant the hotel staff had to carry their breakfast over the road to the theatre, where Stan Laurel and Oliver Hardy sat grimly uncommunicative in their separate dressing rooms.

Subsequent cross-examination of the head hall-porter, Frank Bois, who was there at the time, revealed that it was not the Boys who had argued, but their wives. The compiler of the brochure from whence this story came must have switched the roles for added effect and thus, to his shame, blotted the proud record which Stan and Babe held for never having fallen out in all their years together.

The following night the Water Rats held a dinner at the *Park Lane Hotel* in London. Among those present was Charlie Chaplin, and the highlights of the evening were shown on television. Laurel and Hardy, for whom the occasion would have been an ideal farewell, did not attend, so it is strange to learn that the following night they *were* in London, at the *Prince of Wales Theatre*. As soon as the star of the show spotted them sitting in the front row, he came down off the stage and began clowning around with them. Needless to say, this brought the house down.

After the show Stan and Babe went backstage to congratulate the comic genius on his fantastic success. In 1947, this comedian had been taking his first faltering steps into comedy; now, only five years later, he was headlining a show which was to run for over eighteen months. After their own phenomenal career, Laurel and Hardy's last gesture before they left Britain

Laurel and Hardy pay their respects to Norman Wisdom.
The inscription reads: 'I was very proud to meet them both'.
Prince of Wales, *6 October 1952.*
(By courtesy of Norman Wisdom.) (Author's collection.)

was to go and pass on their best wishes to him – Norman Wisdom had come a long way.

On 9 October the four visitors from America boarded the *Queen Elizabeth* at Southampton Dock for their return trip to New York. Although it had been a totally exhausting tour, and none of them was getting any younger, in less than a year they would be back to do it all over again.

Chapter Fifteen

Paintings in Great Numbers

AFTER six months of inactivity back in Santa Monica, Stan wrote to
Claude Cingalee (The Great Cingalee – Oriental Magician) in England:

> Geo. Lodge the Manager of the theatre in Belfast wanted us to play
> Panto this Xmas in Belfast, but Babe is not too hot about it – too much
> work, so that's out. However we have promised to play Variety for
> him when we come over again.
>
> I understand [show]business has been quiet so far this year, I guess
> they are all saving up for the Coronation DO, and imagine after that,
> things will start moving good.
>
> All here as usual, just taking it easy, but have the feeling to get going
> again. We have a deal pending for Australia and New Zealand and if
> that goes through, we may come to Eng. to play Variety till Dec. and
> then go down there, so don't know as yet what will happen.

When it was finally decided to go ahead with a British tour, restrictions
prevented Hardy from working in Britain until October; but a loophole
was found which allowed him entry into Northern Ireland, where the
comedy duo would write and rehearse their new sketch. So, on 9 September
1953, the *SS America* deposited the Laurels and the Hardys at Cobh, a deep
water port in Southern Ireland, on the Atlantic sea route. It was requested
that there be no advance publicity, and no reception party at the docks; a
request to which the liner company faithfully acceded. This would leave
Stan and Babe free to walk quietly down the gangplank and drive away

The Laurels and the Hardys on board the SS America, *totally unaware of the reception awaiting them in Cobh.*
(By courtesy of John McCabe.)

unnoticed. What they, the company officials, the police, and their hosts had failed to take into account was the fascination that these two funny men held for little children. As at Christmas time, when children know instinctively that Father Christmas is coming, so it was here that they knew of the coming of two equally adored characters. Thus, almost every child in Cobh had played truant, and neither parents, teachers, nor police were going to send them away before they had set eyes on their screen idols.

Adults and children alike poured down to the quayside in a constant stream, blocking traffic to and from the docks. The air was filled with the noise of sirens, hooters and whistles being sounded by every vessel in dock. Those who had taken to the water in pleasure craft followed the tender from the liner to the dockside, waving and cheering at the party on deck. As soon as their feet touched dry land, Laurel and Hardy were mobbed. Children, greeting them like their favourite uncles, climbed on them, hugged them, kissed them and ruffled their hair; they patted them, squeezed them and

As soon as their feet touched dry land at Cobh, Laurel and Hardy were mobbed.
(By kind permission of Joe Wilson.)

begged for autographs. Policemen stood aside in amusement, as there was nothing to do but just allow the tide of love to wash over the two subjects. Genuinely touched by the display of affection, Stan and Babe made every effort to satisfy the desires of the whole assembly, and to sign as many autographs as physically possible. Before being led away, Hardy confided to a reporter, 'We were absolutely overwhelmed. There scarcely ever was a film scene like it. They are grand children, and Stan and I are grateful to them.'

Still reeling from the unexpected sentiment of the reception, the comedians' emotions finally burst forth when, on their being taken to St. Coleman's Cathedral, the air was filled with the sound of its carillon bells ringing out 'The Cuckoo Song'. Both Stan and Babe wept openly, and later described the moment as one of the greatest thrills of their lives.

Continuing the short but memorable visit, the party was taken to Blarney Castle, in whose walls is embedded the legendary Blarney Stone which, so legend has it, has the powers to impart to those who kiss it the gift of flattering speech. To reach it, one has to lean out and hang down over the ramparts. This was easily achieved by Stan, but Ida and Lucille declined; as did Babe who rightly pointed out, 'Nobody would hold me. I'm too big.' This dubious opportunity being lost – which one can rest assured did not seriously affect Mr Hardy's gift for flattery – the party were next received at the City Hall by the Lord Mayor of Cork, Alderman P. McGrath.

All too soon the impromptu sight-seeing tour came to an end, and the party left the city of Cobh a little later than scheduled, with the sights of the children's faces forever etched in their minds, and the sound of its bells echoing in their ears. Having originally planned to arrive unnoticed, Stan Laurel and Oliver Hardy would not have exchanged this reception for the world. In stark contrast, their arrival at the *Royal Marine Hotel* in Dun Laoghaire, following a train ride to Dublin, went off with a minimum of fuss.

Later, a reporter from the *Irish Times* found the Laurels having dinner there. 'Ollie is resting,' explained Stan. 'We had a terrific heat-wave in New York before we left, and, well, it was just too much for him. He did not quite get over it until a few days out on the boat, and then the journey . . .' The following day it was the turn of the *Evening Mail* to pose the questions, and Lucille to act as spokeswoman. 'We are all very tired after the journey,' she told the reporter. 'We intend to rest a few days before starting work on our new show. We will probably go into town tonight.'

Stocking up with typing paper ready for the writing of Birds of a Feather. Royal Marine Hotel, *Dun Laoghaire.*
9 September – 13 October.

During the next three weeks, writing and rehearsing of the new sketch, *Birds of a Feather*, went off favourably. The basic plot of this is as follows:

The Boys have arranged to meet outside a public house. They arrive individually and go through a much extended version of the routine used on the 1952 tour, whereby they keep 'missing' one another. This is effected by the use of two entrances to the public house, and, like a novelty weather clock, as one partner goes in one door his counterpart comes out of the other, and vice versa.

When finally they confront each other, Stan informs Ollie of a vacancy which might suit them. The job entails tasting whisky, with the incentive appearing to be: 'the more you drink, the more you earn'. The Boys take the job, but strive a little too keenly to fulfill demands, with the result that Ollie ends up in hospital[29] after launching himself through an open window, in an effort to fly.

With the introduction of a doctor, a nurse (a man in 'drag'), and an undertaker, mix-ups occur over just who is the patient and who is the visitor. Confusion is increased by the presence of some eggs in Ollie's bedside cabinet which Stanley brought *for* Ollie, but the nursing staff think were laid *by* Ollie. After being fed birdseed, the Boys end up walking around clucking like chickens, and the pandemonium is added to when the doctor opens the cabinet doors and two pigeons fly out.

Following a blackout, the two comedians come front of tabs and sing 'Trail of the Lonesome Pine' (from their film *Way Out West*), before saying their customary 'goodnight'.

Before starting on the tour proper it was decided, with Laurel and Hardy's typically generous nature, to stage a charity showcase at the *Olympia Theatre*, Dublin, where rehearsals had taken place. So, on Sunday 11 October 1953, *Birds of a Feather* was seen for the first time. The *Evening Herald* reported:

The affection in which Laurel and Hardy are held by young and old was very much in evidence, in the premier of their new playlet. This latest effort, which they will present during their forthcoming tour of

---

29   *Birds of a Feather* is quoted by many as having been based on the Laurel and Hardy film *County Hospital*. In both, Stan goes to visit Ollie in hospital, but there any similarity ends. Again, the script can be found in the book *The Comedy World of Stan Laurel*.

Above: A rare photograph showing the backdrop for the first scene of Birds of a Feather, *on which are the two doors used to perform the 'one in – one out' routine.*
(Kindly loaned by Cliff Temple.)

Right: In scene two, Stan recovers from almost strangling himself with a knotted sheet. Ollie looks on in disbelief.
(By courtesy of John McCabe.)

Britain, sticks closely to the formula that has served them so well over the years. It provides straight-forward knock-about fun and the two comedians worked with their usual earnestness and to the great delight of the audience.

On Tuesday 13 October the Laurel and Hardy 'family' sailed across the sea to England – and thus missed seeing the sun go down on Galway Bay. After four days of relaxation at the *Washington Hotel*, London, Saturday found the Boys in the BBC TV studios, being interviewed on Henry Hall's show, *Face the Music*. They were against performing their act, or any part of it, on television because, as Hardy explained, 'In the States, the innumerable TV stations use up material so fast that there aren't enough gags and acts to go round. A comedian has to put as much into a one-hour television show, as into a theatre show which might run for years.'

Towards the end of the interview, Hardy made a slight mistake: 'We open,' he began, 'for Mr Bernard Delfont at Southampton.' After a surprised look from Stan and a gesture from Henry Hall, Babe corrected himself, 'I'm sorry! that's North . . . ampton.'

The two comedy stars duly travelled to North . . . ampton on Sunday, and booked in at the *Plough Hotel*. At Monday-morning rehearsals at the *New Theatre*, their schedule was interrupted when PC Spiller of the Northamptonshire Constabulary enticed them outside into Abington Street to pose for a photograph. In it, we see Stan with a group of schoolchildren standing by a zebra-crossing, and a rather portly warden – Ollie – holding a huge rectangular sign (a prototype 'lollipop') and directing them across. The picture was for the use of a local newspaper in promoting awareness of a nationwide road safety campaign, aimed at teaching children how to cross the road.

In the evening Laurel and Hardy performed their new stage sketch for the first time in England. The *Chronicle & Echo* reviewed it as follows:

Laurel and Hardy had a warm reception from an audience that was strangely mixed. There were adults who had rocked at Stan and Ollie when the films were literally the 'flicks'. Secondly, there were the children – before the curtain it was almost like a panto matinée – whose acquaintance probably dated from the time the family TV set was installed.

Nostalgia, and a love for a comedy couple re-born – ironically by a medium the experts say will one day kill the stage – these were two

Ecologist, Oliver Hardy, giving advice to father of eight, Stan Laurel.
(By kind permission of the *Northampton Chronicle & Echo.*)

main ingredients in the Laurel and Hardy success. But that was certainly not all. There was for the discerning the pleasure of watching two masters of their craft at work.

Things invariably go wrong on first nights, and the Boys did not beat the jinx. At the first house, when the doctor opened the doors of the bedside cabinet at the end of the sketch, the two pigeons, instead of flying out, merely dropped to the floor and strutted about the stage. Backstage, Laurel suggested to Jack Whitmore, the tour manager, that the pigeons had been fed too much. 'Why, they couldn't even take off,' he grinned. At the first house on Tuesday night, however, one bird took advantage of its new-found freedom and finished up watching the end of the show from a theatre box.

One night, a keen amateur recording enthusiast made a tape of Laurel and Hardy's stage act which turned out so well that Stan considered having it produced commercially. (The tape is now in a secret location.) On Thursday evening, Philip Garston-Jones did an interview with the Boys which was broadcast the following night on Midlands radio, in *What Goes On*. Earlier on Thursday Pathé had filmed a small amount of newsreel footage showing Stan and Babe clowning around in a taxi by the stage door, and then in their dressing room. The tragedy, though, is that even after the presence of such filming and recording equipment and crew, there is not one single audio *and* visual recording of *any* of the Boys' British stagework.

I doubt if the people of Northampton realised that that week they had been hosts to a bit of an historic happening, for Laurel and Hardy had been live on TV; were on at the cinema, in *Fraternally Yours* (the British release of *Sons of the Desert*); had their photograph in the paper; were appearing live at the theatre; had made a radio broadcast and a newsreel film; had had their sketch taped; and were featured most evenings in local newspapers. One would be hard pressed to find another time and place where all these media had been employed over such a short period. Liverpool, the next stopover, certainly wasn't in the competition. The press here neglected to let anyone know that Laurel and Hardy were even in the city, and it was only the stage sketch which received a mention. The *Daily Post* was, however, profound in its assessment:

> When Laurel and Hardy take the stage this week, we have to remember they are not there to be judged – merely to be acknowledged in person, as two of the greatest film comedians the world has ever known. Not they, but thirty years of changing tastes and techniques are on trial, to be guilty of failing to raise more than a few laughs despite Stan and Ollie's tremendous sense of comedy, experienced stagecraft, and slapstick script. Their reputation is established and the tricks on which this was built are there for everyone to see. The crushed bowler hat, the falling flower-pot, the battered brolly – everything but the bag of flour and the custard pie.
>
> The same fautless baby-cries appear on Stan's face – the Lancashire-born comedian has lost none of his skill. Oliver's apoplexy still threatens. But is something missing? Is it that the stage prevents them falling off roofs, or being dragged behind moving cars – or is it that their public has just grown up?

The *Liverpool Echo*, too, thought there was something lacking:

> Laurel and Hardy will always be remembered for those two-reel comedies. It is perhaps as well that this should be so. It may well be that the theatre does not offer the scope in action and change of scene which they require, but, whatever the reason, their stage appearance provides but a glimpse of the great comedians we knew and loved.

The manager of the *Liverpool Empire* had his own strong views as to what was wrong with Laurel and Hardy's act. In his weekly report he wrote:

> Very well received. Wonderful performers and they have a good sketch, but it seems that they are 'dated' – that they get nothing from the audience like they deserve. Liverpool is not a 'children's' town and adult audiences are not falling for this type of comedy. I feel it is a great pity – almost bordering on tragedy – as these artistes are great in their way and deserve a much better welcome.

This assessment seems a little contradictory, and is also unfair to the paying customer, as the manager ended it by saying he would not have them back.

During their next engagement, in Manchester, the rain swept down with a vengeance, causing widespread floods. Inside the theatre, things didn't brighten, either, if the account given in the *Evening Chronicle* is anything to go by:

> A not-so-bright *Manchester Hippodrome* variety bill placed too much responsibility on the shoulders of Laurel and Hardy. Nice to see them back again. Sorry to report that, after twenty-six glorious years of making folk laugh their heads off, that old magic doesn't shine quite so brightly. Still, this act from Lancashire-born Stan and a fatter-than-ever Ollie, was streets ahead of anything else offered.

The *Manchester Guardian* reviewer, however, was quite happy to accept the sketch in the capacity in which it had been conceived; that is, as a vehicle to transpose the comedians' film antics to the stage:

> (. . .) this is genuine clowning which sticks to its mindless principles and has no use for smartness, surrealism, or sex. All we ask is that they should be themselves, and to see them in three dimensions on the stage meets the demand; their two-scene psychological melodrama uses precisely the same technique as that of their pictures. It is the tactics of elephant and mouse. The elephant feels diminished by the tiny creature that spends its time getting on his nerves and under his feet, and has to inflate his dignity to enormous proportions as a defensive compensation.

Comedian Peter Goodwright, who gave such a good in-depth report of Laurel and Hardy's 1947 Manchester appearance, was on hand to give an equally perceptive view of their latest one.

THE CARLISLE JOURNAL

A CHANCE TO MEET LAUREL AND HARDY

--- And prizes for child artists

WOULD you like a chance of shaking hands with those world-famous funny men, Laurel and Hardy? A chance to climb on to the stage of Her Majesty's Theatre, Carlisle, on Saturday, April 24th, and get not only a handshake and an autograph, but a book prize as well? Of course, you would, children! So read below how to go about it:—

All you have to do is fill in the eyes, noses, mouths and expressions of these lovable comics. You can use paints, crayons, pencil or ink—and you must make your faces look as near to life as you can.

Then send your picture—and the form printed below the picture—to the Editor, "Carlisle Journal," 60, English Street, Carlisle. This must reach us not later than first post on Wednesday, April 21st.

Competitors will be divided into three age groups—6 to 8 years, 9 to 11, and 12 to 14.

There will be book prizes. The books will be autographed by Laurel and Hardy, who will personally present them to the winners during the Saturday matinee at Her Majesty's.

Well, there it is, children. Now—start work on those faces and then fill in the form below. Let's be hearing from you.

NAME ....

ADDRESS ....

AGE ....

PARENT'S SIGNATURE ....

V. HAUMSLEY

Another example, this time from the Carlisle Journal, *13 April 1954, of the ever-growing number of painting competitions, which almost totally displaced any interest in the comedians themselves.*

Their welcome on this occasion was fairly enthusiastic, but contained none of the euphoria of the previous appearance. This time the house was not full and Stan and Ollie had to work very hard for their laughs. It was on this occasion, as Laurel and Hardy took their applause that I realised, for the very first time, that I had been watching two men who were no longer young.

As they stood on the stage, Stan looked gaunt with thinning hair, and Ollie was obviously having difficulty in walking. It came as a shock to me, I recall, and I was filled with a sadness that not even the laughter they had created could erase. I remember thinking 'I shall not see them again,' and of course, I never did. No-one has emerged to take their place, but then – who could?

'A Laurel and Hardy painting competition' might be the answer to that, as there were no less than three large features of this nature in the *News and Recorder*, and one in the *Manchester City News*, whereas mention of the comedians in their own merit commanded only half a dozen lines.

The following week at the *Finsbury Park Empire*, London, even worse was to occur when the only mention in the local paper was for the *non*-appearance of Laurel and Hardy. Stan had a serious chill, which incapacitated him for a whole week. From his sick-bed in the *Washington Hotel*, he wrote in a letter: 'Got a very bad cold and was unable to open here at *Finsbury Park* last Monday but hope to be in shape for next week – the cold caused a deafness – can't hear a thing and have two doctors working on me.'

On what should have been Laurel and Hardy's opening night, Hardy went on stage to announce that Stan was indisposed, and tried to encourage the audience to give every appreciation to the replacements; but, much as the audience were in sympathy, they could not hide their disappointment at missing the opportunity of seeing two living legends. Consequently, the stand-ins, comedy double-act Jimmy Jewel and Ben Warriss, had a miserable night, followed by four more nights which were not much better.[30] The only bit of comfort for Jimmy and Ben came from Hardy who, being quite at liberty to absent himself from the theatre, chose to go in every night – firstly to appease the audience, and secondly to provide moral support for the acts. If ever a man's heart were in direct proportion to the size of his body, that man was Babe Hardy.

Around this time, Stan and Babe had a reunion with vivacious Hollywood songstress, Vivian Blaine, who was in the middle of a year-long run in *Guys and Dolls*. Miss Blaine had been a shining light in Laurel and Hardy's 1943 film *Jitterbugs*, but was now eager to describe her thrill at having been on the recent *Royal Variety Performance*. In turn, she was delighted to hear of Stan and Babe's tearful welcome at Cobh, which she was later to reveal to millions of American TV viewers on Ralph Edwards' *This Is Your Life* (see Foreword).

From Finsbury Park, in North London, the Boys popped over the River Thames to Brixton, in South London, where Stan was well enough to start the week. *The Stage* printed a unique review for the show, describing lots of the on-stage action:

> In *Birds of a Feather*, at the *Brixton Empress*, Hardy is a patient in a mental hospital. Laurel visits him with a bunch of lilies, and a jam and onion sandwich.

---

30   On the last night, comedian George Doonan and rag-time pianist Winifred Atwell stood in.

Hardy is indignant at being kept in such a place merely because he tried to fly out of a window after sampling some whisky. (Laurel didn't restrain him because, having had some of the whisky himself, he thought Hardy *could* fly out of the window!) Hardy sends Laurel for a barrister, Laurel returns with a section of bannister, a doctor thinks Laurel must be the patient . . . and so on. Hardy sighs, looks to the audience for sympathy, and generally finds Laurel's friendship very, very trying. On Monday there was a big audience, and plenty of laughter in all parts of the house.

After Stan's illness the previous week it was now Babe's turn; he was given a very bad heart scare and, by rights, should have had himself admitted to hospital. But, following the old adage 'the show must go on', he unwisely continued without resting. The only slight compromise Hardy made was to suspend the radio sketch planned for broadcast that week. As events turned out, the idea was never brought to fruition and the world might have to remain forever in the dark as to what the contents of *Laurel and Hardy Go to the Moon* would have been.

On 23 November the Boys were back at the theatre which had started it all for them in British variety – the *Newcastle Empire*. That week, one of the other acts was just starting off in his new career. Twenty-three-year-old Ray Alan was yet to make his mark as the most technically brilliant ventriloquist of all time but, then, was happy enough to be fulfilling one of his ambitions – meeting his comedy heroes, Laurel and Hardy. In 1988 Ray Alan wrote:

Meeting them for the first time was something of an experience. I had never met such big stars before. As I entered the theatre the first thing to greet me was Stan's voice saying, 'Hello there! You must be Ray. I'm Stan and this is Babe. We don't want any of that "Mister" business, do we? After all we are all pros doing a job, arent we?'

When I got to know them a little better, I mentioned to Babe that I had read somewhere about them not talking to each other. Babe Hardy gave me a hearty chuckle, called Stan into the room, and repeated what I'd just said. Stan grinned and replied, 'Oh yeah! We read that too. I'm glad we did 'cos until then we didn't *know* we weren't talking to each other, did we Babe?' Then the pair of them just laughed.

Of his own spot on the show, Ray Alan revealed:

Stan would watch my act each night and then ask me to his room where he would suggest a line or a movement. I remember him once telling me that I was losing a laugh by not pausing before the punchline. I tried it his way at the next performance, and as always he was right. To Stan, timing was more important than the spoken word. He had a magical way of doing nothing, hesitating, then either saying something or deciding not to. Whatever way he chose was right and I still use the same pause, the look and the 'slow-burn' when I work now with 'Lord Charles', as I did then with the 'cheeky-boy' doll.

The review of the show in the *Evening Chronicle* hardly causes one to pause at all: '*Birds of a Feather* provides just the right medium for comedy film stars Laurel and Hardy to indulge their droll slapstick fun, and they well deserved the welcome they received on their return to the city.'

Just what kind of welcome, if any, Laurel and Hardy received away from the theatre is not evident. On the Monday morning, 'Showman' of the *Shields Evening News* phoned Stan at the *Royal Station Hotel*, in Newcastle, and recorded the following conversation:

'How're y' keepin'?' It was a Geordie voice which greeted me when I telephoned Stan Laurel in Newcastle this morning.
    'Fine,' I replied. 'And you?'
    'Oh, I've had a good rest, put on a little weight and feel much better.'
    'And how is Oliver?'
    'Fatter than ever. He weighs over twenty stone.'
    'Will you be visiting Tynemouth during the week?'
    'I'll probably be down one of these days . . . if so, I'll give you a call.'

The article continued:

Yes, Laurel is back on Tyneside . . . Geordie dialect and all. It is his second visit to the area in twenty months. In March last year, he visited Tynemouth where he spent part of his schooldays.
    'We will be in England six months or so and then we may go to Australia,' Laurel told me.
    'How is everyone in Tynemouth? Give them all my love. Tell them I have not forgotten them. God bless.'

Whether Stan bothered to follow up his rather unenthusiastic-sounding intentions to visit Tynemouth is unrecorded. After the blasé treatment the

Boys had received on their last visit to Tyneside, perhaps Stan's urge to go back to the place to which he felt he belonged had severely diminished.

What *was* seen that week, was Stan and Babe's professional dedication in polishing their act. When a show finishes, most artistes are out of the theatre before the applause has died away; but not Laurel and Hardy. If Stan felt ill-at-ease with a line, or saw an opening for an extra gag, the two of them would stay behind to rehearse. To get the true feel of the sketch, they would even ask the scene-shifters not to strike the set, and often it was left up until the following day. Stan was now in the habit of recording the act and playing back the tape for critical analysis. Sometimes he might feel that a certain line would get a bigger laugh if Babe delivered it and, if so, would turn the dialogue around to suit. Whatever the case, the following evening they would be in the theatre well before curtain-up for another run through, so that, when the new piece was put in the act, it would always fit perfectly.

Billy Marsh and Olga Varona had observed this perfectionism back in 1947, when Laurel and Hardy were first adapting to a stage career, whereas Ray was seeing the same amazing amount of tenacity from the Boys after over two hundred shows (although, admittedly, this sketch was pretty new). The rehearsing obviously paid off, as the manager reported:

> Excellent reception. These two well known stage and screen stars return this time with an entirely new sketch. Their comedy of cross patter and actions receives loud laughter . . . and a big laughable finish.

Ray Alan's final word on his utter respect for the Boys was:

> I don't think Stan and Babe ever refused to say hello to anyone, and I have always believed that thanks to them, the world became a much happier place. Laurel and Hardy were able to remind adults what fun it was to be children.

Birmingham, like Newcastle, was receiving a fourth visit from Laurel and Hardy. History or reputation, though, didn't enter into the review in the *Birmingham Mail*:

> Laurel and Hardy at the *Birmingham Hippodrome* were finding the years jading. They showed all the old quirks in a moderate brief farce, but that was all.

The situation wasn't brightened by Brian Harvey's review in the *Birmingham Gazette*:

For old times' sake I wish I could say that I enjoyed Laurel and Hardy as much as when they entertained me as a child, with their film antics. At their return visit, however, they are not particularly funny nor has their act any originality. Relying too much on a few time-worn mannerisms, these two comedians must have the most unimaginative gag-writers in showbusiness.

The Boys must have been reeling on the ropes when they were hit a third time – this time by the *Birmingham Post*:

Laurel and Hardy have been with us for a long time now, and both the formula and reputation of the partnership are well established. That the pair should still be relying on their old formula is nothing remarkable: successful artistes, having recognised their métier, do well to adhere to it. What is significant is that the two clowns, to judge by their performance, are now living on that reputation.

Because their very names are household words, and their appearance and eccentricities an institution, they do this very plausibly. But it is not really good enough. The sketch is mediocre material as the sort used as make-weight in any of a dozen undistinguished touring revues. It has the slightly sentimental appeal of familiarity, and so has the almost mechanical performance of Laurel and Hardy. The original fire is missing from the drollery, and the pair's enthusiastic reception owed as much, one suspected, to gratitude for past favours, as thankfulness for present laughter.

If ever an ally were needed to champion the cause of Laurel and Hardy, then the timing of one young man was impeccable. John McCabe, an American student, was on his way to Birmingham Library when he stopped outside the *Hippodrome* to observe a poster billing Laurel and Hardy, and, unable to believe that his boyhood heroes were there in person, ventured inside. After watching their performance, a strong urge to meet them led John backstage. In Stan's dressing room he conversed so intelligently on Stan's favourite subject, the structuring of comedy, that he was invited back a few nights running. By the end of the week McCabe had enough notes to write the book *Mr Laurel & Mr Hardy* which, when it was published eight years later, was to introduce thousands of new fans to the world of Laurel and Hardy. When in 1987 he was shown the review from the *Birmingham*

*Stan Laurel suspends writing, in his backstage dressing room, to pause for
reflection. John McCabe (in shadow) holds the moment sacred.*
Hippodrome Theatre, *Birmingham, week commencing 30 November 1953.*
(By courtesy of John McCabe.)

Post, McCabe was angered enough by the phrase 'now living on their
reputation' to retort:

> Utter nonsense! Fatuous nonsense! That reviewer was stupid or inat-
> tentive or both. I saw 'Birds' twelve times, (four in Birmingham), and
> I heard the uproarious laughter during each performance. I heard the
> loud cheering that frequently interrupted the performance itself –
> plain, unadulteratedly funny. Living on their reputation indeed! This
> is ludricous.

McCabe's opinion is backed up by the theatre manager who gave Laurel
and Hardy the following report:

> Very excellent reception. These comedians are presenting a very ex-
> cellent show, which is a 'mental' idea, and the comedy they get out of
> this causes roars of laughter. When this is worked up it will be the best

scene they have ever done. Nevertheless in the state it is now it goes excellently.

With further material obtained from a continuing friendship with Laurel and Lucille Hardy, back in America, McCabe was able to compile three more books (see page 265).

Another important spin-off from this friendship was the founding of the Laurel and Hardy Appreciation Society – *The Sons of the Desert* – for which McCabe's pioneering efforts cannot be too greatly lauded. Thanks to McCabe's forethought and enterprise, thousands of adoring Laurel and Hardy fans can now find a channel for their affections, and the memory of these two beloved comedians will be passed on for generation after generation.

Chapter Sixteen

Merry Christmas, Mother

WHILE in Hull in 1947, Laurel and Hardy had been totally ignored by the press, and six years later, in December 1953, the *Hull Daily Mail* still gave only the briefest credit:

> Laurel and Hardy were accorded a great reception at the *Palace Theatre*. Stan and Ollie do not need to speak to raise a laugh. Facial expressions are sufficient. Stan of course is the foil to the redoubtable Ollie, but the partnership is perfect in its contrasting humour and though their sketch is comparatively short, they extract every laugh from it.

On Wednesday, a private luncheon given by local cinema managers at the *White House Hotel* went unrecorded, and the opening of a jeweller's shop by the two world-famous comedians, in nearby Toll Gavel, Beverley, was given the merest of mentions. An unknown person breaking into the shop would have gained front page headlines.

Nottingham, unlike Hull, had done its homework and gave the fullest of respect to these two living legends; their appearance having been advertised two months before they'd even arrived in England. The Boys now had a free week before the start of their Christmas show at the *Nottingham Empire*, but this was taken up with press and publicity calls, photo sessions and rehearsing. They did, however, find time to call at the *Bull Inn* for dinner with the Healeys, whom they had also recently visited on their way through to Hull from Birmingham.

Even though pantomime is traditional for the Christmas season, *Birds of a Feather* was retained for the *Laurel and Hardy Christmas Show* as, in the words of Bernard Delfont, 'There seemed no need to change it.' The support bill had a heavy leaning towards circus-type acts, with trained pigeons, a 'wonder' horse, performing Pekinese dogs, and jugglers; as well as a ventriloquist, two accordionists and a dance trio. To add to the party atmosphere it was arranged for Stan and Ollie to stay on stage after their sketch and act as hosts to a 'free-and-easy' of party games, competitions and a junior talent show. This sounds like the format for a show that could last all night – and it was, as the review from the *Guardian Journal* verifies:

> They always say the sign of a good party is the length of time it lasts without anyone realising how late it is getting. *Laurel and Hardy's Christmas Party* had such a riotous opening that Hardy had to interrupt the fun and games the children were having, because the second-house queue was getting restive, outside.
>
> The famous pair of film comedians act as genial hosts of this grand family entertainment, and provide thirty minutes of slapstick buffoonery in a brand new but traditional sketch. One exasperated sigh from Hardy, or one twitch from Stan's eyebrow – is still enough to send all the youngsters and their parents into hysterics.

The *Evening Post* offered similar observations, except that the twitch in Stan's eyebrow (the one which sent people into hysterics) now belonged to Ollie. Obviously, Stan had swopped it for a couple of blank stares:

> Shrieks of delight greeted Laurel and Hardy at the *Nottingham Empire*. The twitch of an outraged eyebrow from Ollie, or the whites of Stan's eyes raised mournfully to an unkind Heaven, are the signal for every child and adult in the audience to go into that specially delicious brand of hysterics that only clowns of their calibre can conjure up. How splendid it is to recapture that old rapture 'so funny, it hurts!'
>
> The climax of the show, needless to say, is the party on the stage at the end, when Stan and Ollie invite boys and girls to come up and join in a talent contest, with many exciting prizes. Those who are too shy are not forgotten, and each child leaves the theatre clutching a book, a comic or a balloon, thrilled with a wonderful evening.

The *Evening News* contained some hitherto unknown facts about the actual sketch:

Unable to pay for their Christmas dinner, Stan and Babe are put to work behind the bar of the Bull Inn *at Bottesford. Christmas Day, 1953.* (By courtesy of the *Radio Times*.)

The principal scene is in a hospital ward, with Hardy as a patient and Laurel as a visitor who has brought a bunch of lilies with him – just in case! Other comic characters include the nurse, the undertaker, and a physician who is introduced as Dr Wombat.

To understand one off-stage happening during Laurel and Hardy's stay in Nottingham, it is necessary to reflect on the longevity of their partnership. During their many years together, the Boys had been questioned by tens of thousands of fans and press representatives. The most repeated and, therefore, infuriating question was asked when they weren't together. To Stan they would *always* say, 'Where's Ollie?' and to Ollie, 'Where's Stan?' To have had this happen continually, day after day, for twenty-seven years, was enough to send them into a fit of screaming.

Each evening while in Nottingham, Stan and Babe took a taxi from the *County Hotel* to the theatre, even though the two buildings were less than a hundred yards apart. This might seem a strange thing to do, but one must consider that Laurel and Hardy were able to attract a crowd big enough to stop them covering even this short distance. One evening, Babe decided to give the taxi a miss. Before he'd gone two yards a fan stopped him and asked the inevitable question, 'Where's Stan?' With total disdain Babe replied, 'In my bloody pocket,' and marched on. Mouth agape, the offender reeled away feeling thoroughly chastised.

The day after Boxing Day, Stan wrote in a letter to a friend:

We had a very good week's business here to start off the run, and expect to have a very Big week commencing tomorrow – going to do 3 shows a day, so it's going to be pretty hard, as we do our act and appear in the Xmas Party too – then the last two weeks we do Two matinées a week – shall be glad when it's all over and we get back to Twice Nightly again.

With interest added by the proliferation of prizes and the build-up to the talent finals, the show did tremendous business for the full length of its run. Finally, in the middle of January, Stan got his wish and the show moved down to Portsmouth, where it reverted to its twice-nightly variety format. During the party's return stay at the *Queen's Hotel* in Southsea, Stan Laurel appeared to Dereck Riddell, the night porter, to be a very thin and worried-looking man. Oliver Hardy too, didn't seem at all well. On a visit to take tea to Babe's room, Dereck found him sitting in a chair with his feet in a bowl of hot water and a blanket around him, trying to fight off the effects of a cold. Although this scene has comic overtones, reminiscent of a ploy used by Hardy in the film *Sons of the Desert*, it was the start of what turned out to be a very serious illness.

Meanwhile, the show went on, but the local press hadn't improved their standards and, if it weren't for the review in the *Evening News*, Laurel and Hardy would have passed in and out of Portsmouth like a ship in the night:

Laurel and Hardy strolled onto the stage of the *Theatre Royal* to a delighted roar of welcome. It was as if everyone was thinking: 'Gracious, they haven't changed a bit.' Maybe Oliver has added just a couple of extra chins, and Stan may have a wrinkle or two showing through his greasepaint – but it was the same old imperious heavyweight Hardy and the same nervously plodding Laurel.

Come to that, their style of comedy has hardly changed a bit. With slick patter the usual modern trend, they still rely on their natural visual humour and the beautifully-timed comment. A unique pair, they delighted everybody.

After the show on Monday 18 January 1954, the theatre manager held a surprise party to celebrate Babe's sixty-second birthday. In the company at that time was a young comedy entertainer named Harry Worth. Harry had played three weeks on the 1952 tour, and was now in the fifth week of the fifteen he would spend on the 1953–4 tour. Billed as a ventriloquist, he performed the opening part of his act without the doll, Fotheringay, and it was this comedy patter which was earning him good laughs. Babe Hardy saw in Worth the potential to 'lose' the doll, and develop his own character and, under Hardy's encouragement and guidance, Harry did just that. The spot at the beginning of the act was lengthened bit by bit, until the routine with the doll became a secondary feature. Only a couple of months previously it had been Stan Laurel who had given inspiration to a young ventriloquist – now, it was Babe Hardy. At the end of the tour, the vast improvement was noted by William Willis, manager of the *Palace Theatre*, Plymouth, who wrote:

> Harry Worth earned and deserved a very good reception. He has developed and improved his act tremendously in the past year or so. While as a ventriloquist he may not be outstanding from a technical point of view, his presentation, material, and personality combine to make an act which is very much to the popular taste.

Later, Harry 'lost' the doll altogether, to such effect that for thirty-five years he was one of the most respected character-comedians in Britain, and had his own TV and radio shows. Sad to say, Harry died during the writing of this book, but not before he had revealed the fascination of observing Stan Laurel as he was about to walk on stage:

> There was this tired old man in the wings. On the first note of 'Cuckoo', Laurel became visibly ten years younger. He always made his entrance on the same note – he was such a perfectionist.
>
> At the end of the sketch, Laurel would step forward to make a speech, but would be dismissed by Hardy with a hand movement and a facial gesture which indicated, 'As if he could.'

From Portsmouth, it was up the 'London Road' to the *Chiswick Empire*. The Boys had last played there in 1947 as replacements for The Inkspots, but this time were bill-toppers in their own right. The *Brentford & Chiswick Times* afforded them the following:

> Laurel and Hardy receive a great ovation. This is a riotous act, in which Oliver Hardy is confined in a mental ward because he thinks he is a bird, and which finally ends with both he and Stan Laurel losing their speech and clucking like hens.

The Boys were staying at the *May Fair Hotel* in Berkeley Square for the Chiswick booking and their next one at the *Finsbury Park Empire*. At the latter they fulfilled the week's engagement they had been unable to do earlier owing to Stan's illness. *The Stage* was there to record the event:

> Laurel and Hardy naturally come to this essentially family theatre for the benefit of the many who wish to see them in person, and are very welcome. The most amusing thing about them turns out to be that they are very like themselves after all. Their comedy is gentle and, it must be confessed, not very funny. But it serves to show two familiar figures in characteristic situations that recall, by inference, the joyous laughter of the films, to which, in fact, their humour is naturally more closely attuned.

At the conclusion of this run, the Laurel and Hardy party went on the London-to-Brighton run, at the end of which they booked in at the *Grand Hotel*. Of the show, the *Sussex Daily News* had this to say:

> It is a sentimental journey for many of us – our visit this week to the *Brighton Hippodrome*. If we neglected to pay our homage, convey our regards, it would somehow constitute a base betrayal of our youth. For these two ageing zanies were part and parcel of the life we lived in the 'thirties. They were undisputed sovereigns of Screen Cloud-Cuckoo Land. Above all they were an antidote to the ills we were heir to. And so we just had to go along.

An interesting question was then raised:

> How would it all go down with the teenagers of today, reared on a diet of Martin and Lewis? There were remarkably few of them present in a packed house, but there was a generous sprinkling of exuberant kiddies. Could it be that Ollie and Stan have somehow missed a generation?

The *Southern Weekly News*, too, raised some points pertinent to Laurel and Hardy's longevity:

> Two generations have come under the spell of Laurel and Hardy. They occupy a unique place among the comedians of the century. Their greatness lies in the simplicity and cleanness of their humour. The fact that they are no longer at the peak of their fame is due more to radio

than to the passing years. Nearly all the modern funny men, both in the United States and in England, are the products of pure radio. There was no place in radio for Laurel and Hardy. Visual humour declined, and only the chosen few appeared on film.

Now comes television, and the trend is already going back to slapstick. The microphone-hugging comic will soon become as passé as 'steam radio'. All of which goes to suggest that Laurel and Hardy's very welcome return is not so much a glimpse of the past, as of the future. They were as cleanly funny as ever, and went straight to our hearts and freshened many half-forgotten memories.

Douglas Salmon, the critic for the *Evening Argus* wrote:

Still Masters of Slapstick. They came in with the flapper age, flickered their way through the silent films and on to the talkies. Our grandmas laughed at them; our mums laughed at them; and last night – we laughed at them. So synonymous with fun that we laughed as soon as they walked on. We laughed again at Ollie's disgusted look; we laughed when Stan sat on his hat; and we laughed a rather poignant little laugh when he stood in the corner and cried.

They guyed their way through a simple slapstick farce, but it did not really matter what they did. They were Laurel and Hardy; funny, fanatastic Laurel and Hardy – a snatch of our boyhood days back again.

Douglas Salmon was to say of his meetings with Stan and Babe:

During my ten years in journalism – including Fleet Street – and twenty-five years in television, I have met quite a few people, but I can say with all honesty that Stan and Ollie were among the nicest – lovable is not too strong a word – of them all. They were a delight and being with them was like being in the middle of one of their films. They were kind, really funny – hilarious in fact – and always good humoured.

Following such a fine tribute, the world's favourite comedy duo travelled by train to Norwich, for their one and only visit to the county of Norfolk. At noon on Monday 16 February, a reporter caught them outside the *Royal Hotel* about to get into a black Jaguar car to go to rehearsals. The pair of them were wearing heavy overcoats and berets. Even so they were feeling the cold, but not as much as Lucille, who was in bed with a chill. On their way to the theatre the two stars took an interest in the local architecture, and seemed most impressed by the City Hall. At the theatre they jokily informed the driver, 'The stage door please – not the front entrance. That is reserved for ladies and gentlemen.'

Booking Laurel and Hardy was a very ambitious project for the management of the *Hippodrome*, and the most expensive show they had ever staged. To meet the high cost of the show – £1,750, of which £1,000 went to Laurel and Hardy – the *Hippodrome* did what many theatres before them had been forced to do, and raised their seat prices – by sixpence. 'Even so,' the *Eastern News* defended, 'I imagine there are few places where you could see such world famous stars as Stan and Ollie, at such reasonable prices.' Considering the quality and size of the show, the price increase was, of course, totally justified, as one can judge from the review in the *Eastern Evening News*:

> Here they are, just the same as ever. They're still at the top of the tree, and if the tree is shaking its only with the laughter of their audiences. *Birds of a Feather* is not a sparkling piece in itself, but to see Laurel and Hardy playing it is sheer joy. It is done with all their consummate skill, so quietly, so effortlessly, so effectively. It's great fun. You'll be sorry if you miss it.

To strengthen further the mystique surrounding seeing Laurel and Hardy in person, he added:

> The pair so resembled their film selves that when the curtain went up the audience took a minute or two to realise they were seeing their childhood comedy favourites in the flesh.

The *Eastern Daily Press* was also enthusiastic about the live appearance of Laurel and Hardy:

> Laurel and Hardy on the stage with their vast experience of perfect timing, quaint gestures, grimaces and unexpected repartee are even funnier than in the more remote entertainment of the screen. The audience were still laughing when the curtain fell and the pair said 'Goodnight'.

After warm praise from the people of Norwich, Laurel and Hardy were next to experience a cold shoulder from the press on Tyneside, when they were totally ignored by all but the *Sunderland Echo*:

Although we have seen Laurel and Hardy once before at the *Sunderland Empire*, their visit this week is another clear example of the tremendous change which has taken place in popular comedy style. I am not suggesting that Laurel and Hardy are not funny, but that their humour, illustrated through specially written sketches, is an anachronism. It belongs to the silent film or the immediate post-silent era and there is a great deal the modern shift comedian can learn from that particular approach to the problem of how to make people laugh. The slapstick is thoughtful, wistful, and broad. Messrs. Laurel and Hardy give us nostalgic reminder of a grace long since discarded and lost.

It would appear Laurel wanted to forget all about his visit to Sunderland, for in a letter three weeks later, he wrote:

The bus. [business] was shocking in Sunderland – Worst week of our tour – The audiences were blasé – so a miserable week was had by all.

And the manager's report echoed Stan's claims:

Well received. They are working well indeed, and their material is much stronger than on their previous visit here, but, even so, they are not going more than well in any part of the house, and their ability to attract has greatly diminished.

The manager added he would have them back only with very strong support acts. Four years later, Stan was still harbouring the pain of this appearance, as the extract from a letter of 21 February 1958 shows:

Note the *Empire Sunderland* is still doing bad bus. I can't understand why they keep open and lose money week after week, it doesn't make sense. Am sorry for the acts playing to empty houses, I know how I felt the last time we were there, it was a miserable week, was glad to get out of it.

This was a far cry from Stan's feelings upon leaving Tyneside after the 1932 visit. Then, he had stated: 'God bless everybody. I love them all. Tyneside people do not alter – they are as good as ever.' And just prior to their 1952 appearance in Sunderland, Stan had reiterated: 'There's one thing that remains the same – Northern audiences. They're wonderful.'

But the events of the last two visits had made Laurel realise how wrong he had been: when the Tynesiders had been able to bask in his reflected glory, they had claimed him as their own; now that he was fallen from his high pedestal they made no attempt to put him back but, like a broken statue, totally discarded him. But there is no need to single out Stan to be pitied, for he is only one of many comedians who have had their pride taken away by the treatment meted out by audiences in this part of England. Tyneside has never produced a comedian from inside its boundaries, and has never accepted one from outside.

Stan, by now, must have been totally disillusioned with the way the show was being received, and was still harbouring the pain in September when, back in America, he wrote:

> I have been reading that the show business has been taking a turn for the better and sincerely hope it continues and fully recovers from the slump of last year. We certainly were over there during the worst of it, the business was just shocking, very depressing for all concerned.
>
> Hardy is feeling better, and we have several offers on hand to make TV films also a deal to make a picture in London, which would be in February next. I doubt if we shall come over for anymore Variety tours as Hardy prefers film work, doesn't like the traveling every week.

In Glasgow the following week the Boys faced more cold treatment, for the weather there was comparable with the terrible winter of 1947. The city was affected by snow storms, black-outs and blocked roads, and on the day of their arrival two explosions crippled the power-station. Half of Glasgow was without electricity and, with temperatures below zero, no coal was to be had. Rehearsals at the *Empire* were able to go ahead using an emergency lighting supply, but, in the afternoon, the manager announced: 'Unless the normal supply is resumed by this evening, there will be no show.'

The show did go ahead but, if words were pieces of coal, the reviews wouldn't have provided enough to make a fire. The *Daily Record*, which carried the biggest write-up, said only:

> There was nothing anonymous about 'alcoholics' Laurel and Hardy when they appeared on stage, to inject cheer into the hearts of the chilled victims of the power cut. The good old-timers still get the laughs with the simplicity of mime, direct dialogue, and their much loved style of verbal economy.

The snow, ice and black-outs continued throughout the week, and even though business was badly hit, the Boys were well received. This must have

(Roy Sims Collection.)

made the press coverage a sore disappointment, especially to Stan, whose earlier links with Glasgow had led to his becoming its adopted son. Seeking a shoulder to cry on, he left his 'winter hole' at the *Central Hotel* to go and look up the man to whom he expressed a great debt for his showbusiness success – A. E. Pickard. This great showman was still able to grab headlines, but the one that week was not one of his best: 'Self-styled millionaire Albert Ernest Pickard (79) of 92 Balshagray Avenue, Glasgow, was charged with careless driving.' Then, after also visiting Sir Alex King, Stan sought solace at his beloved *Metropole Theatre*, obviously working on the author's invented adage: 'If the present is hurtful – revert to the past.'

Chapter Seventeen

Keep Right On

IN reviewing the show at Wolverhampton, the *Express and Star* sought to relate Stan and Ollie's heyday in films to their current live appearance:

> For many years before the second world war the names of Laurel and Hardy were synonymous with comedy at the cinema. During the war, a number of new screen comedians came to the fore, and the old team were seen less and less at the cinemas in this country. It is some considerable time since a Laurel and Hardy film has been seen in Wolverhampton or, for that matter any other town. But the reception given them, on their first joint stage appearance in the town, surpassed any at the *Hippodrome* for many years. Their sketch was most amusing and entertaining.

George Knox, who was in the theatre orchestra, said of the Boys: 'They looked really tired, and working against time. Still – they brought the house down'.

On Tuesday, six-year-old Pauline Johnson had tea with the lovable buffoons at the *Queen's Hotel*, Birmingham, as a prize from the *Wolverhampton Chronicle*. Stan and Babe were forever giving little children such treats: they loved to see the look of glee on their faces, and were always proud to think that they could impart so much happiness just by letting the children meet them. Babe, especially, loved little girls. Never having had a child of his own, he would always immediately pick them up and give them a big squeeze.

That same week another little girl was brought backstage as a treat for winning a music award. Accompanied by her father, nine-year-old Barbara Leighton was first taken to meet Stan, who said, 'Come along Barbara Vicki, and say a big hello to Uncle Ollie.' Popping her into Babe's dressing room, Stan returned to join her father, Jack, and revealed that Babe was not too well and was seeing a doctor. Jack expressed his concern at bothering Hardy by bringing Barbara, but Stan told him he had insisted on seeing her.

In his dressing room, Hardy said, 'Come along Barbara, climb up on your Uncle Ollie's knee.' Due to his size, she managed it with difficulty, whereupon he sat hugging her, and asking questions about her piano playing. With a child's innocence Barbara told Mr Hardy that he looked tired, to which he replied that he was *very* tired, and thanked her for her concern. When it was time to go, her father came back to the dressing room and, as Barbara climbed off his knee, Hardy said, 'I'm looking forward to seeing you at your first concert.' When Barbara was gone the tired old comedian remained sitting there. Babe Hardy was crying.

Local boy Ron Mason, who had been to the *Wolverhampton Hippodrome* that week, gave his view of the comedy duo's act as follows:

> I prefer to remember Laurel and Hardy from their films, and not their nights in Wolverhampton. It was a farce – and not a comedy one. They gave us a silly, hard to hear, or grasp, pot pourri of giggly nonsense for about twenty minutes, and then went off. What a huge disappointment it was. Much as my esteem was, and still is, we were stunned. I understand it wasn't just the one bad night, either. People who went on other nights said the same.

At Sheffield, which was next on the tour, a reporter from *The Star* caught the Boys having a pot of tea backstage at the *Empire*. He described them as looking 'cold and miserable'. Of their trip from Wolverhampton Hardy said, 'Not a very good place to have come from.' The account continued:

> They sipped their teas in silence for a few moments, and then Stan Laurel turned a face, wrinkled by years in the service of comedy, and said: 'Don't expect us to be funny off-stage at this time of day.'
>
> 'Yes,' they said, 'it was pleasant to be back in Sheffield. No, it didn't seem like two years since they were last here.'
>
> Oliver Hardy shifted his bulk to a more comfortable position on a small chair. He gave it as his opinion that it was *bloody* cold. Said Stan:

'He gets more English every day. You'd think it was Ollie who is the British citizen, not me.' Both were wearing blue berets. Why? 'Comfort' said Stan. 'I can't get into a small car with a proper hat on,' said Ollie. THEN they moved off towards the stage for a rehearsal. The pot of tea was empty.

Of the show itself, the *Sheffield Telegraph* wrote:

Laurel and Hardy, at the *Sheffield Empire*, fill a sketch with all their endearing old tricks, which is certainly not to say there is anything stale about them. The phrase: 'they haven't changed a bit' is a great compliment to them. It is their sheer genius for comedy that makes them as good as ever.

When Oliver, being lowered out of a window on a knotted sheet, tells Stanley to tie the other end to something, of course he ties it around his own neck. And Oliver remonstrates with him in the way that has made millions of friends for Stanley all over the world – 'You might have killed me.' So there you are. They are very lovable and very funny.

The review in *The Star* betrayed none of the stage action, but was full of compliments:

Laurel and Hardy attempt one of the hardest things imaginable in the world of entertainment – to transfer their well-loved slapstick from screen to stage. The devices of the films, where anything is possible and anything can be hidden, are tried on the all-revealing stage. With a few reservations, the trick can be said to have come off, and the passing of the years has not impaired their impeccable timing. To watch Laurel as he wrecks his partners ponderous schemes by a kind of triumphant diffidence is to watch clowning at its very highest. By the contrast of his example, one is made to realise just how much subtlety of facial expression is neglected by modern music-hall artistes.

At the city hall on Thursday afternoon, the Boys opened the 'Prelude to Spring' hair-fashion preview, where they demonstrated their tonsorial artistry when Stan was seen to draw one model's tresses through his palms, and Ollie stood ready to trim them with garden shears. Fortunately, both handed over to the professionals before the lady became a James Finlayson look-alike.

The tour was scheduled to end on 17 April but, by now, Stan Laurel and Oliver Hardy had become very dispirited with touring Britain; Hardy was constantly tired and found the hours too demanding; Stan seemed to be holding himself together health-wise, but was finding the financial rewards of theatre work insufficient, and threatening to become even less. That week he disclosed to a confidante in a letter written at the *Grand Hotel*:

> We can stay over here till next Sept. but due to slump in Theatre Bus. in general, we have been asked to cut our Guarantee and Percentage – which of course, we are not in favour with. our running cost and expense would be just the same as now, so naturally it wouldn't pay us to stay here for the small amount of profit. However our manager is flying over from Los Angeles to look into an offer we have for a tour in Holland. Belgium and Greece with Australia and New Zealand to follow, which would be more profitable to us than staying in England, as it is new Territory for us and an opportunity to make Big money. Will know more about it in a couple of weeks or so and will let you know. If nothing happens – we shall of course return home to the States and make Pictures for TV.

While awaiting the elusive cloud with the silver lining, and the go-ahead to travel tens of thousand of miles, Laurel and Hardy didn't even move out of Yorkshire for their next engagement in the county-town of York. The *Yorkshire Evening Press*, too, felt no need to exert themselves. Of his backstage encounter, their reporter 'Mr Nobody' (his own title) revealed little:

> 'How do you like working in this country?' I asked Stan. He said he preferred working over here, as for one thing it was less strenuous. 'In America we[31] give four, five, six or maybe seven shows a day, including Sundays,' he told me. 'There, the first show of the day starts at about ten in the morning and the last finishes at about eleven at night.'
>
> Among the places which they hope to visit during their week's stay in York, is the Castle Museum.

Having squeezed every last ounce of information from the two comedians, 'Mr Nobody' allowed T. S. Williams, of the same newspaper, to have a go:

---

31 The 'we' mentioned here refers to American stage performers in general, and not directly to Laurel and Hardy.

The surprising thing about Laurel and Hardy is that they are so much like themselves. Ollie looks as reposed as a heavy man usually does, but being a comic is not easy. There is much action and a great deal of nervous tension all the time one is on the stage. Apart from his stage work, he generally takes things easy.

Stan Laurel does not go sight-seeing much, either. It is a life of hotel and theatre. He shrugged and made a comical face. He laughs suddenly and often offstage, you don't remember him laughing very often in films.

The show itself was also summed up in few words:

Laurel and Hardy at *York Empire* this week, are an argument for the real flesh-and-blood stage against mere pictures on celluloid. Funny as they are on films, they delight still more in their sketch, which is laughter from start to finish.

A different view came from Brian Lazarus, a member of the audience at the same show:

The theatre was half empty, and the sketch wasn't helped any by a poor amplification arrangement. Ollie, in bed centre stage, and Stan, sitting to the left, both had a microphone on a stand and would attempt to speak directly into it. Often though, when turning aside to deliver certain lines, the sound would fall away and the line be lost.

Ronald Nendick, violinist in the orchestra, also had his expectations deflated. On his return home from the theatre after meeting his boyhood idols, Ronald's wife was surprised to see a him with a sad look in his eyes. Ronald explained that the contrast of looking up adoringly at the two mirthmakers on the big screen, to the sight of Oliver Hardy straddling two chairs in a dressing room lit by a single naked bulb, was too great a burden for his mind to accept.

Over at the *Royal Station Hotel*, yet another hidden side was revealed. Billy McCaffrey, a floor-waiter, used to serve the Hardys and the Laurels with breakfast in bed, in their seperate suites. At 10 o'clock, and at hourly intervals thereafter, Billy had to take a double whisky to Hardy, for which he was tipped very handsomely.

For dinner the foursome would dine together in the hotel restaurant and then, after the show, would come back to the hotel bar for a little nightcap.

In all that time, Billy never saw the two comedians out of stage costume or make-up. A similar report also came from their stay at the *Central Hotel* in Glasgow, which would seem to indicate that the Boys, who clearly had not the energy nor the patience to remove their make-up and costumes before leaving the theatre, were, indeed extremely tired.

From York, our weary foursome travelled sixty miles south-east to the fishing port of Grimsby, in the mouth of the River Humber. Here the big attraction, according to the *News Pictorial*, was getting a free seat at the theatre by winning the painting competition, the advert for which ran:

> Children! Here is your chance to meet Laurel and Hardy themselves – the world-famous funny men you have so often laughed at on the screen – and to be given by them an autographed book you will always treasure. This famous pair are appearing at the *Palace*, Grimsby, and at the Saturday matinée twelve lucky boys and girls will meet sad little Stan and outsize Oliver. They will get free seats for the show, too.

Just how the 'lucky twelve' got on, or whether anyone else turned up for Laurel and Hardy's performance, the *News Pictorial* didn't bother to tell. It is to be hoped that a lot more was gained from the presence of the 'world-famous funny men' than the handing-over of twelve books. Part of the answer, at least, was supplied by the *Evening Telegraph*:

> To see Laurel and Hardy in the flesh, on stage, is rather like watching a legend spring to life. Their films have been part of the lives of several generations now, but Hollywood is a long way from Grimsby and its inhabitants a little unreal. But there is nothing unreal about Ollie and Stan. Both look and behave exactly as they do on the screen – which is more than can be said for some other film stars. Their sketch is a textbook example of the art of raising laughs without a single blue gag.

It was some twenty-three years later that the *Grimsby Evening Telegraph* chose to print a more in-depth analysis. Labelling Laurel and Hardy's 1954 visit 'part of their farewell tour of Britain before retirement', they related:

> Stan and Ollie addicts came from all over the county to see them. Even so, their stay, and indeed their whole tour, was comparatively low-key, as they had no wish for show-boosting publicity. They had become somewhat unfashionable, almost has-beens, in the eyes of even many of their old admirers.

Proof that at least twelve children turned up for Laurel and Hardy's show at the Palace Theatre, *Grimsby on 3 April 1954.* (By courtesy of Michael Davie, who is pictured next to Hardy.)

They were ageing, and not in the best of health. Styles were changing, as were tastes. Only their total absence from film-making and, indeed, their deaths would enable television to create a new cult which has introduced fresh generations to the amazing art of Laurel and Hardy and allowed millions more to wallow in glorious nostalgia.

Interviews with some of the people who were around at the time also revealed an, as yet, unseen picture. Hardy was reported as being thoroughly miserable and uncommunicative. Although in the theatre each evening two hours before the start of the show, he totally ignored the backstage staff. When the winners of the children's painting competition went backstage, one noted him blatantly sporting a whisky flask. He would also 'top himself up' in the Palace Buffet Bar, across the connecting passage from the theatre. Stan, who was still abstaining, didn't go with him, apart from the one occasion he posed for a photograph, pulling pints behind the bar.

The Boys and their wives stayed at the *Dolphin Hotel* in the neighbouring costal resort of Cleethorpes, where their rooms were kept like incubators to shield them from the cold. There they kept themselves in total privacy, taking all meals in their rooms and never once going to the dining room. Still dis-satisfied with his lot, Hardy, in Laurel's room one evening while awaiting their taxi, was observed looking out of the hotel window exclaiming: 'What are we doing in a Goddam place like this?' (a reference to Cleethorpes itself, and not to the hotel).

Stan was obviously aware of his partner's lack of tolerance, and his curtness to members of staff, and did all he could to redress the balance.

Both in his hotel room and in his dressing room he kept a pile of half-crowns, and every time someone ran an errand or did a small service, he gave them a generous tip.

Leeds, next on the tour, made it three weeks out of the last four in Yorkshire. After Stan's, and Laurel and Hardy's, long-running working relationship with Leeds, one might have expected the local papers to wax lyrical, but the *Yorkshire Evening Post* was short and sweet:

> That familiar tie-wiggle, that doleful face. What else could these things mean but those two favourites, Laurel and Hardy. With all their old skill, they entertain young and old at *Leeds Empire* and, judging by their reception from the first night audience, they occupy a warm spot in the heart of Leeds audiences.

The theatre manager went a little further, and wrote in his weekly report:

> Although the novelty of their first appearance 'in person' lost a good bit of support, they still prove themselves popular. The sketch is very well received and got good laughs.

World-famous Italian tenor Luigi Infantino, who was in Leeds to perform in concert at the *St George's Hall*, went back-stage to greet his comic heroes. Within minutes, wonderful sounds began to issue from the dressing room as Babe and Luigi duetted in a famous aria. The harmony was soon shattered, however, when Stan added his dulcet tones to the rendition – which in turn prompted Betty Kaye's Pekinese dogs to lend their vocal harmonies, and anyone within earshot must have thought they were witnessing the making of the latest Laurel and Hardy comic opera.

Another backstage visitor that week was George Wilkinson, an old classmate of Stan's from the King James I Grammar School. Laurel was delighted to see him, but very saddened to learn that several of the other pupils had been killed in the First World War. They had a happier time recalling the masters and their nicknames, many of which George claimed young Jefferson had invented. Ida was present, and interested to learn of her husband's schooldays from the boy whom Stan described as having 'taught me all my bad habits'. Stan took George along to see Babe, but found him to be resting, so let him be. Hardy, he told him, was suffering from heart trouble, so the opportunity was missed.

In Edinburgh, next, for their fourth visit. A reporter from the *Edinburgh Pictorial* had this to say:

The two veteran funsters, Laurel and Hardy, are the nicest star team I've ever met. It's not just that they are pleasant and polite, though as far as these two virtues are concerned they could put many of the alleged big stars to shame, it's something far more than that and I can only put it down to that mysterious endearing quality that has kept them favourites for so long.

While waiting for Hardy to join the interview, Stan said how much he had enjoyed the Queen's Coronation (2 June 1953), which he and Hardy had watched on TV[32] before leaving California. On entering the dressing room, Babe first begged an excuse to sit down. This accomplished, he promptly began to extol on the beauty of the fair city of Edinburgh:

'Edinburgh is definitely the nicest part of England,' he said.
'Scotland,' corrected Stan.
'No, England,' asserted Hardy, at which an argument ensued.

Coming back to the subject, Babe said, 'I like Edinburgh. I don't think there is a more restful spot in the world. I just like sitting at the hotel window and looking out at the castle.' Lucille Hardy reiterated her husband's feelings for Edinburgh. While shopping in R. & W. Forsyth's she had remarked to an assistant, 'We didn't care much for Glasgow, but we love Edinburgh.' The interview in the *Pictorial* continued with Babe Hardy saying, 'We think we will be here all week, but we won't know until they have seen tonight's show.' Well, here is what they said after they'd seen it. First, the *Evening News*:

Laurel and Hardy made a welcome return to the *Edinburgh Empire* last night. Their performance was all too brief, but their unmistakable forms created laughs without a word of support. They are naturally beginning to show their years, but proved that they are just as young in heart as when they began as a comedy team twenty-seven years ago.

And back to the *Edinburgh Pictorial* interview, which concluded:

Laurel and Hardy are real off-stage buddies who have tasted the best in film success. Their secret – I would say that they enjoy entertaining as much as the public enjoy being entertained. Couple this happy

---

32   Laurel and Hardy, themselves, were currently to be seen on American television, with a re-run of some of their old films being shown nightly.

Children taken backstage to meet their comedy heroes could always guarantee that they would be entertained. Here, one young girl is shown the ups and downs of showbusiness at the Empire Theatre, *Edinburgh, w/c 12 April.* (By kind permission of *Scotsman Publications.*)

frame of mind with the fact that they have never let success go to their heads, and I'm sure that there lies a substantial part of the answer.

On Tuesday Stan and Babe chose the winners of the *Evening Dispatch's* Lovely Shopgirl competition from photographs sent in by the contestants. The three winners were then brought backstage later in the week to receive their prizes from the comedy couple. That week, from his room in the *Caledonian Hotel*, with its lovely view of the castle, Stan Laurel wrote:

> We had a nice week in Leeds – Bus. good for a change – We opened up good here too, but weather has started to get nice – which is not good for the Theatres as people like to stay outdoors in the warm weather – Don't blame them.
>
> We have a deal on to play a summer season in Blackpool starting end of June – but if it doesn't go through – we shall return to the States. I understand we are now booked up to June 7th – but we have not been notified yet.

With business improving, Laurel was made even happier when his next enagagement took him to the Lake District. Why, before now, Laurel and Hardy had not been booked into a venue near to Stan's hometown of Ulverston is a mystery, especially as there were suitable venues in nearby Barrow-in-Furness. Be that as it may, on Monday the Mayor and Mayoress of Carlisle gave a party for Stan and Babe at *Her Majesty's Theatre*. Godfrey Gate, from the *Carlisle Journal*, was on hand to assess their characters:

'My name is Gate,' I said. 'Mine is Laurel,' said the thin man. 'And I'm Hardy,' added the fat one. As if I didn't know! But this unassuming, almost humble self introduction is, I have found, typical of the modesty of two characters who have held a unique place in entertainment for going on thirty years. No theatrical affectation – just down-to-earth condescension. Only a kind of humble satisfaction and sense of privilege that during their career, they have performed the important service of making millions laugh. That is Laurel and Hardy. I say sincerely, that meeting this oddly-assorted pair, looking off-stage much as they do before the footlights or the camera, has been an experience I shall always wish to remember.

Having such affection for Laurel and Hardy, Gate obviously wasn't going to miss watching their show:

The sketch contains a lot of the slapstick humour of the Laurel and Hardy films. So slickly done and – my! – how easy it all comes. While Stan and Ollie clowned in and out of two bars, vainly searching for each other and, miraculously almost rubbing shoulders without one spotting the other, the lady next to me had hysterics; the two small boys immediately in front jumped in a frenzy of delight; the whole circle seemed to rock with atom-bomb explosions of laughter. Then I knew for certain how worthwhile has been the career of these two funny men who have made so many people so happy.

Dick Allen, of the *Cumberland Evening News*, found that the sketch stood up well to Laurel and Hardy's film reputation:

The show will be remembered by Theatre patrons for another generation. Laurel and Hardy brought back to us all those crazy pictures which have filled cinemas all over the world for almost thirty years. Their act is not new, spectacular, nor even brilliantly written. But it is

the funniest thing I have seen in the live theatre for a long time –
because it is Laurel and Hardy.

After the show, Allen met the Boys backstage. He too found it odd that this
was the double-act's first visit to Carlisle, and Stan added, 'As far as I know,
I have never been here before.' (Stan's memory failed him there – *Sleeping
Beauty*, March 1908.) Between houses, Dick invited the Boys across the
road to the *Howard Arms* for a drink. Stan declined, saying, 'I don't want
a drink.' Whether Ollie had told him to say this because they only had
fifteen cents between them, Mr Allen did not reveal.

On completion of their week in Carlisle, and their stay at the *County
Station Hotel*, the Laurels and the Hardys had a free week which, it is
believed, the Laurels spent in the Lake District. The Boys then met up in
Bradford, where the *Telegraph and Argus* logged their sketch as follows:

> Time does not seem to have changed Laurel and Hardy physically (as
> we saw at the *Alhambra*, Bradford, last night), nor has it altered their
> slapstick technique. Together, they are a team, expert at causing con-
> fusion without effort.

The manager's report revealed that they had been 'Very well received. These
popular film artistes are as laughable as ever but are not proving the box
office appeal of previous visits.' The *Telegraph and Argus* article continued
with some comments of Stan's view of comedy, and Hardy's views of
television. Stan stated:

> 'There is always room for new comedians; there is room for hundreds
> of them. I would certainly like to see more good comedians on stage
> and screen.'
>
> Hardy, on reflecting that few good comedies were being made for
> the screen today, said: 'People want their comedy a little too arty-
> crafty, if you know what I mean,' then added, 'The pace of TV
> competition in America is so strong that Hollywood will feel the blast
> of the wind even more strongly during the next few months. Three-
> dimension [3-D], wide screens, and other gimmicks are no substitute
> for good films. You have to give the public something really good,
> whatever tricks of presentation you use.'

Television sets, though, certainly weren't available to all. At seventy-six
guineas for a table-top model, and a hundred guineas for a free-standing

Laurel and Hardy escort their manager, Ben Shipman, to his hotel room. Ida Laurel says 'hello' before leaving for Paris. Queen's Hotel, *Leeds, w/c 3 May.*
(By courtesy of John McCabe.)

one, advertising phrases such as 'Fitted with the new Emiscope aluminised tube for undistorted pictures of outstanding quality and brilliance' may have sounded impressive, but didn't bring the price within the budget of working-class families. Consequently, theatres and cinemas were still to enjoy a good run before attendance figures were hit by patrons becoming home viewers. Asked why Laurel and Hardy had been given so little television exposure, Bernard Delfont conceded that 'The media thought they were past it, and not worth covering.' How ironic that, almost forty years on, Laurel and Hardy films are still among the most popular shown on TV.

Ben Shipman, who had become the Boys' manager, flew over from America and joined them in Bradford to discuss future plans. To enable them to get on with business they all stayed at the *Queen's Hotel* in Leeds – well away from their Bradford fans. Ida, too, kept out of the way, and flew to Paris again (she had gone there during the Boys' week in Birmingham) to visit relatives. Shipman told the Boys that the Blackpool deal had fallen through, and so arrangements were being made to sail back to the States in mid-June.

Knowing time in England was now limited, Stan took a diversion on the way to the next engagement in Aston, Birmingham, and called in to see his sister at Bottesford. John McCabe also took the opportunity to have more interviews to extend his biographical notes on the Boys, and went backstage, most nights, at the *Aston Hippodrome*. Reporting on Laurel and

Hardy's actual show, the *Birmingham Post* disagreed with those who thought their stage work matched up to their film work:

> If Laurel and Hardy are a little disappointing it is because their style of comedy has been exploited so successfully on the screen and benefits so much from the scope and resources this medium has to offer. Though their dialogue was sometimes an encumbrance, their act is polished and amusing.

From the theatre Stan wrote: 'We have decided to finish our tour in Swansea, week of May 24th. We were to have finished two weeks later but didn't like the dates they offered, so called the whole thing off.'

The scheduled penultimate week, commencing 17 May, was at the town where Sir Francis Drake had finished his game of bowls before going to war with Spain – Plymouth. Whether or not Laurel and Hardy were able to bowl over the people of Plymouth, can be gauged from local reviews. The *Western Morning News* commented:

> Laurel and Hardy are extremely shrewd and efficient funny men. They like to work out their comic situations and perfect them to the final detail, and displayed such craftmanship on their first appearance in Plymouth. All fanciers of Hollywood's comedy couple will rejoice at seeing clowning that is real clowning again. Once seen – some will say endured – they were never forgotten; their personality produced a type of comedy which was unique on the screen and is not less so on the stage. And personality makes good entertainment.
>
> Laurel and Hardy know what they are about. Above all they know the difference between a joke that is funny, and a joke that merely ought to be funny. They have always made it their business to know.

The *Evening Herald* had a similar view:

> Laurel and Hardy at the *Palace Theatre* this week, look a little older, and are not as boisterous as they used to be – perhaps because Oliver Hardy was suffering from a chill and had to have penicillin treatment before the act last night – but all their old cleverness and that delightful craziness is still there.

Little did the critics know it, when penning these reviews, but Laurel and Hardy had played their last performance.

Chapter Eighteen

The Last Farewell

ON Wednesday 19 May 1954 the *Western Morning News* informed its readers:

> The variety show last night at the *Palace Theatre* was without the star turn of Laurel and Hardy. Minutes before the curtain was due to go up, Oliver Hardy had to withdraw because of illness. Despite a high temperature Hardy arrived at the theatre hoping that he would be able to go on, but when his temperature was taken it showed 103.4°F, and he was sent to bed. He was examined by a specialist, and the partnership's manager said it was hoped that Hardy would be fit enough to appear later in the week. Stan Laurel did not go on without his partner, but a full programme was given by the support acts.

Later that same day the position was clear, and the *Evening Herald* announced sadly: 'Laurel and Hardy will not be appearing for the rest of the week. Oliver Hardy who became ill shortly before last night's show is confined to bed, and will not be fit enough to rejoin the company.' On Thursday the *Herald's* latest report on Babe was:

> Mr Hardy was confined to his bed in the *Grand Hotel* today. A specialist who saw him diagnosed a virus infection. Mrs Hardy said her husband was 'slightly better, but still feeling terrible. He will remain in the hotel until he has recovered.'

The following day Hardy's temperature was lower but, as well as a severe bout of 'flu, he was diagnosed as having suffered a mild heart attack. With only one more week of the tour to run, their appearances were cancelled. Joe Church completed the week at Plymouth, and Gladys Morgan & Co. stood in the following week at *Swansea Empire*. Although he didn't go on stage at all, Laurel did go to the theatre each night to give moral support to the acts. In an interview with the *Western Independent* Stan spoke of his regrets for the people of Plymouth:

> I am like a lost soul without Hardy. It has been very unfortunate especially as this is the first time we have been here. Hardy went on on Monday, but he should not have done so. The audience were very pleasant and nice. We had a wonderful reception. It has been very disappointing to us that we could not go on. We are sorry the people have been disappointed.

For the benefit of people who might be wondering why Stan didn't go on alone, he said:

> I would not attempt it. I know it would have been disappointing. I am completely lost without Hardy. We do comedy sketches – situations. I am not a gag-man.

Harry Worth, commenting on Laurel and Hardy's on-stage relationship, made the following observations:

> When Stan wanted to, he could make Ollie laugh any time. And when Ollie started laughing, there was a lot of him to go. Trying to control himself was awful. But, some way or other, Stan conveyed this warmth, this love, this appreciation of his friend to the audience. Once you can join in something going on, on the stage – something that is fun – it goes round. It's a wonderful thing to see. Oliver Hardy thought Stan Laurel was the greatest comedian that ever was, and I think Stan had the same regard for Ollie.

On 24 May, after days spent dealing with correspondence, Stan went off to the *Washington Hotel*, London, to make travel arrangements. Statements were made to the press that Hardy would follow him when well enough. The two would then return to the States where, after a rest period, they would be involved in making a television series.

On 30 May the whole party travelled to Hull where, after a four day stay at the *Royal Station Hotel*, they boarded ship. The merchant ship, the *Manchuria*, with only ten passengers aboard, was bound on a twenty-three day trip for Vancouver, via the Panama Canal, but the captain was charged to drop off the Laurels and the Hardys at Los Angeles.

On 3 June 1954, two ageing comedians went unnoticed as they waved goodbye to England from the stern of a ship bound for America . . . but they were leaving behind them a vast comic legacy and a wealth of happy memories for the people who had seen live on the British stage the greatest comedy duo of all time – STAN LAUREL and OLIVER HARDY.

Acknowledgements

A special mention to:

Roy Sims, whose assistance with the book, from birth to maturity, was invaluable; Bruce Crowther, for guiding me on my first, faltering steps; Billy Marsh, who gave me credibility, and whose memory is astounding; Jean Darling, Jeffrey Simmons and Eric and Joy Dalton, for their encouragement and guidance; Norman Wisdom, who realised my life-time's ambition; Olga Varona and Archie Collins, who put aside illness to write a loving documentation; John and Jean Cooper, Jefferson Woods and Nancy E. Wardell, who so kindly allowed me a family insight; John Jones, for the heart-touching story; Shirley Davies, who painted such poetic pictures; and Eric Nicholson, Ray Alan and Peter Goodwright, for their personal revelations.

Thanks for their extreme generosity to:

Billy Barron*; Dorothea Birch;* Bill Butler, MBE; Charlie Cairoli Jnr and Claudine; Ethel Challands; George Cockayne; John Eddolls; Sybil C. Henderson; Audrey Jenkins; Robert F. Kennedy*; Francis J. Mavin, OBE; A. Nesbitt; Bryn Peters; Nancy Jane Reid; Lt Cdr Richard Swift RN (Rtd); Cliff Temple; Sid A. Singleton; Ronald Thomson.

* indicates 'deceased'.

Many thanks also to:

Mark Adlard; Dr Kathleen Barker*; Ron Berryman; Mrs V. Bolton; Estelle Bond; Allen Bromley; Charlie Brooks; Rod Byrne; Frank Carson; Nora Chadwick; Perce Champin; Charlie Chester; B. D. Cook; L. Crane; Mary Crettol; Mike Davie; Freddie Davies; Norma Devitt; Kim Drinkwater; Joe Ellis; Peg Francis; Alec Frutin*; R. R. Fry; John Galloway; Elizabeth M. Gammage; Malcolm Gilbert; Chris Hawes; Kevin Henriques; Mrs S. M. Hess; Emily Hopper; Terry Johnson; Liddell Johnston; Ron Kerr; George Knox; Edward J. Laker; Brian Lazarus; Jack Leighton; Jimmy Logan; Billy McCaffrey; Veron McGinley; Ron Mason; John Mullinder; J. S. Myers; Mrs R. J. Nendrick; Mrs V. Osmond; Dick Pearce; Ron Pearson; Les Pudney; Dereck Riddell; Johnnie Riscoe; Denise Robertson; Billy 'Uke' Scott; Arthur E. Shorter (Hove); Arthur E. Shorter* (Chester); Giles Squire; George Strzodka; Valerie Sturges; Mrs L. Swindells; Carole Thomas; Herbert D. G. Tinkler; Patrick J. Trainer; Jack Twells; Peggy Valentine; Max Wall*; Gerald H. A. Warr, JP; Ben Warriss*; Elsie Waters*; Jock M. Whitehouse; George Wilkinson; Mrs William Willis; Carole Anne Williams; Bea Winterburn; Ken Woodward; and Mrs Wotherspoon*.

And to the authors and writers:

Dave Bradshaw, Press Officer Butlin's, Skegness, and ex-journalist.
Bill Ellis, *Seaside Entertainers: 100 years of Nostalgia*.
Bill Evans, ex-Journalist, *East Kent Times*.
Leslie Frost, *Thanks for the Memories*.
John Montgomery,* *Comedy Films* – and many others.
Douglas Salmon, ex-journalist and ex-BBC television producer.
Tony Wheatley, TV and radio scriptwriter.
Kate Taylor, *History of Wakefield Theatre Royal & Opera House*.

The 'Sons of the Desert':

Stephen Bolton; Siep Bousma; Jack Delente; Mike Jones; Graham McKenna; Laurence Reardon; Bram Reijnhoudt; Dave Walker; Philip Martin Williams and David Wyatt who shared everything they had.

And to:

Peter Brownlow; Brian Clarry; Rob Lewis; Willie McIntyre and Bill Winfield for their valued assistance.

To the societies and archives of:

Blyth Local History Society – Robert Balmer; The British Film Institute – Tony Widdows and Sue Wilson; The Cinema Theatre Association – David Jones, Leslie Bull, R. Benton, Donald Hickling, Bill Flockney, Fred T. P. Windsor, Barry R. Stevenson; Concert Artistes' Association – Jimmy Perry; Entertainment Artistes' Benevolent Fund – Reg Swinson; Grand Order of Water Rats – John Adrian; Huntley Archives – John Huntley; Northamptonshire Police – Tom Paintain and Jack Spiller; R.C.A.H.M.S. – Ian Gow; Scotland Yard (Black Museum); Scottish Film Council – Janet McBain; Stoll Moss Archives – George Hoare; University of Strathclyde – Dr J. S. McGrath; Theatre Museum – Jonathan Gray and Julia Law; The Theatres Trust – D. F. Cheshire and John Earl; Tottenham Bruce Castle Museum – Jane C. Kimber; Madame Tussaud's, London – Undine Concannon; West Mercia Constabulary – A. W. Sykes; Willesden Grange Museum – Bridget T. Keane; The Wilson Collection – Joe Wilson; Writer's Guild of Great Britain – Nick Dalziel.

And to the hotels:

Savoy, London – Peter Crome and Rosemary Ashbee; Grand, Tynemouth – Mrs J. Richardson; Caledonian, Edinburgh – Allan G. Blest; Westminster, Rhyl – Mrs A. M. Qureshi; Prince of Wales, Southport – John Barrington–Fortune; Park, Cardiff – Doris McIntyre and Frank Bois; Polygon, Southampton – Anne Midgely; Grand, Bristol – Christopher Skidmore; Gleneagles, Scotland – Ian Wilson; Station, Dudley – Mrs E. Stephenson; North Stafford, Stoke – Patsy Ball.

To the libraries, who were helpful in the extreme:

(Central Libraries unless otherwise stated)
Battersea – Richard Shaw; Belfast – Jennifer Grant; Birmingham – Patrick Baird; Blackburn – Mrs M. J. Painter; Blackpool – James K. Burkitt; Bolton Department of Education – Brian Hughes and T. K. Campbell; Bournemouth Local Studies – Mrs R. M. Popham; Bradford – Gina L. Szekely and Elvira M. Willmott; Brighton – Stephanie Green; Bristol – Miss D. Dyer; Bury – Mrs R. Hirst; Cardiff – J. B. Jones; Carlisle – Stephen White; Coventry – A. J. Mealey; Dudley Archives – Mrs K. H. Atkins; Dumfries – John Preston; Dundee – J. B. Ramage; Dunfermline – John Jamieson; Durham County Library – J. Main and Miss A. L. Ward; Ealing

– Miss A. Terre; Edinburgh – Norma Armstrong; Glasgow Mitchell Library – Elizabeth Carmichael and Anne Escott; Glasgow University – Miss E. M. Watson; Greenock Watt Library – Mrs L. E. Couperwhite; Greenwich – Len Riley; Hammersmith Archives – Mrs C. M. Bayliss; Hanley – N. Emery and Miss A. Ormsby; Hartlepool – Miss M. E. Hoban; Hull – Peter J. Ainscough; Ilford; Kenilworth – L. Alexander; Kilmarnock – W. A. Anderson and Anne Geddes; Leamington Spa – Gary Archer; Leeds – Mrs A. Heap and Mrs J. H. Horne; Leicester Information Centre – Aubrey Stevenson; Lewisham Local History Centre – Richard A. Martin; Liverpool Brown, Picton and Hornby – Janet Smith; Longsight – Hilary Pate; Manchester – Helen Foster and David Taylor; Margate – Penny Ward; Motherwell – Ronald Kelsall; Newcastle – F. W. Manders, Patricia Sheldon, and Barbara Heathcote; Newcastle Blandford House – Bruce Jackson; Newcastle James Joicey Museum – Joe Ging; Newport – Mrs S. Pugh; North Shields Local Studies – Eric Hollerton; Northumberland – Mr Burdon, N. J. Baumfield and G. S. Payne; Norwich – C. Wilkins-Jones; Nottingham – Dorothy Ritchie; Oldham – Deidre L. Heywood; Peterborough – R. W. E. Hillier; Plymouth – J. R. Elliott; Pontypridd – Mrs J. P. Pugh; Poplar Bancroft Road – C. J. Lloyd; Portsmouth – John Thorn; Rawtenstall – Susan A. Halstead; Rhyl – Rona Aldrich; Rochdale – Mrs P. Goodman; St. Annes – P. Shuttleworth; Sale – Martin Gaw; Salford Local History – Royston Futter and Tony Frankland; Sheffield – J. M. Olive and Sylvia Pybus; Shrewsbury Local Studies – Anthony M. Carr; South Shields – Rod Hill and T. Graham; Southampton – H. A. Richards; Southport Atkinson Library – J. Hilton; Stafford William Salt Library – Ms P. Davies; Stalybridge Tameside Local Studies – Alice Lock; Stockport – Mrs M. J. Myerscough; Stratford – Howard Block; Sunderland – D. Hinds and Jeffrey Devine; Sutton – Mary Batchelor; Swansea – Brian Thomas; Swindon – D. M. Allen and Roger Trayhurn; Swiss Cottage – Malcolm Holmes; Todmorden – Jane Brierly; Wakefield – John Goodchild; Walsall Local History – Cath Yates; Warrington – David Rogers and Peter Rogerson; Wigan Heritage – Bob Blakeman and A. Gillies; Wigan Record Office – N. Webb; Wolverhampton – Elizabeth A. Rees; Woolwich – Len Riley; York Archives – Mrs R. J. Freedman; York – Elizabeth A. Meline.

Many thanks also to the newspaper companies:

Accrington Observer; *Birmingham Post & Mail* – John R. Daniels, Richard Edmonds and Carol Evans; *Blackpool Gazette* – Tom Ainge, Robin Duke and R. P. Officer; *Bolton Evening News*; *Bournemouth Daily Echo*; *Bradford Telegraph & Argus* – Mike Priestley; *Bristol Evening Post*; *Cumberland News* – Dick Allen; *Daily Mail* – Nigel Davies; *Eastern Evening News* – Derek James; *T. Bailey Forman* – Ralph D. Gee; *Glasgow Evening Times*; *Grimsby Evening Telegraph*; *Edinburgh Evening News*; *Irish News Ltd* – Martina Stewart; *Isle of Thanet Gazette*; *Newcastle Evening Chronicle*; *Northampton Chronicle & Echo*; *Nottingham Evening Post* – Ian Scott; *Peterborough Herald & Post* – Janet Sorrell; *Plymouth Evening Herald* – Mike Miller; *Portsmouth News* – Keith Ridley and Alan Montgomery; *Shrewsbury Chronicle* – Alan Godding; Solo Agency – Danny Howell; *South Wales Evening Post*; *Southern Evening Echo* – Alison Tilley; *Staffordshire Evening Sentinel*; *The Stage* – Graham Ireland and Peter Hepple; *Sunday Sun* – Robin Etherington; *Sunderland Echo* – Chris Storey; *Warrington Guardian*; *Wolverhampton Express & Star*; *York Star* – Peter L. Charlton; *Yorkshire Evening Post* – John Thorpe; *Yorkshire Express*.

Not forgetting:

The Public Record Office, Kew; and the Cunard Archives, Liverpool University who provided the shipping data.

And a massive thank you:

To the staff of the British Newspaper Library, Colindale, who, with unfailing grace, supplied me with literally thousands of newspapers.

With much gratitude, to:

John McCabe for his leadership, encouragement, appraisal of the manuscript, and loan of photographs; and to Bob Spiller, and Alison Grimmer, by whose brilliant perceptions, and much appreciated suggestions, the text was greatly enhanced.

And lastly to:

Lord Delfont and Billy Marsh, who revived the career of two neglected comedians, and without whom there would be no story.

Bibliography

Adeler and West, *Remember Fred Karno* (John Long)

Chaplin, Charles, *My Autobiography* (Bodley Head)

Chaplin, Charles, *My Life in Pictures* (Peerage Books)

Crowther, Bruce, *Laurel and Hardy – Clown Princes of Comedy* (Columbus)

Delfont, Bernard, *East End, West End* (Macmillan)

Gallagher, J. P., *Fred Karno - Master of Mirth & Tears* (Hale)

Guiles, Fred Lawrence, *Stan - the Life of Stan Laurel* (Stein and Day)

Land, Joan, *The Jeffersons in Bishop Auckland* (Bowler Dessert)

McCabe, John, *Charlie Chaplin* (Magnum)

McCabe, John, *The Comedy World of Stan Laurel* (Robson)

McCabe, John, *Mr Laurel & Mr Hardy* (Signet USA)

McCabe, John, *Babe - the Life of Oliver Hardy* (Robson)

Pawson/Mouland, *Laurel before Hardy* (Westmorland Gazette)

Read, Jack, *Empires, Hippodromes & Palaces* (Alderman Press)

Robinson, David, *Chaplin - His Life and Art* (Collins)

Skretvedt, Randy, *Laurel and Hardy - The Magic Behind the Movies* (Moonstone)

Reference works:

Curtains!!! (John Offord)

Howard, Diana, *London Theatres and Music Halls*

Writers' & Artists' Yearbook (A & C Black)

Stan Jefferson's
Residences and Schools

Arthur Jefferson's
Residences and Theatres

1. Manchester
2 Ulverston, Hippodrome
3. Bishop Auckland, Royal/Eden
4. Blyth, Royal and New Royal
5. North Shields, Hippodrome
   and Royal
5b. Wallsend, Royal
5c. Hebburn, Royal
5d. Consett, Royal
6. Glasgow, Metropole
7a. Ealing
8. Bottesford

2. Ulverston
3. Bishop Auckland
3a. Gainford
5. North Shiools
5a. Tynemouth
6. Glasgow
6a. Rutherglen
7. London

Appendix I :

The Jeffersons

ARTHUR – born 12 September 1862, in Manchester.

MADGE (née Margaret Metcalfe) – born 22 October 1860.
   Married – 19 March 1884 at the Holy Trinity Church, in Ulverston.

GEORGE GORDON – born 3 February 1885, at 3 Argyle Street, Ulverston.
   Christened – St. Mary's Church, Ulverston.

ARTHUR STANLEY – born 16 June 1890, at 3 Argyle Street, Ulverston.
   Christened – in the home.
   Re-christened – 21 October 1891, St. Peter's Church, Bishop Auckland.
   Received into the Church – 3 January 1895, St. Peter's Church, Bishop
      Auckland.

BEATRICE OLGA – born 16 December 1894, 66 Princes Street, Bishop Auckland.
   Christened – 3 January 1895, St. Peter's Church, Bishop Auckland.

SYDNEY EVERITT – born 30 April 1899, 8 Dockwray Square, North Shields.
   Christened – Christ Church, North Shields.
   Died – 10 September 1899.
   Buried – Preston Cemetery, North Shields.

EDWARD EVERITT – born 1 April 1900, 8 Dockwray Square, North Shields.

Appendix II :

Arthur Jefferson's Theatres

(*circa*) 1884 – Hippodrome Theatre, ULVERSTON

1889 – Theatre Royal, BISHOP AUCKLAND (later renamed the Eden)

8 August 1892 – Theatre Royal, CONSETT

17 October 1892 – Eden Theatre (formerly Theatre Royal), BISHOP AUCKLAND

7 August 1893 – Theatre Royal, BLYTH

19 August 1895 – Theatre Royal, NORTH SHIELDS

(*circa*) 1899 – Theatre Royal, WALLSEND

5 February 1900 – New Theatre Royal, BLYTH

August 1900 – Theatre Royal, HEBBURN

5 August 1901 – Tynemouth Circus and Novelty Hippodrome, NORTH SHIELDS

5 August 1901 – Metropole Theatre, GLASGOW

(The dates above are the opening dates. From 1889 onwards, Arthur Jefferson's status was 'lessee and manager'.)

H. B. LEVY'S and J. E. CARDWELL'S
Celebrated JUVENILE Pantomime Company
In the Gorgeous New and Original Fairy Spectacle
"The Sleeping Beauty"
Or, "The Prince With The Golden Key"

Specialities by
WEE GEORGIE WOOD
Marvellous Boy Comedian and Mimic
Little JEANNIE BRODIE
Scotland's Premier Dancer
Full Chorus of 60   Augmented Orchestra
THREE GRAND BALLETS

CHARACTERS

Bertie Dalrymple . . . . WEE GEORGIE WOOD
The Queen . . . . J. ARMSTRONG
Dame Asbestos . . . . G. ARMSTRONG
Colonel Dreadnought . . . . JACK GRAHAM
Major Flashlight . . . . BENNY BARRON
Prince Florizel . . . . KITTY TREWITT
Sleeping Beauty . . . . ISA GIBSON
Queen Claribel . . . . Miss FLO EDWARDS
Maligna (The Witch) . . . . Miss BEATTIE TOWNSEND
Sir Alphonso . . . . Miss MARIE LUMBERG
Maid of Honour . . . . TRIXIE WYATT
King's Herald . . . . DAISY THOMPSON WOOD
King Fearnought . . . . Master JACK HARRISON
Julius Caesar (Golliwog 1) . . . . . . Master JACK ADAMSON
Ebeneezer (Golliwog 2) . . . . . . Master STANLEY JEFFERSON
The Nurse . . . . ROSE PALEY

Musical Director   ARTHUR SILVER

THE SLEEPING BEAUTY
(Levy & Cardwell Company)

1907

Sep	30	SUNDERLAND, King's
Oct	7	GREENOCK, Alexandra
Oct	14	MOTHERWELL, New Century
Oct	21	CASTLEFORD, Royal
Oct	28	SWINDON, Queen's
Nov	4	CREWE, Lyceum
Nov	11	DARWEN, Royal
Nov	18	not known
Nov	25	TYLDESLEY, Royal
Dec	2	RAWTENSTALL, Grand
Dec	9	MEXBOROUGH, Prince of Wales
Dec	16	WIDNES, Alexandra
Dec	23	STOCKPORT, Royal (2 weeks)

1908

Jan	6	SALFORD, Regent (2 weeks)
Jan	20	ASHTON -UNDER-LYNE, Royal (2 weeks)
Feb	3	OLDHAM, Collesseum (sic)
Feb	10	STAFFORD, Lyceum
Feb	17	DUDLEY, Royal Opera House
Feb	24	SEACOMBE, Irving
Mar	2	JARROW, New Royal
Mar	9	SEAHAM HARBOUR, New Royal
Mar	16	BLYTH, New Royal
Mar	23	CARLISLE, His Majesty's
Mar	30	NORTH SHIELDS, Royal
Apr	6	CONSETT, New Royal
Apr	13	WEST STANLEY, Royal
Apr	20	WEST HARTLEPOOL, Grand & Opera House

(Stan appeared in all the above.)

THE GENTLEMAN JOCKEY
(Edward Marris Company)

CHARACTERS

Francis Graumer . . . . CECIL W. PARKIN
Frank Snakeworth . . . . WALTER B. NUGENT
David Grayson . . . . HENRY LE MAISTRE
Blodgers . . . . GEORGE BRENTWOOD
Jenny Jarvis . . . . Miss MOLLIE HACKETT
Archie Fitzherbert . . . . CHARLES KING
Kate Graumer . . . . Miss LILLIAN DRAKE
Tony (The Stable Boy) . . . . J. R. TYRELL
Mary Grayson . . . . Miss CECILIA RANSOME

1908

Jun 8   BROUGHTON, Victoria
Jun 15   not known
Jun 22   NEWCASTLE, Tyne & Opera House

(Stan's name not found amongst principal players.)

Stan placed his tour with *The Gentleman Jockey* as 1909. Below are some of the venues which were traced, but again his name was not found in reviews. As most of the 1909 dates clash with *Alone in the World*, which Stan is confirmed as playing, and because he mentioned one of the venues by name (Tyne Theatre, Newcastle), the 1908 tour is favoured as correct.

1909

Jul 19   GRIMSBY, Prince of Wales
Jul 27   not known
Aug 2   GLASGOW, King's

(List discontinued)

THE STAGE   April 16th, 1908

ARTHUR JEFFERSON AND SON'S SKETCHES.

———

"For His Sake", "Home from the Honeymoon",
"Her Convict Lover", "Amateur Fire Brigade",
"An Unwilling Burglar".

Managers and Agents requested to witness
Home from the Honeymoon
Opens Moss and Stoll Tour May 1st, Hackney.

Arthur Jefferson, Ltd.
Presents an entirely New and Original
Farcical Comedy Sketch, entitled:

HOME FROM THE HONEYMOON

1908

May 18	HACKNEY, Empire	(not May 1st as above)
May 25	HOLLOWAY, Empire	
Jun 1	NEW CROSS, Empire	
Jun 8	STRATFORD, Empire	
Jun 15	SHEPHERD'S BUSH, Empire	
Jun 22	not known	
Jun 29	CARDIFF, Empire	
Jul 6	SWANSEA, Empire	
Jul 13	NEWPORT, Empire	
Jul 20	LEICESTER, Palace	
Jul 27	BIRMINGHAM, Empire	
Aug 3	NEWCASTLE, Empire	
Aug 10	SUNDERLAND, Empire	
Aug 17	not known	
Aug 24	EDINBURGH, Empire	

(It is believed that Stan joined the above at Newcastle.)

Mr and Mrs H. B. Levy and Mr J. E. Cardwell's
Juvenile Company
In the GRAND PANTOMIME

"THE HOUSE THAT JACK BUILT"
Or, 'THE OLD WOMAN WHO LIVED IN A SHOE'

Company of 40 Artistes

Full Chorus and Augmented Orchestra
Latest Songs and Dances   Big Specialities

CHARACTERS

Jack	Miss FLORRIE TAYLOR
Jill	Miss EVELYN MAJOR
Fairy Twinkle Star	Miss OLIVE PURCELL
Gretchen (The Little Dutch Girl)	Miss JENNIE MARSDEN
Colin	Miss HETTY JONES
Wee M'Gregor	WEE GLADYS WISE
Scragg & Scraggles	Messrs DOYLE & GIBSON
Aunt Purdy	HORACE HILLERBY
Squire Bounce	PADDY SLOAN
Percy	STANLEY JEFFERSON
Harold	IRELAND CUTTER
Sgt McGinty	Master ADAMS
Cow	JACK ADAMSON
Cat	FRED HAMMOND
Tommy Tucker	Miss PATTIE BLANCHARD
Dolly Dimple	Miss OLIVE WOODBRIDGE
Bella Blot	Miss W. ADAMSON
Maid Marian	Miss ANNIE BRUMBY
Polly Pickle	Miss MOLLY JOHNSON
Musical Director	Mr Hy Mitchell
Producer	Roger Alwyn

THE HOUSE THAT JACK BUILT
(Levy & Cardwell Company)

1908

Dec	7	TYLDESLEY, Royal
Dec	14	CASTLEFORD, Royal
Dec	25	DUDLEY, Royal Opera House

1909

Jan	4	DUDLEY, Royal Opera House
Jan	11	SWINDON, Empire
Jan	18	DARWEN, Royal
Jan	25	SALFORD, Regent
Feb	1	BLYTH, New Royal
Feb	8	CONSETT, New Royal
Feb	15	JARROW, Royal
Feb	22	SEAHAM HARBOUR, New Royal
Mar	1	NEWCASTLE, Empire
Mar	8	DUNFERMLINE, Opera House
Mar	15	KILMARNOCK, King's
Mar	22	not known
Mar	29	DUMFRIES, Royal
Apr	5	WEST STANLEY, Royal

(Stan appeared in all the above.)

Mr Percy Williams Presents the
Latest and Greatest American Success

Alone in the World

A BEAUTIFUL and PATHETIC STORY of CHILD LIFE
by HAL REID

Brimful of Human Interest and altogether
something new in Modern Drama.

Over 3 tons of new Scenery carried.

Strong Dramatic Company of Fourteen.

Now Booking Spring 1910.

CHARACTERS

Robin Hadley – a Boy of Fate . . . . . Little MARIE WILSON
Kitty (Robin's sweetheart) . . . . Miss EDITH DEWS
Ruby Warren . . . . STEPHANIE BARING
Frank Wesley . . . . W. H. GARBOIS
John Warren (the Bank Manager) . . . . CHARLES LEVERTON
Jack Arnold . . . . Mr FRANK COPELAND
Robert Reynolds . . . . GERALD NOLAN
Virginia Arnold . . . . Miss VIOLET VINCENT
Madge Delph (a Creole) . . . . Miss KATHIE BRATBY
P.C. Stoney Broke . . . . STANLEY JEFFERSON
Angel White (1st coon) . . . . Mr HARRY M. VERNON
Jezebel White (2nd coon) . . . . Miss BLANCHE HUBER

ALONE IN THE WORLD
(Percy Williams Company)

1909

Aug 2   PONTYPRIDD, Royal Clarence

Aug 9   MANCHESTER, Metropole

Aug 1   WAKEFIELD, Opera House

Aug 23   BRADFORD, Prince's

          [MANCHESTER, Queen's Park Hippodrome – pulled out]

Aug 30   LEEDS, Royal

Sep 6   vacant date [SALFORD, Hippodrome – pulled out]

Sep 13   TODMORDEN, Hippodrome

Sep 20   HORWICH, Prince's

          [LONGSIGHT, King's – pulled out]

Sep 27   vacant date [KIDDERMINSTER, Opera House – pulled out]

Oct 4   ASHINGTON, Miner's

Oct 9   Tour ended prematurely

          [Cancelled: NEWCASTLE, Palace; SCARBOROUGH;
          WEST STANLEY.]

(Stan is credited in all the above.)

> FRED KARNO'S
> CELEBRATED TROUPE OF COMEDIANS,
> in their Screaming Travesty of Modern Music Hall
> **MUMMING BIRDS**
> The Saucy Serio, The Inebriated Swell,
> The Irate Uncle, the Perky Schoolboy
>
> Archibald Binks (Inebriated) . . . . CHARLES CHAPLIN
> Boy in Eton Collar . . . . MIKE ASHER
> Magician . . . . ARTHUR DANDOE
> Comic Singer . . . . STANLEY JEFFERSON
> Boy's Uncle . . . . BERT WILLIAMS
> Usherette . . . . AMY MINSTER
> Woman Soprano . . . . MURIEL PALMER
> Marconi Ali (the Wrestler)
>
> Supported by the Renowned Karno Troupe of picked London Performers:
> ALBERT AUSTIN, FRED PALMER, GEORGE SEAMAN, EMILY SEAMAN,
> FRANK MELROYD, CHARLES GRIFFITHS, FRED WESTCOTT.
> Manager: for Fred Karno, ALF REEVES.

(The above cast list is incomplete, as it was compiled from the limited information – mainly the 1910 American tour).

MUMMING BIRDS

1909

Dec 6   HULME, Hippodrome

Dec 13   WARRINGTON, Palace   [plus The Casuals]

Dec 20   SALFORD, Royal Hippodrome

Dec 27   Christmas break

1910

Jan 3   WAKEFIELD, Empire   [plus Skating]

Jan 10   LIVERPOOL, Pavilion   [probably when Stan first met Chaplin]

(Stan Jefferson was not found in any reviews of British Fred Karno productions. The lists, therefore, might not accurately represent Stan's appearance, but are as near as probability allows.)

```
( ～～～～～～～～～～～～～～ )
```

Fred Karno's
COMPANY OF COMEDIANS in

SKATING

New and Original Absurdity on the Latest Craze

CHARACTERS

Archibald Binks . . . . CHARLES CHAPLIN
Miss Zena Flapper . . . . JOHNNY DOYLE

And a cast of 30 including:
ERNIE STONE, GERTIE JACKSON, TED BANKS,
M. SCHOFIELD, STANLEY JEFFERSON, JIMMY BERESFORD.

SKATING
(Fred Karno Company)

1910

Jan	17	ROCHDALE, Hippodrome [plus *Early Birds*]	
Jan	24	BURY, Royal [plus *Early Birds*]	
Jan	31	WIGAN, Hippodrome [plus *The Casuals*]	Charles Chaplin (lead)
		HULME, Hippodrome	[probably same company as above]
Feb	7	ILFORD, Hippodrome	
Feb	14	LEEDS, Hippodrome	Charles Chaplin (lead)
Feb	21	BIRMINGHAM, Hippodrome	Charles Chaplin (lead)
Feb	28	SHEFFIELD, Hippodrome	Charles Chaplin (lead)
Mar	7	LIVERPOOL, Royal Hippodrome	Sydney and Charles Chaplin
Mar	14	NEWCASTLE, Pavilion	Sydney and Charles Chaplin
Mar	21	ECCLES, Crown	Sydney Chaplin and Jimmy Russell
Mar	28	LONGSIGHT, King's	Charles Chaplin and Stan Jefferson
Apr	4	HACKNEY, Empire	

(Charlie Chaplin is listed where there is confirmation, but both Chaplin *and* Jefferson
appeared in all the above – as far as can be ascertained.)

FRED KARNO'S LATEST:

THE THRILLING ADVENTURES OF

JIMMY THE FEARLESS

'THE BOY 'ERO'

AN ELABORATE REALISATION OF THE BOYS' 'PENNY DREADFUL'

Charlie Chaplin as 'Jimmy'

CHARACTERS

Jimmy . . . . Mr CHARLES CHAPLIN
Alkali Ike . . . . Mr BERT WILLIAMS
Jimmy's Father . . . . Mr ARTHUR DANDOE
Jimmy's Mother . . . . Miss EMILY SEAMAN
Mike . . . . Mr MIKE ASHER
Washti Wampa . . . . Mr ALBERT AUSTIN
Bartender . . . . Mr ERNEST STONE
Chinaman . . . . Mr HARRY DANIELS
Gwendolen . . . . Mrs BERT WILLIAMS

Supported by hand-picked members of the Karno Company, including:
STAN JEFFERSON, JIMMY BERESFORD, TED BANKS,
FRED JORDAN, and T. RUDD.

Scene 1: . . . . . . A Hearty Supper and its After-Effects – The Nightmare.
Scene 2: . . . . The Dog's Nose Drinking Salon, Deadman's Gulch.
Scene 3: The Rocky Mountains – The Attack – The Hand-to-Hand Fight –
. . . . Saving the Girl – The Rescue – Jimmy Triumphs.
Scene 4: . . . . Then He Awoke!

Produced by: Charles Baldwin and Frank O'Neill (Company Manager),
in conjunction with Fred Karno.

JIMMY THE FEARLESS
(Fred Karno Company)

1910

Apr 11	EALING, Hippodrome [rehearsals]	
Apr 18	EALING, Hippodrome	Stan Jefferson (lead)
	WILLESDEN, Hippodrome	Stan Jefferson (lead)
Apr 25	STRATFORD, Empire	
May 2	HOLLOWAY, Empire	
May 9	SHEFFIELD, Empire	
May 16	SOUTH SHIELDS, Empire	
May 23	NEWCASTLE, Empire	
May 30	GLASGOW, Coliseum [*Mumming Birds*, not *Jimmy the Fearless*]	
Jun 6	GLASGOW, Coliseum	
Jun 13	WALSALL, Her Majesty's	
Jun 20	LEICESTER, Palace	
Jun 27	CARDIFF, Empire	
Jul 4	NEWPORT, Empire	
Jul 11	SWANSEA, Empire	
Jul 18	LEEDS, Empire	
Jul 25	BIRMINGHAM, Empire	
Aug 1	HULL, Palace	
Aug 8	LIVERPOOL, Empire	
Aug 15	ARDWICK GREEN, Empire	
Aug 22	NOTTINGHAM, Empire	
Aug 29	BRADFORD, Empire	
Sep 12	TOTTENHAM, Palace	

[Stan appeared in all the above. Chaplin appeared from April 25 onwards.]

[The above information on *The Wow-Wows* was compiled from the limited sources
available – mainly the 1910 American tour.]

FRED KARNO presents his
Latest and Greatest Laughable Production

THE WOW-WOWS

CHARACTERS

Archibald Binks . . . . CHARLES CHAPLIN
Charlie Blazen . . . . ARTHUR DANDOE
Fred Brunton . . . . BERT WILLIAMS
Jack Denton . . . . FRANK MELROYD
Jimmie Bottlie . . . . MIKE ASHER
Percy . . . . FRED PALMER
Lady Binks . . . . MURIEL PALMER
Lydia Scotch . . . . AMY MINSTER

Supported by the Renowned Karno Troupe of picked London Performers:
ALBERT AUSTIN, STAN JEFFERSON, FRED WESTCOTT, GEORGE SEAMAN.
Scene I: . . . . 'The Nook', Depicting River Life with its beauty and gayety.
Scene II: . . . . Entrance to the Secret Society's Chamber of Horrors.
Scene III: . . . . Interior of the Chamber of Horrors. The Initiation.
Manager for Fred Karno   ALF REEVES

THE WOW-WOWS

1910

Sep 5   WOOLWICH, Hippodrome

Sep 12   *TOTTENHAM, Palace
            [*Jimmy the Fearless*, not *The Wow-Wows*] Charles Chaplin (lead)
            *SHOREDITCH, Olympia
            *ILFORD, Hippodrome

Sep 22   Charles Chaplin and Stan Jefferson sail for America.

    * It is highly probable that the same company performed at all three venues.
       (Stan and Chaplin appeared in all the above – as far as known.)

1932 Tour Route Map

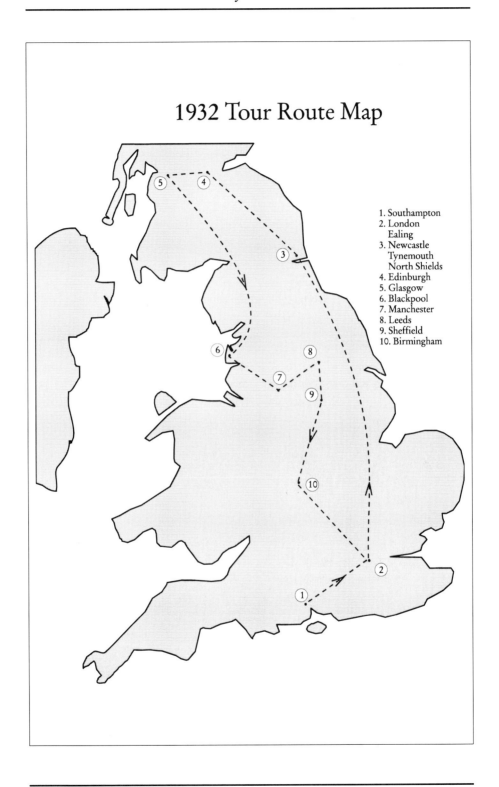

1. Southampton
2. London
   Ealing
3. Newcastle
   Tynemouth
   North Shields
4. Edinburgh
5. Glasgow
6. Blackpool
7. Manchester
8. Leeds
9. Sheffield
10. Birmingham

DATE SHEET
1932

Jul 16   Sail from NEW YORK on the *Aquitania*.

Jul 23   (Saturday) Arrive SOUTHAMPTON, England.
Train to Waterloo Station, LONDON.
Afternoon: press reception, *Savoy Hotel*, LONDON.

Jul 24   (Sunday) *Drury Lane Theatre*, LONDON.

Jul 25   (Monday) 9 p.m. *Empire Theatre*, LEICESTER SQUARE.

Jul 26   (Tuesday) 10.35 p.m. BBC radio broadcast, LONDON.
Strand Theatre, LONDON.

Jul 27   (Wednesday) Dinner at Screen Artistes Federation, LONDON.
Overnight train to NEWCASTLE.

Jul 28   (Thursday) Arrive NEWCASTLE Station 5.49 a.m.
Car to *Grand Hotel*, TYNEMOUTH.
Civic reception, Mayor's Parlour, Town Hall, NORTH SHIELDS.
Luncheon: *Albion Assembly Rooms*, NORTH SHIELDS.
3 p.m. Assemble *Grand Hotel*, TYNEMOUTH,
     for *Tynemouth Plaza*.
9 p.m. *Queen's Hall*, NEWCASTLE.
Stoll Picture House, NEWCASTLE.

Jul 29   (Friday) 11.10 a.m. NEWCASTLE Central Station.
1.35 p.m. Arrive at Waverley Station, EDINBURGH.
Staying at *North British Station Hotel*, EDINBURGH.
Afternoon: visit Scottish National War Memorial and Castle.
7.30 p.m. *Edinburgh Playhouse*.
9.30 p.m. Caledonian Station, EDINBURGH – train for Glasgow.
10.47 p.m. Arrive Central Station, GLASGOW. *Central Hotel*.

Jul 30   9 a.m. Hardy – Western Gailes Golf Course.
4 p.m. *La Scala Cinema*, Sauchiehall Street (both), GLASGOW.

Jul 31   (Sunday) Hardy – Gleneagles Golf Course.

Aug 1   (Bank Holiday Monday) 10.05 a.m. GLASGOW Central Station.
2.20 p.m. arrive PRESTON. Car to BLACKPOOL – *Metropole Hotel*.
Evening: *Winter Gardens, Palace Theatre*, and *Tower Ballroom*.

Aug 2   (Tuesday) Morning: Depart North Station, BLACKPOOL.
Arrive Victoria Station, MANCHESTER.
     Staying at *Midland Hotel*.
6.30 p.m. *New Oxford Cinema*, MANCHESTER.
Manchester Opera House.

Aug 3   (Wednesday) 1.07 p.m. Arrive New Station, LEEDS.
Staying at *Queen's Hotel*, LEEDS.
7.30 p.m. *Majestic Cinema*, LEEDS.

Aug 4   (Thursday) 11 a.m. Train leaves for SHEFFIELD.
12 noon. Arrive SHEFFIELD. Staying *Grand Hotel*.
6.30 and 9.00 p.m. *Cinema House*, Fargate.

Aug 5   (Friday) 1.26 p.m. arrive New Street Station, BIRMINGHAM.
Staying *Queen's Hotel*, BIRMINGHAM.
Afternoon: Council House, BIRMINGHAM.
Evening: *Gaumont Cinema*, and *West End Dance Hall*.

Aug 6   (Saturday) 8.40 a.m. Leave for LONDON.
Staying *Savoy Hotel*, LONDON.

Aug 8   (Monday) Dad's – 49 Colebrook Avenue, EALING.
8 p.m. *Walpole Cinema*, and *Walpole Hall*, EALING.

Aug 10   (Wednesday) Morning: Victoria Station, LONDON –
     for boat train to FRANCE.
Staying at *Claridge's Hotel*, PARIS.

Aug 18   (Thursday) Return to LONDON, England.
Columbia Recording Studios, LONDON.

NOTE: Must visit Elstree Film Studios.

Aug 24   (Wednesday) Return to AMERICA. Sailing on *S.S. Paris*.

1947 Tour Route Map

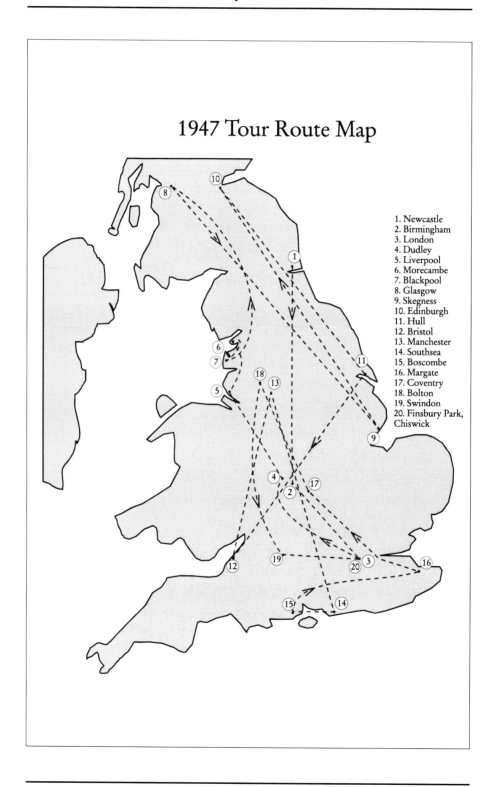

1. Newcastle
2. Birmingham
3. London
4. Dudley
5. Liverpool
6. Morecambe
7. Blackpool
8. Glasgow
9. Skegness
10. Edinburgh
11. Hull
12. Bristol
13. Manchester
14. Southsea
15. Boscombe
16. Margate
17. Coventry
18. Bolton
19. Swindon
20. Finsbury Park, Chiswick

PROGRAMME
Commencing March 10th, 1947

1. OVERTURE - - - - "All Set"

2. THE ELWARDOS - - Hand-springing Acrobats

3. LEN & BILL LOWE - - From the R.A.F Gang Show

4. LOUISE and her DOGS - - From
Bertram Mills' Olympia Circus

5. TOMMY FIELDS - - London's Lancashire Comedian

6. BILLY COTTON and his BAND

BILLY COTTON - Conductor

Saxophones :- FRANK KENYON, STAN QUIDDINGTON,
CHAS. SWINNERTON, KEN DRYDEN

Brass :- ABE HUNTERMAN, EDDIE LEVER, RAY LANDIS,
RUBE STOLOFF, ELLIS JACKSON

Pianist and Arranger :- CLEM BERNARD

Violinist :- PHIL PHILLIPS   Drums :- REG BRYANT

Guitar :- BILL HERBERT   Bass :- ERIC FIELD

Vocalist :- ALLAN BREEZE   Dancer :- ELLIS JACKSON

INTERMISSION

"Ballet Memories" ... ... *Delibes*
THE LONDON PALLADIUM ORCHESTRA
Under the Direction of George Steele

PROGRAMME CONTINUED

7. THE DOLINOFFS and RAYA SISTERS *Dancing Dellusions*

8. JACK TRAIN - - Colonel Chin-strap from I.T.M.A
"I DON'T MIND IF I DO"

9. RONALD CHESNEY - - - *Harmonica Virtuoso*

10.
Bernard Delfont presents

Stan   Oliver
LAUREL & HARDY
Hollywood's Famous Screen Comedy Couple
Assisted by HARRY MORENY

11. RICHARDO - - - *Thrills on the Wire*
& ASSISTANT

STAN   OLIVER
LAUREL & HARDY
ARE APPEARING HERE
FOR 3 WEEKS ONLY
POSITIVELY LAST PERFORMANCES
SATURDAY, MARCH 29th

PLEASE NOTE—PHOTOGRAPHING IN THE THEATRE IS FORBIDDEN

In the interest of Public Health this Theatre is disinfected throughout with JEYES FLUID

THIS THEATRE IS FULLY LICENSED.   SMOKING PERMITTED.

Typical programme layout and bill for Laurel and Hardy's 1947 tour.
London Palladium, week commencing 10 March 1947.

Typical newspaper advertising block for Laurel and Hardy's 1947 tour. (By kind permission of the Swindon Evening Advertiser.)

PROGRAMME BILLS
1947

Feb 24   Empire, NEWCASTLE
The Three Redheads; Miss Louise & her Dogs; Slim Rhyder; Johnson Clark; Erikson; Mariora; Bob Lloyd & Betty; Keefe Bros & Annette.

Mar 3   Hippodrome, BIRMINGHAM
The Three Redheads; Miss Louise & her Dogs; Slim Rhyder; Erikson; Johnson Clark; Bob Lloyd & Betty; Keefe Brothers & Annette; Olga Varona.

Mar 10   (3 weeks)   Palladium, LONDON
The Elwardos; Len & Bill Lowe; Miss Louise & her Dogs; Tommy Fields; Billy Cotton Band; The Dolinoffs & Raya Sisters (replaced Marilyn Hightower); Jack Train; Ronald Chesney; Richardo.

Mar 24   (3rd week)   Palladium, LONDON
The Elwardos; Len & Bill Lowe; Miss Louise & her Dogs; Tommy Fields; Billy Russell; Damora Ballet; Jack Train; Ronald Chesney; Charley Wood; Richardo; Two Beels.

Mar 31   Wimbledon, LONDON
The Four Bobrics; Len & Bill Lowe; Miss Louise & her Dogs; Mariora; Slim Rhyder; Johnson Clarke; Norman & Vonnie Munro.

Apr 7   Hippodrome, LEWISHAM
The Lai Founs; Len & Bill Lowe; Slim Rhyder; MacKenzie Reid & Dorothy; Jimmy Bruce; Palette's Dogs; Norman & Vonnie Munro.

Apr 14   (4 weeks)   Coliseum, LONDON
The Five Aussies; Tessa Deane; George Lacy; Rawicz & Landauer; Tommy Jover, Raf & Fe; Slim Rhyder; Elsie & Doris Waters; Darmora Ballet; Newman Twins.

Apr 27   (1 night)   Victoria Palace, LONDON
Betty Blackler; George Doonan; Henry Lytton; Terry Wilson; Clarkson Rose; N'Gai; Bert Weston; Arthur Prince; Jack Martell; Binnie Hale; Noele Gordon; Neville Kennard; Vera Lynn; Will Fyffe; Norman Wisdom.

May 12   Hippodrome, DUDLEY
The Three Redheads; Len & Bill Lowe; Bob Lloyd & Betty; Olga Varona; Slim Rhyder; Mariora; Ann Yeaman's Sporting Dogs.

May 19   Empire, LIVERPOOL
The Three Redheads; Ivor E. Keys with Betty Ross; Slim Rhyder; Erikson; The Newman Twins; Terri Carol; MacKenzie Reid & Dorothy; Ann Yeaman's Sporting Dogs.

May 26   Victoria Pavilion, MORECAMBE
The Three Redheads; Connie Graham & Hal Scott; Newman Twins; Olga Varona; Johnson Clark; Slim Rhyder; MacKenzie Reid & Dorothy.

Jun 2   Palace, BLACKPOOL
Vic Ray & Lucille; Velda & Vann; Olga Varona; Paul Rogers; Slim Rhyder; Bobbie Kimber; Cynthia & Gladys; Levaine Bros.

Jun 9   (2 weeks)   Empire, GLASGOW
Newman Twins; Victoria Barna & Alec Brook; Carl & Roger Yale; Donald MacKay; Olga Varona; Slim Rhyder; Johnson Clark; MacKenzie Reid & Dorothy; The Three Garcias.

Jun 23   Gaiety, Butlin's, SKEGNESS
The Three Redheads; Slim Rhyder; Len Clifford & Freda; Mariora;
Olga Varona; Jimmy Bruce; Ross Bayard Dancers.

Jun 30   Empire, EDINBURGH
The Three Redheads; Bob Lloyd & Betty; Olga Varona; Claude
Chandler; Slim Rhyder; MacKenzie Reid & Dorothy; Baker & Verek.

Jul 7   New Theatre, HULL
The Three Redheads; Ivor E. Keyes; Olga Varona; Paul Rogers; Slim
Rhyder; MacKenzie Reid & Dorothy; the Perfectos.

Jul 14   Hippodrome, BRISTOL
The Three Redheads; Carl & Roger Yale; Jimmy Bruce; Palette's Dogs;
MacKenzie Reid & Dorothy; Mariora; Olga Varona.

Jul 21   (1st week)   Palace, MANCHESTER
Les Silvas; Olga Varona; the Raymonde Sisters & Allan; Johnson Clark;
Musical Derricks with Tony; Slim Rhyder; Rita Bernard & Lena Brown.
(support acts changed after first week).

Jul 28   (2nd week)   Palace, MANCHESTER
Vickers Twins; Ivor E. Keyes; Terri Carol; Bob Lloyd & Betty; Slim
Rhyder; Mills & Paulette; Young China Troupe; Yeaman's Dogs.

Aug 4   King's, SOUTHSEA
Norman & Vonnie Munro; Ivor E. Keyes; Terri Carol; Peter Raynor;
Slim Rhyder; MacKenzie Reid & Dorothy; Olga Varona; Palette's
Dogs.

Aug 11   Hippodrome, BOSCOMBE
The Three Redheads; Ivor E. Keyes; Reading & Grantly; Len Clifford
& Freda; Slim Rhyder; MacKenzie Reid & Dorothy; Olga Varona.

Aug 18   Winter Gardens, MARGATE
The Three Redheads; Peter Raynor; Frank Marx & Iris; Len Clifford
& Freda; Slim Rhyder; the Musical Derricks & Tony; Palette's Dogs.

Aug 25   (2 weeks)   Hippodrome, COVENTRY
The Three Redheads; Bob Lloyd & Betty; Olga Varona; Carl & Roger
Yale; Slim Rhyder; Jack & Mary Kinson; MacKenzie Reid & Dorothy;
Cynthia & Gladys.

Sep 8   Lido, BOLTON
The Three Redheads; Jackie & Partner; Lorraine; Olga Varona; Slim
Rhyder; MacKenzie Reid & Dorothy; Len Clifford & Freda.

Sep 15   Empire, SWINDON
The Three Redheads; Peter Raynor; Yeaman's Dogs; Slim Rhyder; Lorraine & Partner; Olga Varona; MacKenzie Reid & Dorothy; Two Pirates.

Sep 22   Empire, FINSBURY PARK
The Three Redheads; Johnson Clark; Olga Varona; Carl & Roger Yale; Ronalde; Slim Rhyder; MacKenzie Reid & Dorothy; The Skating Merinos.

(doubled)   Empire, CHISWICK
Ray & Madge Lamar; Marie Wilson; Eddie Bayes; Jackie & Betty Lambert; Johnnie Riscoe & Violet Terry; Dennis Lawes; Bex & Bex; Reg Redcliffe.

Royal Variety Performance

Nov 3   Palladium, LONDON
My Hazel; Marilyn Hightower; The Three Shades; Valerie Tandy; Bobbie Tranter & Tony Hulley; The Three Astaires; Hortobagyi Troupe; Billy Russell; Wilson, Keppel & Betty; Norman Evans; Borrah Minevitch's Harmonica Rascals; Mervyn Saunders; Mona & Olivier; Wally Boag; The Crazy Gang; Jack Durant; Robert Wilson; The Dagenham Girl Pipers; Vic & Joe Crastonian; Terri Carol; Cynthia & Gladys; The Three Garcias; Levanda; Maria Kouise; Mariora; Olga Varona; Eva May Wong; Bobbie Kimber; Dolores Gray & Bill Johnson; STAN LAUREL & OLIVER HARDY; Les Zoris; Tommy Trinder; Gracie Fields.

Harry Moreny played the cop in Laurel and Hardy's sketch throughout the 1947 British tour, and accompanied them on the European tour. (See page 157).

The stay at each venue is Monday to Saturday inclusive unless otherwise stated.

The cast isn't necessarily in order of appearance. Laurel and Hardy were the penultimate act on all their own shows.

1952 Tour Route Map

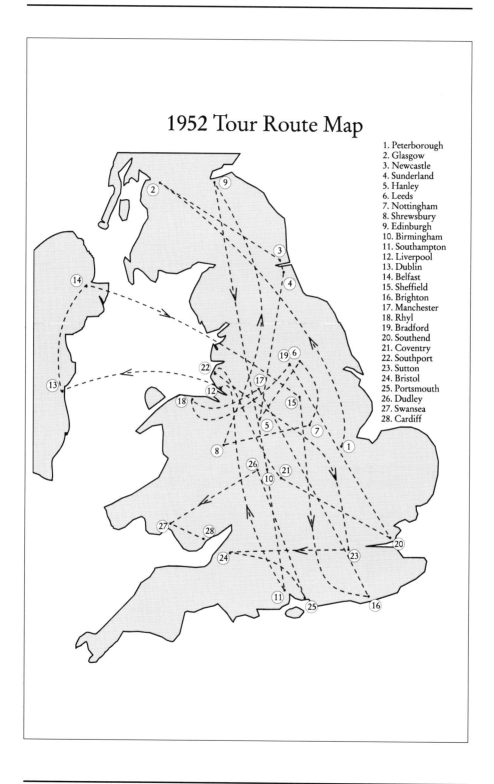

1. Peterborough
2. Glasgow
3. Newcastle
4. Sunderland
5. Hanley
6. Leeds
7. Nottingham
8. Shrewsbury
9. Edinburgh
10. Birmingham
11. Southampton
12. Liverpool
13. Dublin
14. Belfast
15. Sheffield
16. Brighton
17. Manchester
18. Rhyl
19. Bradford
20. Southend
21. Coventry
22. Southport
23. Sutton
24. Bristol
25. Portsmouth
26. Dudley
27. Swansea
28. Cardiff

—— PROGRAMME ——

for week commencing MONDAY, APRIL 7th, 1952
USUAL PERFORMANCES ON GOOD FRIDAY

1. OVERTURE - - - The Empire Orchestra

2. CLAYTON & WARD - - - Open the Show

3. LORRAINE - - - Singing Cartoonist

4. THE KENWAYS - - - Thrills in the Air

5. "DAISY MAY" - - - The Captivating Starlet
   Assisted by SAVEEN

6. VOLTAIRE - - - Out of this World

INTERMISSION
"THE FIREFLY" . . . . Rudolf Friml
THE EMPIRE ORCHESTRA
Under the direction of RONALD A. ROBERTS

FULLY LICENSED BARS
in all parts of the Theatre
FAVOURITE PROPRIETARY BRANDS
at POPULAR PRICES
WHISKY   GIN   PORT & SHERRY
2/-   1/9   2/-
BEERS & MINERALS AT MODERATE PRICES

Programme continued overleaf

—— PROGRAMME ——
Continued

7. CLAYTON & WARD - - - Steps in Rhythm

8. JIMMY ELLIOTT - - - Animal Mimic

9. IRVING & GIRDWOOD - - - Musicale Moderne

10. Bernard Delfont presents
    STAN   OLIVER
    LAUREL and HARDY
    in "A SPOT OF TROUBLE"
    A Comedy Sketch in Two Scenes
    Locale : A Small Town in the U.S.A.
    Scene 1: Waiting Room at the Railway Station
    Scene 2: The Chief of Police's living-room
    Officer (a small town cop with a mind smaller
       than the town) .... Leslie Spurling
    The Chief of Police (a fiery blustering type)
                                        Kenneth Henry
    Two Gentlemen en route   STAN   OLIVER
                             LAUREL and HARDY

The Management reserves the right to refuse admission to the Theatre, and to
change, vary or omit, without previous notice, any item of the programme

In accordance with the requirements of the Leeds City Council:
(a) The public may leave at the end of the performance by all exit and entrance doors, and
such doors must at that time be open. (b) All gangways, passages and staircases must be kept
entirely free from chairs or any obstructions. (c) Persons shall not be permitted to stand or
sit in any of the intersecting gangways, or stand in any unseated space in the auditorium,
unless standing in such space has been specially allowed by the Watch Committee. A Notice
is exhibited in that part of the auditorium in which standing has been sanctioned. (d) The
safety curtain must be lowered and raised once immediately before the commencement of
each performance so as to ensure its being in proper working order.

HERE MONDAY, APRIL 21st
RONDAY PRODUCTIONS LTD. present
STARS OF
★ RADIO TIMES ★
A MUSICAL COCKTAIL WITH A GREAT CAST INCLUDING
The   From
Famous Comedian MAX WALL "Variety Band-Box"
DICK • BERYL • THE HEDLEY
JAMES   REID   WARD TRIO
Singing Star   Radio's "Monica"   From "Educating Archie"

Typical programme layout and bill for Laurel and Hardy's 1952 tour.
Leeds Empire, week commencing 7 April 1952.

*Typical newspaper
advertising block for
Laurel and Hardy's
1952 tour.*
(By kind permission of the
Southend Echo.)

PROGRAMME BILLS
1952

Feb 25   (2 weeks)   Embassy, PETERBOROUGH
Cynthia & Gladys; Lorraine; Ray & Madge Lamarr; Saveen & 'Daisy
May'; Ted & George Durante; Jimmie Elliot; Roy & Ray.

Mar 10   Empire, GLASGOW
Lonsdale Sisters; Lorraine; Walthon & Dorraine; The Great Cingalee;
Saveen & 'Daisy May'; Jimmy Elliot; MacKenzie Reid & Dorothy.

Mar 16   (1 night)   Gaumont Cinema, NORTH SHIELDS
Eric Nicholson; Northumbrian Serenaders; Frankie Burns; Betty Hart;
Tony Rowley; James Metcalf; Dick Urwin; Billy 'Uke' Scott.

Mar 17   Empire, NEWCASTLE
Skating Sayers; Lorraine; Medlock & Marlowe; Saveen & 'Daisy May'; Aerial Kenways; Jimmie Elliot; MacKenzie Reid & Dorothy.

Mar 24   Empire, SUNDERLAND
The Three Adairs; Lorraine; Saveen & 'Daisy May'; Voltaire; Aerial Kenways; Jimmie Elliot; MacKenzie Reid & Dorothy.

Mar 31   Royal, HANLEY
Shane Sisters; Jackley & Jee; Aerial Kenways; Saveen & 'Daisy May'; Jimmie Elliot; Reggie Redcliffe.

Apr 7   Empire, LEEDS
Clayton & Ward; Lorraine; Aerial Kenways; Saveen & 'Daisy May'; Voltaire; Jimmy Elliot; Irving & Girdwood.

Apr 14   Empire, NOTTINGHAM
Avril & Irene; Lorraine; Lou Folds; Saveen & 'Daisy May'; Aerial Kenways; Skating Websters; Jimmy Elliot; MacKenzie Reid & Dorothy.

Apr 21   Granada, SHREWSBURY
The Three Adairs; Lorraine; Aerial Kenways; Saveen & 'Daisy May'; Newman Twins; Jimmie Elliot; MacKenzie Reid & Dorothy.

Apr 28   Empire, EDINBURGH
Merle & Marie; Lorraine; Aerial Kenways; Saveen & 'Daisy May'; Newman Twins; Skating Sayers; Jimmie Elliot; MacKenzie Reid & Dorothy.

May 5   Hippodrome, BIRMINGHAM
Clayton & Ward; Lorraine; Aerial Kenways; Saveen & 'Daisy May'; Newman Twins; Jack Melville; Jimmie Elliot; MacKenzie Reid & Dorothy.

May 12   Gaumont, SOUTHAMPTON
Lonsdale Sisters; Lorraine; Aerial Kenways; Saveen & 'Daisy May'; The Great Cingalee; Newman Twins; MacKenzie Reid & Dorothy.

May 19   Empire, LIVERPOOL
Lonsdale Sisters; Lorraine; Aerial Kenways; Saveen & 'Daisy May'; The Great Cingalee; Jimmie Elliot; MacKenzie Reid & Dorothy.
(George Pughe replaced Kenneth Henry in Laurel & Hardy's sketch).

May 27   (2 weeks)   Olympia, DUBLIN
Lonsdale Sisters; Lorraine; Archie Elray & Co; Aerial Kenways; The Great Cingalee; Jimmie Elliot; MacKenzie Reid & Dorothy.

Jun 9   (2 weeks)   Grand Opera House, BELFAST
Lonsdale Sisters; Lorraine; Archie Elray & Co; Ariel Kenways;
The Great Cingalee; Jimmie Elliot; MacKenzie Reid & Dorothy.

Jun 30   Empire, SHEFFIELD
Lonsdale Sisters; Lorraine; Aerial Kenways; Archie Elray & Co; The
Great Cingalee; Jimmy Elliot; MacKenzie Reid & Dorothy.

Jul 7   Hippodrome, BRIGHTON
Les Valettos; Lorraine; Aerial Kenways; Joan Turner; Voltaire; Jimmie
Elliot; MacKenzie Reid & Dorothy.

Jul 14   Palace, MANCHESTER
Ray & Madge Lamar; Lorraine; Aerial Kenways; Archie Elray & Co;
The Four Fredianis; Pepino's Miniature Circus; Jimmie Elliot;
MacKenzie Reid & Dorothy.

Jul 21   Queen's, RHYL
Lonsdale Sisters; Lorraine; Aerial Kenways; Archie Elray & Co;
The Great Cingalee; Jimmie Elliot; MacKenzie Reid & Dorothy.

Jul 28   Alhambra, BRADFORD
Lonsdale Sisters; Lorraine; Aerial Kenways; Harry Worth; The Great
Cingalee; Jimmie Elliot; MacKenzie Reid & Dorothy.

Aug 4   Odeon, SOUTHEND
Lonsdale Sisters; Lorraine; Aerial Kenways; Archie Elray & Co; The
Great Cingalee; Jimmie Elliot; MacKenzie Reid & Dorothy.

Aug 11   Hippodrome, COVENTRY
Lonsdale Sisters; Lorraine; Aerial Kenways; Harry Worth; The Great
Cingalee; Jimmie Elliot; MacKenzie Reid & Dorothy.

Aug 18   Garrick, SOUTHPORT
Lonsdale Sisters; Lorraine; Aerial Kenways; Archie Elray & Co; The
Great Cingalee; Jimmie Elliot; MacKenzie Reid & Dorothy.

Aug 25   Granada, SUTTON
Lonsdale Sisters; Lorraine; Aerial Kenways; Archie Elray & Co;
The Great Cingalee; Jimmie Elliot; MacKenzie Reid & Dorothy.

Sep 1   Hippodrome, BRISTOL
Lonsdale Sisters; Lorraine; Aerial Kenways; Archie Elray & Co; The
Great Cingalee; Jimmie Elliot; MacKenzie Reid & Dorothy.

Sep 5   (1 night)   Grand Spa Hotel, CLIFTON (charity show)
Western Brothers; Fayne & Evans; Len Marten; Fred Ferrari; Ken Morris.

Sep 8
                         Royal, PORTSMOUTH
Lonsdale Sisters; Lorraine; Aerial Kenways; Harry Worth; The Great
Cingalee; Jimmie Elliot; MacKenzie Reid & Dorothy.

Sep 15
                      Hippodrome, DUDLEY
Lonsdale Sisters; Lorraine; Archie Elray & Co; The Great Cingalee;
Jimmie Elliot; MacKenzie Reid & Dorothy.

Sep 22
                       Empire, SWANSEA
Lonsdale Sisters; Lorraine; Aerial Kenways; Archie Elray & Co; The
Great Cingalee; Jimmie Elliot; MacKenzie Reid & Dorothy.

Sep 29
                   New Theatre, CARDIFF
Lonsdale Sisters; Lorraine; Aerial Kenways; Archie Elray & Co; The
Great Cingalee; Jimmie Elliot; MacKenzie Reid & Dorothy.

Assistants in Laurel & Hardy's sketch were Leslie Spurling and Kenneth Henry, unless
otherwise stated or not known.

Laurel & Hardy's act was last on the bill.

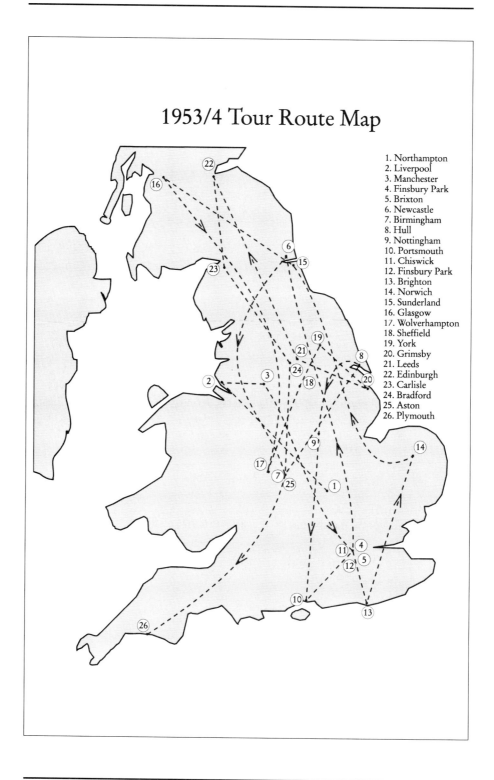

1953/4 Tour Route Map

1. Northampton
2. Liverpool
3. Manchester
4. Finsbury Park
5. Brixton
6. Newcastle
7. Birmingham
8. Hull
9. Nottingham
10. Portsmouth
11. Chiswick
12. Finsbury Park
13. Brighton
14. Norwich
15. Sunderland
16. Glasgow
17. Wolverhampton
18. Sheffield
19. York
20. Grimsby
21. Leeds
22. Edinburgh
23. Carlisle
24. Bradford
25. Aston
26. Plymouth

PROGRAMME BILLS
1953

Oct 11   (1 night)   Olympia, DUBLIN (charity performance)
Billy Banks; Anne Jamison; Paddie Crosbie; Freddie Doyle; Elizabeth Carroll; Neil Phelan; Eddie Lambert; Capitol Theatre Dancers.
(Laurel & Hardy assisted by: Gordon Craig; Gerald Lennan; Donald McCollum.)

Oct 19   New Theatre, NORTHAMPTON
Jill Jill & Jill; Freddie Harris & Christine; Ursula & Gus; Fred Lovelle; Krista & Kristel; Keefe Bros & Annette; Roy & Ray.
(Laurel & Hardy assisted by: Gordon Craig; Gerald Lennan; Bernard Newson.)

Oct 26   Empire, LIVERPOOL
Jill Jill & Jill; Derek Rosaire & Tony – the Wonder Horse; Mundy & Earle; Ursula & Gus; Ronnie Leslie; Seaton & O'Dell; Roy & Ray; Betty Kaye's Pekinese.
(Laurel & Hardy assisted by: Gordon Craig; Gerald Lennan; Reginald Newson.)

Nov 2   Hippodrome, MANCHESTER
Jill Jill & Jill; Ronnie Leslie; Ursula & Gus; Fred Lovelle; Derek Rosaire & Tony – the Wonder Horse; Betty Kaye's Pekinese; Roy & Ray; Laurel & Hardy closed the show. (Assisted by: Gordon Craig; Gerald Lennan; Bernard Newson.)

Nov 9   Empire, FINSBURY PARK
Jill Jill & Jill; Seaton & O'Dell; Ronnie Leslie; Roy & Ray; Ursula & Gus; Bobbie Kimber; Derek Rosaire & Tony – the Wonder Horse; Betty Kaye's Pekinese. (Jewel & Warriss replaced Laurel & Hardy).

Nov 16   Empress, BRIXTON
Jill Jill & Jill; Bobbie Kimber; Newman Twins; Ursula & Gus; Keefe Bros & Annette; Freddie Harris & Christine; Roy & Ray.

Nov 23   Empire, NEWCASTLE
Jill Jill & Jill; Fe Jover & Jack; Freddie Harris & Christine; Ursula & Gus; Ray Alan & 'Steve'; Derek Rosaire & Tony – the Wonder Horse; Roy & Ray; Betty Kaye's Pekinese.
(Laurel & Hardy assisted by: Gordon Craig; Leslie Spurling; Reginald Newson.)

Nov 30   Hippodrome, BIRMINGHAM
Jill Jill & Jill; Fe Jover & Jack; Freddie Harris & Christine; Roy & Ray; Derek Rosaire & Tony – the Wonder Horse; Paul & Peta Page; Ursula & Gus; Betty Kaye's Pekinese.

Dec 7   Palace, HULL
Candy Sisters & Eddie; Freddie Harris & Christine; Nicol & Kemble; Fred Lovelle; Ursula & Gus; Roy & Ray; Betty Kaye's Pekinese.
 (Laurel & Hardy assisted by: Gordon Craig; Leslie Spurling; John Sullivan.)

Dec 21   (4 weeks)   Empire, NOTTINGHAM
Jill Jill & Jill; Ursula & Gus; Harry Worth; Derek Rosaire & Tony – the Wonder Horse; Bob Bemand's Pigeons; Roy & Ray; Betty Kaye's Pekinese.

The newpaper advertising block for Laurel and Hardy's last ever show.
(By courtesy of the *Plymouth Evening Herald*.)

PROGRAMME BILLS
1954

Jan 18   Royal, PORTSMOUTH
Jill Jill & Jill; Alan Rowe; Ursula & Gus; Harry Worth; Derek Rosaire & Tony – the Wonder Horse; Paul Arland; Roy & Ray; Betty Kaye's Pekinese.
(Laurel & Hardy assisted by: Gordon Craig; Gerald Lennan; Reginald Newson.)

Jan 25   Empire, CHISWICK
Jill Jill & Jill; Alan Rowe; Ursula & Gus; Harry Worth; Derek Rosaire & Tony – the Wonder Horse; Paul Arland; Roy & Ray; Betty Kaye's Pekinese.

Feb 1   Empire, FINSBURY PARK
Charmony Three; Alan Rowe; Newman Twins; Arthur Worsley; Victor Julian & Pets; Nick & Pat Lundon; Paul Arland; Krandon & Karna.
(Laurel & Hardy assisted by: Gordon Craig; Leslie Spurling; John Sullivan.)

Feb 8   Hippodrome, BRIGHTON
Lorraine; Ursula & Gus; Harry Worth; Derek Rosaire & Tony – the
Wonder Horse; Paul Arland; Roy & Ray; Betty Kaye's Pekinese.

Feb 15   Hippodrome, NORWICH
Jill Jill & Jill; Lorraine; Ursula & Gus; Harry Worth; Derek Rosaire &
Tony – the Wonder Horse; Paul Arland; Roy & Ray; Betty Kaye's
Pekinese.
(Laurel & Hardy assisted by: Gordon Craig; Leslie Spurling; John
Sullivan.)

Feb 22   Empire, SUNDERLAND
Jill Jill & Jill; Alan Rowe; Ursula & Gus; Harry Worth; Derek Rosaire
& Tony – the Wonder Horse; Paul Arland; Roy & Ray; Betty Kaye's
Pekinese.

Mar 1   Empire, GLASGOW
Jill Jill & Jill; Alan Rowe; Ursula & Gus; Harry Worth; Derek Rosaire
& Tony – the Wonder Horse; Paul Arland; Roy & Ray; Betty Kaye's
Pekinese.
(Laurel & Hardy assisted by: Gordon Craig; Leslie Spurling; John
Sullivan).

Mar 8   Hippodrome, WOLVERHAMPTON
Jill Jill & Jill; Alan Rowe; Audrey Jeans; Harry Worth; Derek Rosaire
& Tony – the Wonder Horse; Paul Arland; Roy & Ray; Betty Kaye's
Pekinese.

Mar 15   Empire, SHEFFIELD
Jill Jill & Jill; Alan Rowe; Ursula & Gus; Harry Worth; Derek Rosaire
& Tony – the Wonder Horse; Keefe Bros & Annette; Roy & Ray; Betty
Kaye's Pekinese.

Mar 22   Empire, YORK
Jill Jill & Jill; Alan Rowe; Ursula & Gus; Peter Raynor; Derek Rosaire
& Tony – the Wonder Horse; Keefe Bros & Annette; Roy & Ray; Betty
Kaye's Pekinese.

Mar 29   Palace, GRIMSBY
Jill Jill & Jill; Alan Rowe; Ursula & Gus; Nicol & Kemble; Derek
Rosaire & Tony – the Wonder Horse; Keefe Bros & Annette; Roy &
Ray; Betty Kaye's Pekinese.
(Laurel & Hardy assisted by: Gordon Craig; Leslie Spurling; John
Sullivan).

Apr 5   Empire, LEEDS
Jill Jill & Jill; Alan Rowe; Ursula & Gus; Bobbie Kimber; Derek Rosaire & Tony – the Wonder Horse; Peggy Cavell; Roy & Ray; Betty Kaye's Pekinese.

Apr 12   Empire, EDINBURGH
Jill Jill & Jill; Alan Rowe; Ursula & Gus; Bobbie Kimber; Derek Rosaire & Tony – the Wonder Horse; Dunn & Grant; Dorothy Reid & Mack; Betty Kaye's Pekinese.
(Laurel & Hardy assisted by: Gordon Craig; Leslie Spurling; John Sullivan).

Apr 19   Her Majesty's, CARLISLE
Jill Jill & Jill; Jimmie Elliot; Ursula & Gus; Bobbie Kimber; Derek Rosaire & Tony – the Wonder Horse; Lorraine; Dorothy Reid & Mack; Betty Kaye's Pekinese.

Apr 26 (week off)

May 3   Alhambra, BRADFORD
Conway & Day; Alan Rowe; The Skylons; Harry Worth; Derek Rosaire & Tony – the Wonder Horse; Peggy Cavell; Dorothy Reid & Mack; Betty Kaye's Pekinese.
(Laurel & Hardy assisted by: Gordon Craig; Leslie Spurling; John Sullivan).

May 10   Hippodrome, ASTON
Mary & Michael Mills; Alan Rowe; Harry Worth; Derek Rosaire & Tony – the Wonder Horse; Trio Botando; Dorothy Reid & Mack; Betty Kaye's Pekinese.

May 17   Palace, PLYMOUTH
Shane & Lamar; Alan Rowe; Trio Botando; Harry Worth; Derek Rosaire & Tony – the Wonder Horse; Lorraine; Dorothy Reid & Mack; Betty Kaye's Pekinese.
(Laurel & Hardy appeared on first night only. Joe Church finished the week.)

May 24   Empire, SWANSEA – cancelled.

Birds of a Feather was the penultimate act – unless otherwise stated.

FILM FOOTAGE

1932 Jul 28   TYNEMOUTH – Grand Hotel and Plaza.   (pages 54, 76)
(J. G. Ratcliffe)

1932 Jul 29   EDINBURGH – Castle, and Playhouse Theatre.   (page 56)
(Alan J. Harpur)

1947 Feb 10   SOUTHAMPTON – arrival on *Queen Elizabeth,*   (page 84)
Interviewed by John Parasols. Talk about forthcoming tour and proposed film *Robin Hood*. Do the 'standing on the foot' gag. Robert Taylor and Barbara Stanwyck also seen.
(Pathé Newsreels)

1947 Mar 16   LONDON – Daily Mail Ideal Home Exhibition.   (page 99)
Tessie O'Shea and Vera Pearce sit on Hardy's knee. Stan grins and is kissed by Tessie.
(Pathé Newreels)

1947 Mar 21   KENT – Romney Hythe & Dymchurch Railway.   (page 99)
Laurel and Hardy are welcomed at New Romney Railway Station. Do business of opening train shed doors, with huge key. Fool about with engine controls, then get into one of Pullman cars, and set off for Dungeness.   (Gaumont and Paramount)

1947 Apr 13   LONDON – 'Comedians at the Apollo'.   (page 107)
Laurel and Hardy, Sid Field, The Crazy Gang, Tommy Trinder and George Robey, dressed in farmers' smocks, selling programmes outside the venue prior to a charity show.
(Pathé Newreels)

1947 Apr 28   LONDON – Daily Mail Film Awards, The Dorchester.   (page 109)
Laurel and Hardy arrive late and interrupt Lady Rothermere presenting an award to Margaret Lockwood.   (Pathé Newreels)

1947 Nov 2   KENT – Aboard the French boat train.   (page 153)
The Laurels and the Hardys en route from Paris to London to attend the Royal Variety Show.   (Pathé Newsreels)

1952 Jan 31   LONDON – Variety Club Luncheon, Empress Club.   (page 162)
The Boys at a charity dinner, with Eamonn Andrews, Freddie Mills, Charlie Chester and CoCo the clown.   (Pathé Newreels)

1953 Oct 22   NORTHAMPTON – New Theatre.   (page 219)
Laurel and Hardy's car arrives at stage door, and they do business of getting in and out. In dressing room, Laurel brushes Hardy's coat, and catches his chin, then traps Hardy's coat in trunk.
(Pathé Newreels)

BROADCASTS

RADIO

1932 Jul 27   NATIONAL – interview in London BBC Studio.   (page 48)

1947 May 29   NORTH – *Morecambe Night Out* – interview by Reg Smythe in dressing room of *Pavilion Theatre*, Morecambe.   (page 118)

1952 Jun 17   BBC BELFAST – broadcast from the *Grand Opera House* – link up with an 'on air' talent show at the *Tonic Cinema* Bangor, for which Laurel and Hardy acted as judges.

1953 Oct 23   MIDLAND – *What Goes On* – interview by Philip Garston-Jones, at the *New Theatre*, Northampton.   (page 219)

1957 Aug 14   AMERICA – *Turning Point* – Laurel interviewed by Arthur B. Friedman, just one week after the death of Hardy.   (page 154)

1959 Jan   AMERICA – *Voices from the Hollywood Past* – Stan Laurel interviewed by Tony Thomas.

TELEVISION

1952 Feb 20   BBC – *Picture Page* – interview by Leslie Mitchell.   (unconfirmed)

1953 Oct 17   BBC – *Face the Music* – interview by Henry Hall.   (page 218)

1955 Oct 9   BBC – *This is Music Hall* – a live transmission of a Gala Variety Show presented by the Grand Order of Water Rats during which a short recorded sequence was shown of Laurel and Hardy sending greetings from America. (Recorded 29 September in California)

GRAMOPHONE

1932 Aug 18   *Laurel and Hardy in London* (Columbia CAX 6488 DX370).   (page 78)

All the above recordings are British unless stated otherwise.

*Where it all started, 3 Argyle Street – virtually unchanged over one hundred
years after Stan Laurel was born there.*
(By kind permission of Paul Wain.)

THE BRITISH LOCATIONS

This section is designed to assist readers who may wish to visit some, or all, of the extant theatres which Stan Jefferson and/or Laurel and Hardy played, and the hotels at which they stayed. It is arranged in geographical order, beginning at Stan's birthplace and ending with the theatre where Laurel and Hardy played their last ever performance.

KEY: The theatres which Stan Jefferson and/or Laurel and Hardy played, and the hotels at which they stayed are listed below, on the left. In brackets is the capacity, followed by the address. Their current state, or whatever now occupies their former sites, is on the right-hand side. The date in brackets is the year the venue was demolished.

    It was impracticable to list every theatre, public house, company, civic venue, hotel, etc., to which Laurel and Hardy paid a casual visit, but most are referred to in the text.

    (*) Indicates Stan Jefferson solo.

    (!) Indicates Stan Jefferson solo, plus later appearance with Hardy.

    (+) Indicates properties owned, or leased, by Arthur Jefferson.

CUMBRIA

3 Argyle Street, ULVERSTON.	occupied house (!)
County Station Hotel, Court Square, CARLISLE.	Cumbrian Hotel

Demolished:

CARLISLE, Her Majesty's (1,300) Lowther Street.	(1970s) car park (!)

SCOTLAND

DUMFRIES, Royal (550) 66-68 Shakespeare Street.	(façade only original) theatre (*)
KILMARNOCK, King's (2,200) King Street.	(shell, only, is original) Cannon Cinema (*)
GLASGOW, Panopticon and Britannia Music Hall, 115 Trongate.	(Grade A listed) derelict (*)
42 Buchanan Drive, RUTHERGLEN.	occupied house (*)
185 Stonelaw Road, RUTHERGLEN.	occupied house (*)
17 Craigmillar Road, Battlefield, GLASGOW.	well preserved (*)
Stonelaw High School, Stonelaw Road, RUTHERGLEN.	unaltered (*)
Queen's Park Secondary School, Grange Road, QUEEN'S PARK.	still a school (*)
GLASGOW, La Scala (1,300) 155 Sauchiehall Street.	disused
Central Hotel, Gordon Street, GLASGOW.	working hotel
GLASGOW, Coliseum (2,890) 85-97 Eglington Street.	cinema (*)
MOTHERWELL, New Century (2,000) Windmill Street.	(original portions only) amusement centre (*)
EDINBURGH, Playhouse (3,131) 18-22 Greenside Place/Leith Walk.	rock concert venue
North British Station Hotel, Prince's Street, EDINBURGH.	Balmoral Hotel
EDINBURGH, Empire Palace (2,016) Nicholson Street.	(refurbished 1992) Festival Theatre (!)
Caledonian Hotel, Prince's Street, EDINBURGH.	working hotel

Demolished:

GREENOCK, Alexandra (1,500) West Blackhall Street.	(1972) roadway (*)
GLASGOW, Metropole (2,000) Stockwell Street.	(1961) car park (*)
GLASGOW, Empire (2,500) 31-35 Sauchiehall Street/West Nile Street.	(1963) shops
DUNFERMLINE, Opera House (1,250) Reform Street.	(dismantled 1988, rebuilt in Florida) shops (*)

NORTH EAST

NEWCASTLE, Stoll Picture House (1,389) 111 Westgate Road NE1.	Tyne Theatre & Opera House (!)
NEWCASTLE, Pavilion (1,600) Westgate Road.	(converted 1990 – façade remains) flats (*)
Royal Station Hotel, Neville Street, NEWCASTLE.	working hotel
TYNEMOUTH, Plaza (713) Grand Parade.	nightclub/skating rink
Grand Hotel, Percy Gardens, TYNEMOUTH.	unchanged
NORTH SHIELDS, Gaumont Cinema (1,790) Russell Street.	bingo
Town Hall, Saville Street, NORTH SHIELDS.	unaltered
SOUTH SHIELDS, Empire Palace (1,412) King Street.	derelict (*)
SUNDERLAND, Royal (2,500) Bedford Street.	(original façade only) bingo (*)
SUNDERLAND, Empire (1,550) High Street.	intact, inside and out (!)
SUNDERLAND, Villiers Institute (900) Villiers Street.	builder's merchants (*)
CONSETT, New, Front Street.	Freemason's Hotel – ballroom (*)

Demolished:

ASHINGTON, Miner's (1,422) Station Road.	(1990 vacant lot (*)
(+) BLYTH, Royal (1,500) Waterloo Road.	(1989) Keel Row Centre – shops
(+) BLYTH, New Royal (2,000) Trotter Street.	(1983) Keel Row Centre car park (*)
NEWCASTLE, Queen's Hall (1,400) Northumberland Street.	(1983) shopping arcade
NEWCASTLE, Empire Palace (1,849) Newgate Street.	(1963) Swallow Hotel (!)
(+) NORTH SHIELDS, Royal (1,800) 25 Prudhoe Street.	(1939) Theatre Place – housing (*)
(+) NORTH SHIELDS, Tynemouth Hippodrome, Rudyerd Street.	(1910) housing
(+) Albion Assembly Rooms, 19 Norfolk Street, NORTH SHIELDS.	(1985) wasteland
(+) Ayton House, Ayres Terrace, NORTH SHIELDS.	new houses (*)
(+) Gordon House, 8 Dockwray Square, NORTH SHIELDS.	new houses (!)
(+) WALLSEND, Royal (1,200) Portugal Place.	(1906) housing and clinic (*)
(+) HEBBURN, Royal (1,500) Carr Street.	(burned down 1950s) housing
(+) JARROW, Royal (991) Market Square.	(1962) housing (*)
SUNDERLAND, King's (2,000) 13 Crowtree Road.	(1954) shops (*)
(+) CONSETT, New Royal (200) Trafalgar Street.	(1901) busman's canteen (*)
WEST STANLEY, Royal (1,400) Station Road.	(1930) open land (*)
SEAHAM HARBOUR, New Royal (1,005) Green Street.	(1975) Co-op store (*)
WEST HARTLEPOOL, Grand & Opera House (2,500) Lambton Street.	(1950s) wasteland (*)

BISHOP AUCKLAND

St. Stephen's Church, Prince's Street.	well preserved (*)
(+) 66 Prince's Street.	well preserved (*)
King James I Grammar School, South Church Road.	King James I Comprehensive School (*)

Demolished:

(+) EDEN (1,550) Fairless Street/Newgate End.	(1974) road junction
(+) Theatre Royal	(1892 – became Eden Theatre, above)
(+) 15 Tenter Street.	(c.1981) office
Gainford Academy, North Terrace, GAINFORD.	no records (*)

The original Gainford Academy building was in High Row, and is extant – as flats. In 1899 the Academy transferred to premises in North Terrace, for which there are no records.

YORKSHIRE

YORK, Empire (1,000) Clifford Street.	Grand Opera House
Royal Station Hotel, Station Road, YORK.	Royal York Hotel
HULL, New (1,200) Kingston Square.	working theatre
Royal Station Hotel, Ferensway, HULL.	Royal Hotel
Dolphin Hotel, Alexandra Road, CLEETHORPES.	working hotel
LEEDS, Majestic Cinema (2,392) City Square.	bingo/leisure centre
Queen's Hotel, City Square, LEEDS.	(built on site of old one – 1937)
BRADFORD, Empire (1,320) Great Horton Road.	(entrance only original) working theatre (!)
Midland Hotel, Cheapside, BRADFORD.	bar/restaurant
BRADFORD, Alhambra, (1,480) Morley Street.	renovated 1980s
WAKEFIELD, Theatre Royal & Opera House (600) Drury Lane.	live theatre (*)

Demolished:

HULL, Palace (1,800) Anlaby Road.	(1965) flats (!)
GRIMSBY, Palace (1,509) Victoria Street.	(1979) car park
CASTLEFORD, Royal (980) Albion Street.	(1964) supermarket (*)
LEEDS, Empire Palace (1,750) 108 Briggate.	(1962) Empire Arcade – shops (!)
Queen's Hotel, City Square, LEEDS.	(1935 – see earlier entry)
LEEDS, Hippodrome (3,000) King Charles Croft.	(1967) Schofield's shopping centre (*)
LEEDS, Royal, King Charles Croft/Lands Lane.	(1957) Schofield's shopping centre (*)
BRADFORD, Prince's (2,900) Little Horton Lane.	(1964) road and greenery (*)
WAKEFIELD, Empire (977) 115 Kirkgate.	(c.1960) supermarket (*)
MEXBOROUGH, Prince of Wales (1,000) High Street.	(1939) car park (*)
SHEFFIELD, Cinema House (763) Fargate.	(1961) Fountain Precinct – shops
SHEFFIELD, Empire Palace (3,000) Charles Street.	(1959) shops (!)
SHEFFIELD, Hippodrome (2,760) Cambridge Street.	(1963) Grosvenor House Hotel (*)
Grand Hotel, Church Street, SHEFFIELD.	1974) Fountain Precinct – shops

MANCHESTER

HULME, Hippodrome (2,000) Preston Street (now Chichester Street), M15.	(Grade II) disused (*)
New Oxford Picture Theatre (1,150) Oxford Street.	Macdonald's
Midland Hotel, Peter Street.	working hotel
Palace (2,000) Oxford Street.	working theatre
Grand Hotel, 8 Aytoun Street.	working hotel
OLDHAM, Colleseum (576) Fairbottom Street.	Coliseum (*)
SALFORD, Opera House (2,070) Quay Street.	Grade II listed
ECCLES, Crown (2,500) Church Street.	bingo (*)

Demolished:

Brooklands Hotel, Hope Road/Marsden Road, SALE.	(1972) office block
STOCKPORT, Royal (3,000) St. Peter's Square.	(1962) Co-op Bank (*)
LONGSIGHT, King's, Stockport Road/Shepley Street.	(1973) Social Services Department (*)
ARDWICK GREEN, Empire (3,000) Hyde Road.	(1935 – became New Hippodrome below) (*)
ARDWICK GREEN, New Hippodrome (2,100) (former Ardwick Green Empire).	(1964) roadway (!)
OPENSHAW, Metropole, 505 Ashton Old Road, M12.	(1962) recreation ground (*)
ASHTON-UNDER-LYNE, Royal (3,000) Oldham Road.	(1960s) car park (*)
SALFORD, Regent (2,684) Regent Road/Cross Lane.	(1963) Ship Hotel car park (*)
SALFORD, Royal Hippodrome (3,000) Cross Lane/Peel Street.	(1962) Thorn Court – flats (*)

LANCASHIRE

TODMORDEN, Hippodrome (1,600) Halifax Road.   run by Amateur Operatic Dramatic Society (*)
BOLTON, Lido (1,800) Bradshawgate.   Cannon Cinema
MORECAMBE, Victoria Pavilion (2,960) Winter Gardens, Marine Road.   derelict and decaying
     Elms Hotel, Prince's Crescent, BARE.   working hotel
BLACKPOOL, Tower Ballroom, Promenade.   restored 1956
BLACKPOOL, Empress Ballroom (3,000) Winter Gardens.   restored to original
BLACKPOOL, Baronial Hall, Winter Gardens.   perfectly preserved
     Metropole Hotel, Princess Parade, BLACKPOOL.   Butlin's Hotel
SOUTHPORT, Garrick (1,600) Lord Street.   bingo
     Prince of Wales, Lord Street, SOUTHPORT.   working hotel

     Demolished:
ROCHDALE, Hippodrome (1,800) Newgate.   (1930) Newgate House – DSS offices (*)
BURY, Royal (2,000) Market Street.   (c.1986) Halifax Building Society (*)
RAWTENSTALL, Grand (1,600) Cheapside.   (1938) Fire Station (*)
DARWEN, Royal (1,500) Railway Road.   (1960s) garage (*)
BLACKPOOL, Palace (2,012) Central Beach.   (1961) Lewis's store
BLACKPOOL, Picture Palace Pavilion (1,972) Central Beach.   (1961) Lewis's store
     Majestic Hotel, St. Annes Road West, ST. ANNES.   (1974) Majestic Court – housing
TYLDESLEY, Royal (980) John Street.   (pre-1979) houses (*)
HORWICH, Prince's (1,400) The Arcade, Lee Lane.   (1962) supermarket car park (*)
WIGAN, Hippodrome (1,300) 43 King Street.   (c. 1956) supermarket (*)

LIVERPOOL

Empire (2,293) Lime Street.   working theatre (!)
     Adelphi Hotel, Lime Street.   Britannia Adelphi Hotel
Pavilion (2,050) Lodge Lane/Beaumont Street, L8.   disused (*)
SEACOMBE, Irving (2,500) Victoria Road (now Borough Road).   King's Theatre bingo (*)
     Demolished:
Royal Hippodrome (3,200) West Derby Road, EVERTON.   (1984) builder's yard (*)

IRELAND

DUBLIN, Olympia (1,750) 72 Dame Street.   restored 1974
     Gresham Hotel, O'Connell Street, DUN LAOGHAIRE.   working hotel
     Royal Marine Hotel, DUN LAOGHAIRE.   working hotel
BELFAST, Grand Opera House (1,050) Great Victoria Street, B12.   restored 1980
     Midland Hotel, Whitla Street, BELFAST, BT15.   Midland Building – offices

NORTH WALES/SHROPSHIRE/CHESHIRE

WIDNES, Alexandra (2,000) Alexandra Street.   (gutted by fire 1948) industrial workshop (*)
WARRINGTON, Palace and Hippodrome (2,100) Barbauld Street.   bingo (*)
RHYL, Queen's (1,300) Promenade.   amusement arcade
     Westminster Hotel, East Parade, RHYL.   working hotel
SHREWSBURY, Granada (1,456) Castle Gates.   bingo
     Demolished:
     Raven Hotel, Castle Gates, SHREWSBURY.   (1960) Woolworths
CREWE, Lyceum (1,250) Russell Street/Heath Street.   (destroyed 1911) rebuilt (*)

STAFFORDSHIRE/WEST MIDLANDS

HANLEY, Royal (1,800) Pall Mall.   restored 1982
 North Stafford Hotel, Station Road, STOKE.   working hotel
 Demolished:
STAFFORD, Lyceum (800) Martin Street.   (1920) County Analysts (*)
WOLVERHAMPTON, Hippodrome (1,960) Queen Square.   (1956) Poundstretcher
WALSALL, Her Majesty's (2,000) Town End Bank/Park Street.   (1937) cinema (*)

NOTTINGHAM/LINCOLNSHIRE/LEICESTER

Plough Inn, West Street, BARKSTON.   reconverted to house
 Bull Inn, 5 Market Street, BOTTESFORD.   working pub
SKEGNESS, Gaiety (1,800) Butlin's.   working theatre
 Demolished:
NOTTINGHAM, Empire (2,200) South Sherwood Street.   (1969) Royal Centre (!)
 County Hotel, Theatre Square, NOTTINGHAM.   (1975) Royal Centre
LEICESTER, Palace (2,750) Belgrave Gate.   (1960) shops and offices (*)

CAMBRIDGESHIRE/NORFOLK

PETERBOROUGH, Embassy (1,500) Broadway.   disused
 Great Northern Hotel, Station Road, PETERBOROUGH.   working hotel
 Royal Hotel, Prince of Wales Road, NORWICH.   restored 1989
 Demolished:
NORWICH, Hippodrome (1,836) St. Giles Street.   (1966) car park

NORTHAMPTONSHIRE/MIDLANDS

COVENTRY, Hippodrome (1,982) Trinity Street.   bingo
 Clarendon Hotel, The Parade, LEAMINGTON SPA.   Clarendon Court – offices
 Abbey Hotel, Priory Road, KENILWORTH.   (converted 1982) flats
BIRMINGHAM, Hippodrome (2,000) Hurst Street.   original façade and foyer (!)
 Midland Hotel, New Street, BIRMINGHAM, B5.   working hotel
DUDLEY, Hippodrome (1,500) Castle Hill.   bingo
 Station Hotel, Castle Hill, DUDLEY.   working hotel
 Demolished:
NORTHAMPTON, New Theatre (2,000) Abington Street.   (1960) Primark Store
 Plough Hotel, Bridge Street, NORTHAMPTON.   Mulliners Hotel
BIRMINGHAM, Empire Palace (2,000) Hurst Street.   (1950) shops (*)
BIRMINGHAM, Gaumont Cinema (2,200) Steelhouse Lane.   (1983) Wesleyan Insurance Company
 Queen's Hotel, New Street, BIRMINGHAM.   (1966) Pallasades shops
ASTON, Hippodrome (1,800) Potters Lane.   (1981) Astra Hippodrome
DUDLEY, Royal Opera House (1,680) Castle Hill.   (1936) Dudley Hippodrome built on site (*)

SOUTH WALES

PONTYPRIDD, Royal Clarence (1,000) High Street.   bingo (*)
CARDIFF, New (1,600) Park Place.   touring theatre
    Park Hotel, Park Place, CARDIFF.   working hotel
    Demolished:
SWANSEA, Empire (963) Lower Oxford Street.   (1960) Primark Store (!)
    Mackworth Hotel, High Street, SWANSEA.   (c.1971) Oldway House Arcade
CARDIFF, Empire (1,726) Queen Street.   (1962) C & A's (*)
NEWPORT, Empire (2,500) Charles Street.   (1942) shops and offices (*)

AVON/WILTSHIRE/BERKSHIRE

BRISTOL, Hippodrome (2,000) St. Augustine's Parade, BS1.   working theatre
    Royal Hotel, College Green, BRISTOL.   re-developed 1989
    Grand Hotel, Broad Street, BRISTOL.   working hotel
    Bear Hotel, Charnham Street, HUNGERFORD.   working hotel
    Demolished:
BRISTOL, Broadweir Hall (1,200) 7 Broadweir.   (1959) Job Centre (*)
SWINDON, Empire (1,470) Clarence Street.   (1959) Lloyd's Chemists (!)
SWINDON, Queen's, Clarence Street.   (1907 – became Empire, above)

LONDON

    Drayton House, 49 Colebrook Avenue,
    Drayton Green, EALING, W13.   occupied house (!)
WIMBLEDON, Wimbledon (1,700) The Broadway, SW19.   working theatre
    Burford Bridge Hotel, Box-Hill, DORKING.   working hotel
Victoria Palace (1,600) 126 Victoria Street, SW1.   working theatre
LEICESTER SQUARE, Empire (3,226) WC2.   (façade, only is original) cinema
Drury Lane (2,283) Catherine Street, WC2.   working theatre
ALDWYCH, Strand (1,193) WC2.   working theatre
Coliseum (2,400) St. Martin's Lane, WC2.   London Coliseum
    Savoy Hotel, 189 The Strand, W1.   working hotel
Palladium (2,300) Argyll Street, W1.   working theatre
    Washington Hotel, Curzon Street, W1.   refurbished 1989
    Dorchester Hotel, Park Lane, W1.   working hotel
Apollo (893) Shaftesbury Avenue, W1.   working theatre
    May Fair Hotel, Berkeley Square, W1.   working hotel
Prince's (1,392) Shaftesbury Avenue, WC2.   (restored 1986) Shaftesbury Theatre (*)
HACKNEY, Empire (2,218) 381 Mare Street, E8.   refurbished theatre (*)
TOTTENHAM, Palace (1,783) Tottenham High Road, N17.   bingo (*)
    Demolished:
WILLESDEN, Hippodrome, High Street, Harlesden, NW10.   (1957) D.S.S. (*)
EALING, Hippodrome (1,260) 21, The Broadway, W5.   (1958) W.H. Smith (*)
EALING, Walpole Cinema, Bond Street, W5.   (1981) office block
CHISWICK, Empire (2,154) Chiswick High Road, W4.   (1959) Empire House
SUTTON, Granada (2,000) Carshalton Road.   (1979) Sutton Park House
BRIXTON, Empress (1,900) Brighton Terrace, SW9.   (1992) flats
LEWISHAM, Hippodrome (3,492) 153–9 Rushey Green, CATFORD, SE6.   (1960) Eros House

HOLLOWAY, Empire (1,210) 564 Holloway Road, ISLINGTON, N19.　(c.1976) office block (*)
FINSBURY PARK, Empire (2,000) St. Thomas's Road, N4.　(1965) Vaudeville Court – flats
SHOREDITCH, Olympia (1,845) 203 Shoreditch High Street, E1.　(1940) S. Syedown & Co. (*)
STRATFORD, Empire (1,500) Broadway, E15.　(1958) office block (*)
WOOLWICH, Hippodrome (1,680) Wellington Street, SE18.　(1939) night club (*)
ILFORD, Hippodrome (2,500) High Road/Ilford Lane.　(1957) shops and offices (*)

ESSEX

SOUTHEND, Odeon (2,750) Elmer Approach.　working cinema
　　Palace Hotel, Pier Hill.　refurbished 1988

SOUTH COAST

MARGATE, Pavilion (1,533) Winter Gardens, Fort Crescent.　working theatre
　　St George's Hotel, CLIFTONVILLE.　Butlin's Hotel
　　ROMNEY, HYTHE & DYMCHURCH RAILWAY, KENT.　fully operational
BRIGHTON, Hippodrome (1,850) Middle Street.　bingo
　　Grand Hotel, King's Road, BRIGHTON.　refurbished hotel
PORTSMOUTH, Royal (1,050) Guildhall Walk, PO1.　restored 1989
SOUTHSEA, King's (1,780) Albert Road, PO5.　working theatre
　　Queen's Hotel, Clarence Parade, SOUTHSEA.　working hotel
SOUTHAMPTON, Gaumont (2,251) Commercial Road.　Mayflower Theatre
　　Polygon Hotel, Cumberland Place, SOUTHAMPTON.　working hotel
BOSCOMBE, Hippodrome (1,350) Christchurch Road.　The Academy
　　Chine Hotel, Boscombe Spa Road, BOURNEMOUTH.　working hotel
PLYMOUTH, Palace (1,200) Union Street.　The Academy
　　Grand Hotel, Elliott Street, The Hoe, PLYMOUTH.　working hotel

Happy Hunting!

Index

List of Subscribers

JANET THWAITE
ROBERT CLEARY
WILLIE McINTYRE
KENNETH P. McNAMARA
ANGUS McCHESNEY
ROY WALTON
JANET McBAIN
PATRICK J. TRAINER
CHARLES LEWIS
DAVID WALKER
RONALD THOMSON
DOUGLAS KELLETT
COLIN HOLMAN
MARGERY CRAIG
R. STAFFORD
PATRICIA McMANUS
SUNDERLAND EMPIRE
GARY & SUE DENT
GRAHAM E. ANDERSON
JOHN TAYLOR
COLIN GREENWELL
IAN WATSON
J. S. MYERS
A. MITCHEL
DAVID OYSTON
JIM STEPHENSON
RON PEARSON
BARRY CHEESE
JOHN V. ROTSEY-SMITH
PATRICK ALLEN
MICHAEL JOWLE
JOHN A. BURTON
JOHN T. HURST
ANDREW PATTINSON
KATE TAYLOR
GRAHAM McKENNA
DYLAN SMITH
STEVE MULLIN
JOHN STOKES
STEVE WORTHINGTON
ROSS F. WAGMAN
TREVOR WILSON
MARK SLATER
FRED MOLYNEUX
JOHN A. COWELL
TONY WHIPP
JIM SIDEBOTHAM
A. A. ASHTON
ANDY FLANAGAN
NIGEL LAWRENCE
REBECCA A. F. SMITH
SCRUFFY DOG
PHIL BARKER
KEN APPLETON
MRS B. CROSBY
JIM BARTON
CHARLIE CAIROLI Jnr.
CLAUDIA CAIROLI Jnr.
CYRIL CRITCHLOW
PHILIP ELLIS
GRAHAM PEARCE
BOB SPILLER
ADRIAN C. BRAILSFORD
G. M. PENLINGTON
GLYN ROBERTS
NANCY JANE REID

LOUIS & MARIE REA
RORY & MARY O'DONNELL
JACK L. WHITELEY
HARRY THOMAS
MARY SHORTER
DAVID SHEPHARD
JOHN LOVE
MARK HANCOCK
GORDON LOMAS (BMHS)
ROBERT BURFORD
HOWARD PARKER
GRAHAME & ANNI MORRIS
KENNETH J. TAYLOR
BRYAN BARBER
GRAEME HARDY
BRIAN CHEETHAM
DAVID PIPER
ALLAN BROMLEY
BILL JOHNSON
DAVID & SHARRON
    JOHNSON
ANDREW MENNELL
DAVID MARLOW
CHRIS HARPER
PHIL RUSHTON
KIM DRINKWATER
PAUL A. REEKS
JOHN ULLAH
BARRIE H. FINNEY
WAYNE ROBINSON
JOHN W. NICHOLLS
MARK BURNS
JACK TWELLS
TERRY PRICE
MUNRO JACK
GINO V. DERCOLA
RICHARD C. PARKER
DICK PEARCE
D. KENTEN
PAUL HUNT
DOUGLAS SALMON
JOANNA HEMBLEN
JOHN ROCHE
PETER C. NEWMAN
ROBERT POWELL
D. C. POPE
DAVID MARSHALL
BRISTOL LIBRARY
C. ROGERS
STEVE GORE
PETER JOHN ANDREWS
ALAN P. J. BEER
VANESSA COOMBES
Dr RICHARD BROWN
JIM SALISBURY
JEFFREY HOLLAND
PETER GOODWRIGHT
G. D. WALKER
PAUL A. TREGELLES
R. J. GALE
J. V. SMITHSON
JOHN M. LEAK
GARETH EVANS
ROCKY JACQUES
CHRIS HARE
R. SELLERS

IAN WREN
ALISON GRIMMER
ROGER ROBINSON
MIKE JONES
JOHN HUNTLEY
MARK CHAPMAN
DAVID F. CHESHIRE
KEVIN HENRIQUES
LAURIE MANSFIELD
GEORGE HOARE
RICHARD BRIERS
CHRISTOPHER BRAN
NAOMI DEARSLEY
JIMMY PERRY
ANNA REGI
MICK WOODS
M. JOHNSON
DAREN BUTTERFIELD
DAVID KIBBLE
RAY ANDREW
FRED JEFFREY
DAVE TURNER
JOHN T. WILLIAMS
H. A. DEEKS
PERRY SMITH
TERRY MOORE
JEFF & BARBARA BINES
BRUCE GRAHAM
GUY EGERTON
DAVID HANRAHAN
DANIEL KNIBB
S. MILLHOUSE
DAVID BROXHAM
A. G. STREETER
MRS J. N. COOPER
BRIAN A. TAYLOR
RON QUIBELL
FRED EDWARDS
R. SELLER
DEVON COUNTY LIBRARY
NORTH SHIELDS LIBRARY
PIET ADRIAANSE
EDWARD HEYNE
PETER J. KOK
RICHARD SCHUURMAN
HANS LIGTENBERG
TOM SCHERMER
S. SCHOUTEN
R. W. RADEVAN
ALPHONS BAKKER
ARNOUD ALDERLIESTE
ANDRE ROUWENHORST
H. G. C. SCHATTENBERG
W. LAGERMAN
EMYL MIJNHOUT
FRANK VERBRUGGHE
PEETERS WIM
MARC DE CONINCK
HUGO GIELEN
ERIK VANDEN EECKHOUT
JOHAN VERMEULEN
EMMANUEL VAN DOOREN
ROBERT MERHOTTEIN
RON YOUNG